Praise for
Then They Came for Me

"A well-told story of faith, personal courage and repentance that speaks to a nation's journey through delusion and horror to contrition. With skill that weaves his deep research and knowledge of German history into a finely-knit biography, Matthew Hockenos takes us swiftly through Martin Niemöller's nine decades, from his origins in a family of monarchist, anti-Semitic, Lutheran ministers through his career as a naval officer and U-boat commander, from his early support for the Nazis to his disillusionment and 8 years in concentration camps through his evolution into a pacifist icon and moral authority in turbulent post-war Germany."

—ETHAN MICHAELI,
author of *The Defender*

"In this engaging biography, Matthew Hockenos explores the many lives of Martin Niemöller as he evolved from U-boat captain to clergyman to critic of Hitler to defender of the German people. Combining historical empathy with honest critical analysis, Matthew Hockenos masterfully demonstrates how a deeply flawed religious activist challenged an authoritarian political leader and changed the course of history."

—MATTHEW A. SUTTON,
author of *American Apocalypse*

THEN
THEY CAME
FOR ME

ALSO BY MATTHEW D. HOCKENOS

A Church Divided:
German Protestants Confront the Nazi Past

THEN THEY CAME FOR ME

MARTIN NIEMÖLLER, THE PASTOR WHO DEFIED THE NAZIS

Matthew D. Hockenos

BASIC
BOOKS
New York

Basic Books
Hachette Book Group
1290 Avenue of the Americas, New York, NY 10104
www.basicbooks.com

Printed in the United States of America
First Edition: September 2018

Published by Basic Books, an imprint of Perseus Books, LLC, a subsidiary of Hachette Book Group, Inc. The Basic Books name and logo is a trademark of the Hachette Book Group.

The Hachette Speakers Bureau provides a wide range of authors for speaking events. To find out more, go to www.hachettespeakersbureau.com or call (866) 376-6591. The publisher is not responsible for websites (or their content) that are not owned by the publisher.

Print book interior design by Linda Mark.

The Library of Congress has cataloged the hardcover edition as follows:

Names: Hockenos, Matthew D., 1966– author.
Title: Then they came for me : Martin Niemoller, the pastor who defied the Nazis / Matthew D. Hockenos.
Description: First edition. | New York : Basic Books, 2018. | Includes bibliographical references and index.
Identifiers: LCCN 2018008433 (print) | LCCN 2018022869 (ebook) |
 ISBN 9780465097876 (ebook) | ISBN 9780465097869 (hardcover)
Subjects: LCSH: Nieméoller, Martin, 1892-1984. | Lutheran Church—Germany—Clergy—Biography. | Bekennende Kirche.
Classification: LCC BX8080.N48 (ebook) | LCC BX8080.N48 H63 2018 (print) | DDC 284.1092 [B] —dc23
LC record available at https://lccn.loc.gov/2018008433

ISBNs: 978-0-465-09786-9 (hardcover), 978-0-465-09787-6 (ebook)

LSC-C

10 9 8 7 6 5 4 3 2 1

For Alexandra and Oscar

In memory of
Warren J. Hockenos (1930–2010)
and
John S. Conway (1929–2017)

Contents

Introduction

*First they came for the Communists, and I did not speak out—
    because I was not a Communist.*

*Then they came for the Trade Unionists, and I did not speak out—
    because I was not a Trade Unionist.*

*Then they came for the Jews, and I did not speak out—
    because I was not a Jew.*

Then they came for me—and there was no one left to speak for me.

O N A WINTRY NOVEMBER DAY IN 1945, A SIMPLY DRESSED, WHITE-haired woman huddled beside a gaunt, somber man as they read a plaque affixed to a tree. The middle-aged German couple, man and wife, had suffered greatly during the war, and although the man looked particularly haggard, it was his wife who was close to fainting. The plaque itself was plain-looking: a white-painted board with black letters and numbers. The inscription, however, was anything but ordinary: "Here in the years 1933–1945, 238,756 people were cremated." Overwhelmed, the woman leaned into her husband for support. She was visibly shaken, knowing that he could have been one of them. Her husband was Martin Niemöller. They were standing at the entry of the crematoria at Dachau concentration camp outside Munich, where he had been an inmate from 1941 to 1945.[1]

Martin Niemöller said that, upon reading the inscription, "a cold shudder ran down my spine." But for him, unlike for Else, his wife, it was not only the number of people murdered that was upsetting. He was even more taken aback by the dates: 1933–1945. Dachau had opened in March 1933, when the Nazis began incarcerating their enemies, just one month after Hitler came to power. Niemöller had been a free man at that time, a prominent pastor of an influential parish, and he remained at liberty until his arrest in 1937. Imprisoned in a Berlin jail and a concentration camp from 1937 to 1941, Niemöller and other famous camp inmates were transferred by the Nazis to Dachau in 1941. "My alibi accounted for the years 1937–45," he told a German audience a few months after he and his wife visited Dachau. "But God was not asking me where I had been from 1937 to 1945 but from 1933 to 1945 . . . and for those [earlier] years I did not have an answer."[2]

There is little doubt that the sentiments expressed in Niemöller's famous confession emerged from this revelatory moment at Dachau. Throughout 1946, he repeated the confession frequently to his German compatriots, modeling for them how to admit to and repent one's complacency toward and complicity in the Nazi era and the Holocaust.

The popularity of what is known as the "Niemöller confession" spread in the United States in the late 1970s and early 1980s with the rise of the human rights movement. Today it is frequently invoked by a multitude of activists and others. Though it reflected Pastor Niemöller's particular circumstances in Nazi and post-Nazi Germany, groups and organizations ranging from Black Lives Matter to the Tea Party have appropriated the quotation for their causes. Secondary school teachers employ it to instruct American youth on the virtues of diversity and good citizenship. College students adorn their dorm-room walls with posters bearing the German pastor's words. Politicians and pundits on the left invoke it in response to crackdowns on undocumented immigrants and minorities, while the United States Holocaust Memorial Museum in Washington and the Holocaust Memorial in Boston prominently display the confession.

Despite the wide use of Niemöller's confession, its author's life story remains largely unknown. Previous biographies (two in German and three in English, to date) have done little to probe the depths of this complicated man, preferring instead to present him in a mostly heroic light. Would his admirers in the American public embrace the confession so enthusiastically if they knew of Niemöller's support for Adolf Hitler during his rise to power from the 1920s into the early '30s? The Nazis' stigmatization and persecution of minorities did not initially trouble Niemöller. He said nothing when the Gestapo arrested Communists, Socialists, and Jews—and not because he was timid. As we will see, he was anything but. He was silent because he shared the belief that these groups were anti-Christian and disloyal to Germany.

Then They Came for Me is a revisionist biography that weaves together Niemöller's personal story with the great dramas of the twentieth century that drove his moral and political evolution. It seeks neither to vilify him nor to add to the existing hagiographies, but rather to understand him and his confession and to reveal what his transformation from Nazi sympathizer to committed pacifist tells us about how and under what circumstances such reversals are possible.

Born in 1892, Martin Niemöller lived to ninety-two, witnessing two world wars and the Cold War. He grew up during the German monarchy's struggle for world recognition and served proudly as a submarine officer in Kaiser Wilhelm II's Imperial Navy in World War I. After the war and the socialist revolution that overthrew the Hohenzollern monarchy, Niemöller entered the seminary. Ordained a Lutheran pastor in 1924, he remained an archconservative nationalist during Germany's short-lived liberal republic, the Weimar Republic, casting his ballot for the Nazis in 1924 and again in 1933.

Although he welcomed the appointment of Hitler as head of the German government in January 1933, Niemöller soon recognized that Hitler and his followers sought to transform Luther's church into a Nazi-led church—where Nazi storm troopers could pray to a blond-haired, blue-eyed, Aryan Jesus. It was this intrusion into church affairs and Nazi attacks on the Old Testament that sparked Niemöller's turn. A stubborn Westphalian by nature and a skilled manager and administrator since his days as a naval officer, Niemöller took command of the Protestant Church's opposition to Hitler's repressive church policy and remained its undisputed leader until his arrest in July 1937. His unlikely survival after nearly a decade in concentration camps gave Niemöller the opportunity to remake himself and his reputation in postwar Germany.

The wiry, bespectacled, five-foot-eight Lutheran pastor lived for another four decades. In the immediate postwar years, he took the lonely stance of acknowledging the complicity of the German Protestant churches in the Nazi era, and indeed he confessed his own egregious failure to combat anti-Semitism. An outspoken critic of West Germany and its Cold War patron, the United States, he wholeheartedly embraced pacifism and called for a united, neutral Germany. As a leader in the growing ecumenical movement that sought better relations between churches with diverse traditions and from different countries, he spent the rest of his life campaigning against war, nuclear weapons, and Western imperialism.

Niemöller's detractors remained skeptical that his postwar evolution was as thorough as the former U-boat commander and anti-Semite implied. In fact, Niemöller's correspondence from the immediate postwar years confirms that his rejection of anti-Semitism did not come easily or quickly, despite his public comments. While the speed and extent of Niemöller's conversion in the years immediately after World War II are debatable, one cannot deny the long-term changes.

On his ninetieth birthday, Niemöller joked that he had started his political career as "an ultraconservative" who loyally served the kaiser. Now he was "a revolutionary," he said. "If I live to be a hundred, maybe I'll be an anarchist." While this tongue-in-cheek prophecy never came to pass, he had indeed embarked on tangled political and personal journeys. "Niemöller was always 'on his way,'" Karl Barth, the world-renowned Swiss theologian, said of the pastor's propensity for change. Martin Niemöller's persona never quite changed, but his causes, all of which he served selflessly and passionately, did. He did not take them up haphazardly; there was a clear direction to his life. His transformation from nationalist to internationalist, from militarist to pacifist, and from racist and anti-Semite to champion of equality all evinced a more general transformation—from provincial, narrow-minded chauvinist to compassionate, open-minded humanitarian. In this, Niemöller is to be admired and his evolution celebrated. Committed as most of us are today to particular beliefs, we would do well to engage with the life of a man who changed his—even if that effort ultimately falls short of the truly heroic.[3]

– ONE –

With God for King and Fatherland
(1892–1914)

MARTIN NIEMÖLLER GREW UP IN THE SHADOW OF THE CHURCH—literally. "Its bells ushered in and closed each of our days," he later recalled of his father's church, "and we grew to love it as our second home." Heinrich Niemöller was pastor of a small Protestant parish in rural Lippstadt, a town of thirteen thousand in Germany's northwestern state of Westphalia. Lippstadt's farmers were more likely to supply Germany's nearby Rhine-Ruhr industrial hub on the Belgian-Dutch border with dairy products and farm produce than they were Germany's distant metropolises of Munich and Berlin. The faithful parishioners of Heinrich's church, the Great Church of St. Mary, were especially proud that their town had been the first in the region to accept the teachings of Martin Luther, in 1521. St. Mary's, with its distinctive steeple and bell tower, was originally Catholic, consecrated to the Virgin Mary; in the years of the Reformation the church became Lutheran but kept its old name. The Niemöller home was a two-hundred-year-old parsonage on Brüderstrasse, next to another Protestant church, the Church of Brethren (Brüderkirche), where Heinrich occasionally preached, and just down the street from St. Mary's. As an adult, Martin Niemöller said he understood the importance of the Christian spirit that pervaded his parents' household and how it had influenced the direction his life would take.[1]

"The Lippstadt parish," Martin's younger brother Wilhelm remembered, "was father's first love," and his parishioners returned that love. His passionately delivered sermons with no ornamentation or deviations from Scripture earned him the respect and devotion of his flock. "God's Word itself came to life," Wilhelm reminisced, "and in such a way that parishioners understood it and absorbed it."[2]

Heinrich, born in 1859, was typical of Protestant pastors at the time in that his devotion to God was matched only by his reverence for the Prussian-German Hohenzollern monarchy. In 1871, Wilhelm I—a member of the Hohenzollern dynasty who had been king of Prussia since 1861—became emperor (*kaiser*) of the German Empire (*Deutsches Reich*) and was known as Kaiser Wilhelm. "The national ideal was always foremost in Martin's upbringing," a friend explained. Asked later in his life by the journalist Günter Gaus if he had ever rebelled against this upbringing, Niemöller conceded, "No, I can't say I ever did." There were two reigning dogmas in his parents' house that no one could even imagine questioning: "a good Christian is a good citizen and a good Christian is a good soldier." Commenting on the politics of the church during the years of the Hohenzollern monarchy, Niemöller explained, "There was an unseen motto engraved above the church door: 'for monarchists only' or 'for nationalists only.' A Social-Democrat could not be a real Christian and a real member of the church. His conviction was regarded as incompatible with the Christian faith."[3]

Heinrich instilled his love of throne and altar in his six children, five of whom survived to adulthood. He and his wife Paula nee Müller named their first son, born in 1890, after Heinrich. Their subsequent sons Martin, born in 1892, and Wilhelm, in 1898, were named after the two towering figures in their lives: Martin Luther and the current Hohenzollern emperors, Wilhelm I and Wilhelm II. The three daughters were Magdalene (1894), Pauline (1896), and Maria (1901). The Niemöllers were Protestant and Prussian through and through.[4]

Martin inherited his nearly black eyes and dark complexion from his mother's side. Though Paula Müller herself was Westphalian, her Huguenot ancestors had been strangers to the region, having emigrated from southern France to escape the religious persecution inflicted upon Protestants by the Roman Catholic Church. Paula's father ran a general store in the town of Wersen near Osnabrück. Heinrich, who was nine years older than his wife, had met her when she was a child. The Müllers were inordinately proud of their Huguenot heritage, which emphasized intellectual and artistic interests, and which no doubt was a factor in Martin's success in school. Paula's knowledge of Latin came in handy when she helped the children with their homework. Although artistically inclined herself, and endowed with inexhaustible energy, Paula was confined to the role of a pastor's wife; Heinrich told her early in their marriage that her main duties were in the home.

Martin was an imaginative, self-sufficient, curious, outspoken boy who spent his days outdoors and taught himself all manner of things, including the names of the constellations. Before he was old enough to attend the local primary school, he had mastered numerals by using his mother's tape measure and scribbling with chalk on stone slabs in front of their home. In a letter from later in their lives, Magdalene, his younger sister by nearly three years, wrote that playing in the garden of the Lippstadt parsonage was akin to playing in paradise, and that her older brother was her godlike hero. "I was convinced he could do anything." Martin played the piano and the French horn, led the school band, taught his siblings to swim ("Just jump in. I will save you"), excelled at gymnastics, and always got the best grades in school.[5]

A small, thin boy with large protruding ears, Martin most enjoyed playing sailor along the Lippe River, a branch of which flowed through the parsonage garden, and exploring his neighbors' farms. It was an idyllic childhood for the most part, the major exception being his older

Eight-year-old Martin Niemöller with siblings Wilhelm and Magdalene. (Zentralarchiv der EKHN, Darmstadt)

brother's untimely death at the age of three and a half. Niemöller maintained at the end of his life that the death of his older brother had a lasting impact on his life because it stimulated his earliest thoughts about Jesus Christ and heaven. Heini died on Martin's second birthday, which left Martin the oldest of the Niemöller children.[6]

Animals, large and small, were part of their daily lives in Lippstadt and of great interest to Martin, who made fast friends with the neighboring farmers' horses. It was a small creature, however, that took center stage in Niemöller family lore. Martin, like most young boys of the era, eagerly collected cockchafers, a European beetle (and pest). On the occasion of a doctor's visit having to do with an injury to Martin's nose, one of the beetles escaped from its hiding place in a box under Martin's shirt. Not wanting it destroyed, Martin yelled, "That's mine, that's mine," as the beetle flew about the examining room. Finally, when the doctor asked how Martin had injured his nose, the boy said he had fallen on it. "You definitely did not fall on your mouth," the doctor responded.[7]

But Martin's interest in nature came second to his love of the sea. By the age of five, he knew he wanted to be an officer in the kaiser's navy, and like many German boys, he would wear a sailor's uniform every Sunday. When asked what he wanted for Christmas, marine calendars and nautical posters topped the list. He shared with his siblings—perhaps foisted upon them—his enthusiasm for games of ships played in bed, using sheets for sails. He expected his sisters to memorize the types and names of ships in the German fleet from the large poster in his bedroom. Indeed, you could not see the wallpaper for the newspaper clippings, postcards, and photos of ships that covered it. Heinrich hoped that his son would take an interest in the priesthood, but during his early years Martin never wavered from his goal of a career on the high seas.[8]

Foremost, of course, in the pastor's household was the time set aside daily for Bible stories and prayers to the image of Jesus above Martin's bed. Magdalene later recalled the importance of religious holidays in their lives, with Christmas, Easter, and Whitsun (Pentecost) being celebrated with reverence and festivities. Their mother's special biscuits were Martin's greatest material delight at Christmas; his share usually disappeared on Christmas Eve. Acting a supplicant, he'd approach the other children with an empty plate saying, "A poor beggar asking for a small donation."[9]

As pastor in Lippstadt from 1885 to 1900, Heinrich did his part to uphold the Reformation tradition in a region that was not always friendly to Protestants. Westphalia and its western neighbor, the Rhineland, acquired by Prussia at the Congress of Vienna in 1815, were strongly Roman Catholic. Protestants, who made up two-thirds of all Germans but less than half of Westphalians, felt outnumbered and were not particularly enamored of their Catholic neighbors. The feeling was mutual. Catholics, always conscious of being a minority in the new Germany, were still smarting over Bismarck's anti-Catholic initiatives during the *Kulturkampf*—the state's legal persecution of the Catholic Church during the 1870s—and the continued underrepresentation of Catholics in higher public offices.[10]

Jews made up less than 1 percent of the population in Germany—approximately six hundred thousand people—and a mere twenty thousand lived in Westphalia. "I remember I was not a friend of the Jews,"

Martin Niemöller admitted after World War II. "I had no hatred against Jews but this whole atmosphere of noncooperation with the Jews was just that in which everybody grew up." Asked by Günter Gaus in the 1960s about his attitude toward Jews during his youth, Niemöller responded, "In my native Tecklenburg [a region of Westphalia near Osnabrück] there were many farmers who were in debt to Jewish moneylenders and livestock traders. At that time, the mood in this area was not systematically anti-Semitic, but it was intuitively and traditionally so, and I never especially questioned it." In that, he was traditionally Protestant as well.[11]

The Germany of Niemöller's youth was eager to flex its muscle on the international scene. "Like an unbridled wild stallion" is how one German historian described its posture at the turn of the century. The death of Kaiser Wilhelm I on March 9, 1888—two weeks shy of his ninety-first birthday—ushered in Germany's *Dreikaiserjahr*: the year of the three emperors. His first successor was his only son, Crown Prince Friedrich III. Fritz, as he was known, and his "English" wife, Crown Princess Victoria—named after her mother, Queen Victoria of Great Britain—were notorious liberals in the deeply conservative Hohenzollern court. At the time of his ascension, Fritz was suffering from terminal throat cancer. He ruled just ninety-nine days, most of which he spent in bed. His death at the age of fifty-six left the crown in the hands of his impetuous and conservative twenty-nine-year-old son, Wilhelm II.[12]

There was little optimism regarding Wilhelm II's suitability for the role. The new emperor's own mother described him as "chauvinistic and ultra-Prussian" and confided to a friend that he was "stuck up, vain, proud, narrow minded, insolent & oh—so ignorant." Chancellor Otto von Bismarck, a compatriot of Wilhelm I, groaned, "Alas, my poor grandchildren." And Friedrich von Holstein, a diplomat in the German Foreign Office, wrote in his diary in May 1888 that Wilhelm II's reign would be "the nemesis of world history."[13]

Holstein would prove prescient. Convinced that the Hohenzollerns ruled by divine right and that God had appointed him emperor so that he could carry out the divine will, Wilhelm envisioned himself leading the

German people on a Protestant crusade for global dominance. Instead, he led them into the abyss of war, humiliating defeat, and socialist revolution.

MARTIN NIEMÖLLER'S EARLIEST years coincided with the beginning of Wilhelm II's reign. The 1890s witnessed unprecedented economic, scientific, and technological advance in Germany. But rapid modernization did not come without costs. All appearances aside, the unification of Germany in 1871 had not brought economic, political, and social unity. Economic advance and the concomitant emergence of a workers' movement brought strife. Conservative industrial barons and politicians tried to rally the workers to their nationalist cause but had little luck. Rally the workers did, but not to the government's conservative agenda. Instead, they joined the opposition Social Democratic Party of Germany in droves. On the eve of the First World War, the Social Democrats were the largest party in the German parliament. Class antagonisms threatened to undermine Wilhelm's hegemonic aspirations.

Wilhelm's was a personal style of rule: he ignored the responsible organs of government and made the vast majority of decisions based on his gut and the advice of his conservative entourage. The result was a zigzag course in foreign affairs as Germany lurched from crisis to crisis. Erratic, disruptive, and unpredictable as he was in handling Germany's neighbors, Wilhelm remained steadfast on one matter: strengthening the armed forces until Germany was the supreme power in Europe.

Martin Niemöller was truly a child of Wilhelmine Germany, which yoked nationalism to Christianity. He shared the monarchy's faith in the empire's providential glory, and he was hardly unusual in his zeal. Many Germans encouraged their leaders to seek great-power status, which, at the time, meant colonial expansion. Racism and ethnic nationalism propelled German imperialism. Wilhelm and his supporters saw empire as their right and destiny, but fulfilling that destiny would require a transformation of the state and its priorities.

Where Bismarck had championed cautious *Realpolitik*, Wilhelm's "new course" was one of *Weltmachtpolitik*—global power politics, characterized by sea power and colonies. Once on the throne, he began building a world-class navy to challenge the British. In one of his first acts of international diplomacy, Wilhelm refused to renew the Reinsurance Treaty with Russia, opening the way for a Franco-Russian military alliance a few years later and the dreaded threat of a two-front war against Germany.

Wilhelm loved pomp and ceremony; contemporaries called his rule the "age of festivities and speeches." When he couldn't be found sailing the seas aboard the royal yacht *Hohenzollern*, where he spent approximately one-third of his reign, the emperor was crisscrossing his realm toasting his and his ancestors' birthdays, laying foundation stones at new churches, christening ships, attending parades, and always preening for the cameras. The stream of national commemorations and official holidays had a clear purpose: to shore up Hohenzollern rule during a period of rapid change when domestic discord, including challenges to the very idea of monarchy, was mounting.[14]

Wilhelm sought whenever possible to make explicit the ties binding the German people to Martin Luther and the Protestant Church. Especially important to him was the supposedly unique role of Germans in the coming of God's kingdom. To this end in 1892, the Hohenzollerns made elaborate plans for the 375th anniversary of Martin Luther's alleged nailing of his ninety-five theses to the doors of the *Schlosskirche* (Castle Church) in Wittenberg on October 31, 1517, inaugurating the Protestant Reformation. Wilhelm's father and grandfather had embarked first on the partial rebuilding and later the complete renovation of the historic *Schlosskirche*, which had been damaged by fire during the Seven Years' War (1756–1763) and again during the Wars of Liberation (1813–1814). The younger Wilhelm and his advisers spared no expense making the rededication of the church on October 31, 1892, a moment of national prestige.[15]

Accompanying Wilhelm to Wittenberg were the empress, three of their young sons, the Duke of York, the Crown Prince of Sweden, and several German princes. At the head of the procession from the railway station to the church were all the highest clergy of the German Protestant Church, followed by pastors of lesser rank, military generals and officers in uniform, ministers of state, and government officials. The kaiser and his entourage brought up the rear, surrounded by the imperial guard. Throngs of well-wishers lined the streets. As the royal entourage approached Wittenberg's center square, where two huge statues of Luther and his collaborator Philip Melanchthon stood, trumpeters belted out Luther's most famous hymn, "A Mighty Fortress Is Our God" ("Ein feste Berg ist unser Gott").

With the crowds cheering, a young pastor in his robe and collar, overwhelmed by the patriotic religious experience, hurled his hat toward the kaiser's entourage, where it landed amid the honorary guard. The captain in charge called to the pastor, "Herr Pfarrer! Enthusiasm is all very well, but you've spoiled my dressing!" The guilty pastor, now full of apologies, was Martin Niemöller's father, Heinrich. Years later, when recounting the episode, he concluded, "But I would do the same again!" As far as Heinrich was concerned, his participation in the rededication of Luther's church—in the presence, no less, of His Majesty, who also served as the supreme bishop of the church (*summus episcopus*)—was made possible by the will of God alone.[16]

The year of Martin's birth, 1892, the German emperor set off on an ambitious effort to refashion Germany's place in the world. Wilhelm II's administration submitted to parliament a bill seeking the highest ever peacetime investment in the army. The emperor felt strongly that the threat of a two-front war against France and Russia justified drastically increasing the number of men in uniform. But even more important was a naval buildup. Also that year, Wilhelm appointed Alfred von Tirpitz chief of staff of the navy executive command. Tirpitz convinced Wilhelm that the British Royal Navy was the main obstacle to Germany's power, necessitating construction of many new battleships.

Until Wilhelm's ascension to power, the navy had been the nation's "junior service," commanded by army generals. But the new Imperial German Navy—the High Seas Fleet—would be the darling of the young kaiser, the source and symbol of *his* globe-spanning might. Where Wilhelm I had used the Prussian army to make Germany a great power

(*Grossmacht*), Wilhelm II intended to use the German navy to make Germany a world power (*Weltmacht*). That these initiatives alienated other powers on whose good graces Germany relied did not concern Wilhelm. The consequences for Germany and for the world would be dire.

The fleet was built at lightning speed, as demanded by Tirpitz's "risk strategy." The grand admiral did not believe that Germany actually had to be stronger than Britain on the high seas, only that it had to be strong enough to scare the British off from a direct encounter. He assured Wilhelm that once the naval buildup was completed, Britain would have "lost all inclination to attack us." As late as April 1914, Tirpitz maintained, "The pressure exerted on England, just by the presence of our fleet—the threat to their position as a world power—better than anything else, ensures peace." Moreover, a large and powerful German fleet, Tirpitz argued, would have "alliance value"; that is, it would convince the British that it was in their best interests to ally with Germany against Russia and France. And if both deterrence and alliance should fail, Tirpitz assured Wilhelm, by 1920 Germany could build the high-quality ships, develop the superior tactics, and train the qualified officers it would need to have a real chance of victory over the British navy in the North Sea.[17]

The attempt to inspire alliance through competition proved self-defeating. Where Bismarck had advised keeping off the seas in order to ensure Britain's good graces, Wilhelm's saber-rattling led to the very thing it was intended to head off: confrontation. "I have no desire for good relationship with England at the price of the development of Germany's navy," he proclaimed. Britain accepted the challenge, and the naval arms race was on.[18]

The maritime expansion from the 1890s to 1914 electrified the German middle class, which took great pleasure in the spectacles of modern shipbuilding, launches of new warships, and ceremonial fleet reviews presided over by the kaiser. The race to build more and better ships, the cult of the uniform, and the naval mania in the popular media bolstered their patriotism. Tirpitz's Naval Office carried out its own public relations campaign aimed at influencing popular opinion and the legislative process. Active and retired officers, writers, and friendly academics—

so-called fleet professors (*Flottenprofessoren*)—disseminated naval propaganda through books, brochures, newspaper articles, and lectures. A young Martin Niemöller gobbled it all up.[19]

Several ultranationalist lobby groups founded in the 1880s and 1890s—including the German Colonial Society, the Pan-German League, and, most important, the German Navy League—also sought to shape public opinion and pressure the government to pursue aggressive *Weltmachtpolitik* through naval expansion. Members of the German Navy League were predominantly middle-class and represented a new form of right-wing politics from below. In addition to organizing an extensive lecture circuit, the league published leaflets, posters, postcards, and a newspaper, *Die Flotte*, with a circulation of 750,000. A pioneer in propaganda, the league was also an early adopter of the new medium of cinema.[20]

The Franco-Russian alliance of 1894, which followed Wilhelm's rejection of the Reinsurance Treaty, should have been warning enough to stay on good terms with Britain. After all, Bismarck's advice that Germany be "one of three [great powers] . . . when there are five" had proved sound. But Wilhelm and his advisers remained convinced that Britain would eventually be drawn into an alliance with Germany because English colonial interests clashed with those of France and Russia and were best served by partnership with the continent's supreme industrial and military power. This vision might have been realized had German foreign policy been more restrained. But Wilhelm's imperial pursuits and the naval arms race exasperated England. As British foreign secretary Sir Edward Grey lamented, "The German kaiser is ageing me; he is like a battleship with steam up and screws going, but with no rudder, and he will run into something some day and cause a catastrophe."[21]

WILHELM'S PENCHANT FOR stirring up trouble in faraway places, including his infamous telegram to President Paul Kruger of the Transvaal in support of the Boers against the British in 1896, was on ostentatious display during his historic trip to the Middle East in 1898. The stated purpose of the "expedition to the Orient" was to inaugurate a Protestant church in Jerusalem, the Lutheran Church of the Redeemer, on Reformation Day, October 31. Constructed in the 1890s according to Wilhelm's preferred Romanesque Revival style, the church had a bell tower, designed by the kaiser himself, that offered panoramic views of the Old City. Wilhelm intended the monumental tower to serve "as a symbol of German Protestant presence at the holy places of Jerusalem."[22]

Since his boyhood, Pastor Heinrich Niemöller had dreamed of visiting the Holy Land. After learning of the trip, he was eager to join, though the mere thought of spending time in the presence of the emperor was more than he could fathom. How would an "ordinary mortal" like himself manage a berth on the ship that was to carry the leaders of the German Protestant Church? Evidently Heinrich had earned great respect in his Lippstadt church, for his parishioners and presbytery donated most of the 1,500 marks he needed to make the trip. In a further stroke of good fortune, the president of the Protestant Consistory of Prussia granted the small-town pastor the final berth. "Das war Gottes Finger!" Heinrich proclaimed. On October 17, 1898, Heinrich and more than two hundred German pilgrims set sail for Haifa from Genoa on—ironically enough— the British steamer *Midnight Sun*. Although nearly one-third of the pilgrims were women, mostly wives accompanying their husbands, Paula was not among them. When Heinrich set off on this month-long adventure, Paula was left tending the home fires with four very young children, including six-month-old Wilhelm.[23]

Given the tensions in the Middle East, it would have been a good time for Wilhelm II to heed Bismarck's famous quip that the entire Orient wasn't worth the life of a single Pomeranian grenadier. But instead of the sober diplomacy "the Eastern Question" demanded, Wilhelm engaged in bombastic theater. For Kaiser Wilhelm, the inauguration of the church was an opportunity to practice *Weltmachtpolitik*. With the Ottoman Empire in decline, he saw a chance to secure a German Protestant foothold in the Holy Land. Traveling by sea in his palatial white yacht *Hohenzollern*, with an escort of German warships, Wilhelm began his grand tour of the Orient with a stop in Constantinople to meet with Sultan Abdul Hamid II. From there he continued to Haifa, where the imperial couple disembarked for a dusty ride to Jaffa and then Jerusalem.

Although they were guests of the Ottoman sultan, the Germans entered the Holy Land with the air of conquerors. Huge crowds gathered to witness the imperial procession—120 carriages, 1,300 horses and mules, 100 coachmen, 600 drivers, 12 cooks, 60 waiters, and 230 tents, followed by Turkish lancers, German hussars, and the emperor's entourage. In his dedication speech, Wilhelm underscored the mythical relationship between Germany and the Holy Land, declaring, "From Jerusalem came the light in splendor from which the German nation became great and glorious; and what the Germanic peoples have become, they became under the banner of the cross, the emblem of self-sacrificing charity."[24]

The pastor from Lippstadt looked on in awe. The German Protestant pastorate claimed that it was apolitical and above party politics, but in fact the vast majority of pastors were intensely loyal to the Hohenzollern monarchy and supported right-wing anti-Semitic parties. To celebrate Reformation Day in Jerusalem in the presence of His Majesty was an unforgettable benchmark in Heinrich Niemöller's life. That his trip was as much a celebration of German power and prestige as a religious pilgrimage is evident in certain entries in his ornate memory book, *Up to Jerusalem*. On October 18, he noted the anniversary of Napoleon's 1813 defeat at Prussian hands in the Battle of the Nations at Leipzig. On October 22, the birthday of Wilhelm II's wife, Empress Augusta Victoria, Heinrich recorded, "We must thank God that our people are led by a royal couple whose marriage is so holy and pure." The consecration of the Redeemer Church itself was a milestone in the history of German Protestantism, "an evangelical manifestation of a sort which had not been seen in modern times," according to Heinrich. Nothing could better demonstrate the alliance of throne and altar, in his view, and that of many others.[25]

When Heinrich returned by ship and train to Germany, Martin accompanied his mother to the station to meet him. A month is a long time for a six-year-old boy to be separated from his father. On his way to the station, Martin's big worry was whether he would still recognize his father, and vice versa.

Shortly after his return, Heinrich moved his family from tranquil Lippstadt to bustling Elberfeld (today a subdivision of Wuppertal) in the industrial Rhineland. The family balked at leaving their own little Eden, but Heinrich cited Elberfeld's superior schools as his reason for this unpopular decision; he may also have been eager for a more challenging pastorate.

Although the two locations were not even seventy miles apart, the family suffered from culture shock. "In place of the most beautiful Westphalian churches from the pre-Reformation period," Wilhelm remembered, "we found a somewhat frightening brick gothic; in place of the intimate parsonage, a less cozy row house; in place of our rich and well-kept garden we got a garden, but with such lack of light and air neither roses nor potatoes could flourish." Although the homesickness eventually wore off, Martin would remember the eight years he lived in Lippstadt as the high point of his youth. During the most miserable time of his life, in Sachsenhausen concentration camp in the late 1930s, he wrote his parents reflecting on his "idyllic childhood in Lippstadt."[26]

Although both sons held their father in great esteem, Heinrich was often too busy tending to his parish to spend time with them. It was their mother, Paula, who took charge of their education and upbringing. Wilhelm found a male role model in Martin. "He was six years older than I was, and that is a great deal when you are young. At that time he would hardly have realized that I loved him," Wilhelm recalled in his forties. "It would never have occurred to me to say such things."[27]

"In Elberfeld," Martin would recall, "the parish was an industrial one in which the old families were but a small minority in the ceaseless flow of immigrants who came from eastern Germany." With rapid industrialization came economic volatility, unemployment, poor working conditions, the turn to class consciousness among common laborers, and increasing indifference to religion. Other factors that added to demographic disorder and Protestant anxiety included emigration from Germany to the United States, the internal migration of Protestants into traditional Catholic territories, and the migration of Catholics into traditional Protestant territories. In addition to his increased pastoral duties, Heinrich spent untold hours with the Gustav Adolf Union, an organization designed to spread the Protestant faith where it was under threat from Catholicism, and the Rhenish Missionary Society, which sent Protestant missionaries to Africa. With Paula ruling the roost, the family thrived in spite of Heinrich's absence.[28]

Wilhelm Niemöller, the historian in the family, claimed that his father made more than two thousand house visits every year offering his parishioners counseling and prayers. He witnessed broken marriages, prostitution, children born out of wedlock, alcoholism, criminality, unemployment, and child labor—sometimes with young Martin in tow. One home visit made a lasting impression on the boy. He accompanied his father to the home of a poor weaver dying of tuberculosis. As his father prayed with the man, Martin eyed on the wall a framed piece of cloth stitched with gold-colored beads that read, WAS WÜRDE JESUS DAZU SAGEN? What would Jesus say? This was Martin's introduction to the "social question"—what would Jesus say about the poor, the sick, the infirm, the victims of the industrial revolution in Elberfeld?[29]

In the Niemöller household, the answer to this question was not settled. Certainly Jesus would say that a Christian has the responsibility to address social misery through prayer and pastoral counseling. But there were also signs that Heinrich agreed with the views of Pastor Adolf Stoecker, who founded an ultraconservative and anti-Semitic political party that advocated addressing the origins of social misery through legislative reforms. Most pastors, however, viewed the class hierarchy as God-given and therefore as not to be challenged by mere mortals.

When it came to the plight of the poor, Protestant church officials, including Wilhelm II, the supreme bishop, held the view that "pastors should busy themselves with the souls of their parishes and cultivate brotherly love, but keep politics out of it." A year earlier, in 1895, conservative church leaders had affirmed the "Doctrine of Two Kingdoms," whereby the state deals with earthly matters and the church with spiritual. Officially, political activism was said to "divert the church from the goals set by the Lord of the church: generating spiritual happiness." Of course, that Wilhelm himself was the supreme bishop, and that he tried so hard to bind German Protestantism to German nationalism, suggested that this was a selective understanding of the issue.[30]

While Heinrich tended to his flock, the Niemöller children attended the Elberfeld grammar school. At that time, secondary school or gymnasium began after four years of elementary school, but Martin was so bright that he was promoted to gymnasium after three grades. He was good in mathematics, in physics, in Latin, and so proficient in Greek that he and several fellow students formed a society to read Greek poetry for fun. He also loved gymnastics, which had been popular in Germany since the gymnastics movement (*Turnbewegung*) got its start as a means for physically preparing for the Wars of Liberation in the early nineteenth century. And Martin had the opportunity to travel. When he was sixteen, his parents arranged for him to spend part of his summer vacation in London as the guest of a British family, the Lumbs. The steamship voyage to England was his first experience of the sea. For a month he crisscrossed London, devouring its museums, galleries, and architecture and especially enjoying the bustling traffic he spied on the Thames River, all the while referring to the English-language dictionary that never left his hand. The Lumb family reinforced Martin's English studies in the evenings with Shakespeare readings. Two years later, in 1910, he graduated from gymnasium at the top of his class. His formal, classical education was behind him. He was off to join the navy.

"AFTER GRADUATING FROM high school," Niemöller explained, "I left my parents' house to enter the Imperial Navy and to realize the ardent longing which had filled me since childhood." Shortly before Niemöller entered the Flensburg-Mürwik Training College north of Kiel on the Baltic Sea, none other than Kaiser Wilhelm had appeared in person to inaugurate the college and celebrate the cadets' choice of career. "I love the profession, which you, my young comrades, have chosen," he announced at the opening of their new training facility. Wilhelm mused that the honor and prestige of a naval career distinguished the officer cadets from the "unpatriotic louts and scoundrels" in the German parliament.[31]

By the time Niemöller joined the navy, the arms race was in full swing. The British had upped the ante in 1905 with the construction of the 17,900-ton battleship *Dreadnought*. Mounted with ten huge cannons, the ship was nonetheless capable of high speed—twenty-one knots— thanks to its state-of-the-art steam turbine. Kaiser Wilhelm and Admiral Tirpitz responded with rapid construction of their own "dreadnoughts" and increasingly efficient U-boats (*Unterseeboot*, or undersea boat).

The growing size and sophistication of the fleet placed new demands on officers and sailors. Between 1897 and 1914, the number of naval officers grew threefold. Some 85 percent were middle-class, and most, including Niemöller, had completed the *Abitur* (college entrance exam). That the navy was the "melting pot" of Germany, as Tirpitz put it, was an exaggeration, but the navy's middle-class officer corps stood in sharp contrast to the caste-ridden army, dominated as it was by nobility. Even Tirpitz, the son of a judge, lacked noble status until Wilhelm granted it in 1900. Still, officers behaved with intolerance toward noncommissioned officers and enlisted men, many of whom were artisans with technical skills—and union members.[32]

The two hundred or so naval cadets in Niemöller's class were much like him: educated, relatively affluent, and Protestant. (One of Niemöller's middle-class Protestant classmates, Karl Dönitz, would become commander-in-chief of Hitler's navy and briefly succeed the führer as German head of state in 1945.) The cost of attending the naval training college was significant—approximately 2,000 marks per year—ruling out the lower classes, who were not, at any rate, viewed as officer material. To ensure social homogeneity, the sons of Social Democratic or trade unionist homes were barred, along with Jews, even if they could afford tuition. The number of cadets in Niemöller's class who were Catholic could be counted on one hand.[33]

Shortly after joining the navy, Niemöller and his fellow cadets took the oath of loyalty to the emperor at the Garrison Church in Kiel:

> I, Martin Niemöller, swear a personal oath to God the Almighty and
> All-knowing that I will faithfully and honorably serve His Majesty
> the German Kaiser, Wilhelm II, my Supreme War Lord, in all and any
> cases, on land and at sea, in peacetime and in wartime, regardless of
> where this may be . . . and will act in a manner proper and suitable for
> a righteous, intrepid, honor- and duty-loving soldier.

For devout and patriotic men such as Niemöller, an oath to God and kaiser was sacrosanct. Niemöller would say later in life that he considered
his oath to the kaiser binding until Wilhelm's death in 1941.[34]

Training and instruction for naval cadets took about three years. In
the first, Niemöller received six weeks of infantry training, followed by
over ten months on "school ships." He learned the arts of navigation, en-
gine tending, and stoking. During his time on the training ship *Hertha*,
his crew called at ports in the Baltic and North Seas, the Atlantic Ocean,
the Mediterranean, and the Adriatic, including such exotic locations as
Tangiers, Port Said, and Haifa. Although there was little meaningful in-
teraction with the locals in these places, just being so far from home was
an education for a young cadet raised in Lippstadt and Elberfeld.

On one voyage during his first year of training, while off the coast of
Norway, Niemöller had a pleasant surprise. When the British steamer
Midnight Sun sailed past the *Hertha*, Niemöller recorded in his log, "In
this ship my father took part in the emperor's visit to Palestine in year
1898." But his reaction to an encounter with the kaiser's yacht that same
year on the high seas was even more thrilling. As the *Hertha*'s crew
scrambled to acknowledge the passing *Hohenzollern* with a thirty-three-
gun salute, Wilhelm could be seen saluting in return from his bridge—a
moment that filled the young cadets with pride.

The second year of naval training was spent mostly at the Flensburg-
Mürwick Training School on the border of Denmark and included instruction in everything from navigation and seamanship to gymnastics
and dancing. There were even English- and French-language lessons. But
it was not as though Niemöller enjoyed a liberal arts education. Cadets

Cadet Martin Niemöller with good
friend, Herman Bremer, 1910.
(Zentralarchiv der EKHN, Darmstadt)

learned virtually nothing about politics, socioeconomic issues, or foreign cultures. When, at year's end, Niemöller took executive officer examinations, he again finished at the top of his class.

More specialized training followed in gunnery and torpedo warfare, among other areas. During his final year, Niemöller was scheduled to join the twenty-three-thousand-ton battleship *Thüringen* for additional experience at sea, but having caught the eye of superiors, he was singled out for training as a torpedo officer and, upon successful completion of this course, promoted in September 1913 to lieutenant. At the age of twenty-one, Niemöller received his officer's uniform and sword.[35]

The year 1913 was a festive one for German patriots, filled with celebrations, parades, and military pomp. Wilhelm II kicked it off with festivities marking his fifty-fourth birthday on January 27. It was also the silver jubilee of his ascendency to the throne in 1888 and, more important, the centennial of the Battle of Nations in 1813, when Prussia and her allies defeated Napoleon at Leipzig. Wilhelm announced that he wanted the festivities "to remind us in the present what we owe the Fatherland" and to stimulate in the population the same loyalty and unity their forefathers had displayed a hundred years earlier.[36]

The first major commemoration of the victory over Napoleon took place in Berlin on March 10, one hundred years to the day after King Friedrich-Wilhelm III gave his famous address "To My People," urging them to "make great sacrifices" in the war against Napoleon's Grand Army. Whereas Friedrich-Wilhelm III had addressed his message to all Prussians, Wilhelm II's 1913 address wasn't aimed at all Germans: its title was "To My Army." The emperor declared it a "holy duty" to revive the memory of the people's devotion to the Hohenzollern monarchy displayed in the "holy crusade" against Napoleon. Following subsequent commemorations in Bavaria and Leipzig, a journalist noted, "the common people completely disappear behind the spiked helmets and bayonets."[37]

Wilhelm's attempt to control the masses was only partially successful. His reign witnessed the emergence of grassroots mobilization on the left and right, political forces that were not easily harnessed by the governing elite. Wilhelm's adoration of hierarchy, evident in so much of what he said and did—"I am the sole master of German policy and my country must follow me wherever I go"—undermined any sense of genuine harmony between the monarchy and the nation. As the German Navy League enthusiast Hermann Heydweiller observed, "We are not vassals, but free citizens who are come of age."[38]

As if to punctuate this growing disconnect between state and society, the festive year of 1913 ended with a scandal, the Zabern Affair. The controversy began on October 28, when a lieutenant in the army's 99th Regiment, stationed in the Alsatian town of Zabern, used the derogatory term "*Wackes*" to refer to the local Alsatian population and encouraged his soldiers to use their bayonets if "attacked" by them. Among the native-French locals, resentment had been building since the annexation and occupation of Alsace-Lorraine by the Germans in 1871, and they did not appreciate the army's frequent troop maneuvers, military parades, and commemorations, especially on Sedan Day (*Sedantag*), when the Germans celebrated Prussia's victory over Napoleon III in 1870.[39]

Two local newspapers reported the derogatory comments. Alsatians demanded an apology. Instead, the army declared a state of emergency and arrested two dozen peaceful protesters on charges of insolence and ridiculing the military in public. When Alsace's civilian leadership and a majority of German Reichstag delegates demanded that the monarchy intercede and punish those responsible for the illegal acts, the kaiser and his generals stood solidly behind the army. Only after Chancellor Bethmann-Hollweg intervened did Wilhelm agree that the officers in charge should be held accountable, but hardly anyone was surprised when the military courts merely transferred a few of the offending officers. The Zabern Affair demonstrated the utter contempt in which the monarchy, the armed forces, and the conservative-nationalist elite held the middle and lower classes and their aspirations for a stronger voice in government.[40]

Despite the divisions, by early 1914 Germany was the leading industrial nation on the continent. It boasted the strongest army, and its naval power was second only to Britain's. It was one of the leading trading nations in the world and an active colonial master in Africa and Asia. In short, Germany was a world power. But Wilhelm's colonial expansion, naval buildup, and diplomatic blunders had alienated most European countries, in particular Britain, France, and Russia, which came together to form the Triple Entente against the Dual Alliance of Germany and Austria-Hungary. Bismarck's dictum "when there are five, try to be one of three," was lost on Wilhelm II. When war broke out in the summer of 1914, Germany was one of two, and the second was an empire in decline.[41]

Martin Niemöller wasn't concerned about this imbalance. After all, Germany had defeated France twice on the battlefield in the past century, and there was no reason to think that Russia's plodding, old-fashioned army was a match for Germany's mechanized one. The British navy might have been more powerful on paper, but the High Seas Fleet, every German sailor believed, had superior officers and discipline. Moreover, Niemöller understood that his years of naval training as well as the lessons of his father's parsonage had prepared him for the physical and spiritual challenges of the coming war. Thus, when Wilhelm II declared war against Russia on August 1 and France on August 3, Lieutenant Niemöller eagerly awaited the call to man the torpedoes and defend Germany's rightful place on the world stage.

– TWO –

Serving the Kaiser on the High Seas
(1914–1918)

T O NIEMÖLLER'S DISMAY, HE WAS STUCK DURING THE FIRST YEAR AND A half of the war keeping watch on a battleship, the *Thüringen*, moored in the North Sea port of Wilhelmshaven. "We junior sub-lieutenants dreamed of submarines, of destroyers, of airships," Niemöller recalled. It seemed unfair and dishonorable for an officer to be stranded in port, contributing so little to the war effort, while his comrades-in-arms in the army "waged the war which was draining the lifeblood of all young Germany." Some naval officers were so ashamed and frustrated that they asked for transfers to the army. At long last, in December 1915, Niemöller's hopes were finally realized. He was ordered to report on December 1 for submarine duty in Kiel, the naval port on the Baltic Sea.[1]

For the German monarchy and its supporters, the war was a struggle between the principles of Prussian-German conservatism, monarchism, and Protestantism, on the one hand, and English capitalism, French egal-itarianism, and Russian czarism, on the other. It was nothing less than a clash of civilizations. Wilhelm II's pronouncements at the beginning of the war—including "We shall show our opponents what it means to provoke Germany" and "We are all German brothers"—resonated with many in the middle and upper classes. For them, the war was an op-portunity for Germany to stand up to its hostile neighbors and achieve its rightful place as hegemon in a "new" Europe—its providential place, some thought. When we fight for victory, a Silesian pastor preached in 1914, "we are not fighting only for our people and nation, no, we are fighting in the cause of law and truth, culture and education, humanity and Christianity." Martin Niemöller shared that view.[2]

Yet, while Wilhelm II's war speeches intoxicated Niemöller and many patriotic Germans, the nation was hardly unified behind the monarchy and the coming war. Sentiment in the summer of 1914 varied across geo-graphic regions, classes, confessions, and political ideologies. Farmers in Bavaria, city dwellers in Hamburg, and townspeople in Freiburg all expressed this ambivalence. Gender was also a dividing line. The young men who voluntarily enlisted saw the war as "a rite of passage to fully fledged masculinity," but mothers, sisters, and wives feared what the war would mean for those same men eagerly rushing off to fight in it. Work-ers in particular were absent from patriotic demonstrations, choosing in the tens of thousands to attend socialist antiwar protests. The main worker party, the Social Democratic Party (SPD), voted for war financing on August 4—as did all the political parties—but unenthusiastically and without much support from the rank and file. Social Democratic leaders justified the vote as a Hobson's choice: amid the threat of "hostile inva-sion" and "Russian despotism," war was an "inexorable fact."[3]

Wilhelm II counted on the support of Protestant churches, and he got it. As Martin's younger brother later said, "In the Protestant parish houses across Germany the love of Fatherland was self-evident." Protes-tant pastors across the fatherland hailed the Reichstag's unanimous vote for war financing as the work of the Holy Spirit. One such clergyman, Pastor Walter Lehmann from Holstein, told his congregation that Germans could march off to war confident that "we have God on our side." And, lest they forget it, the young men heading off to war could look down at their belt buckles, which were inscribed with the phrase *Gott Mit Uns*—"God is with us."[4]

But military chaplains were not always popular among the troops, especially after the first months of the war. Their unabashed enthusiasm for a war they didn't have to fight left many young men in the trenches feeling misled. "The field preachers," one soldier carped, "should at least once not talk about the war, battle, courage, and trust in God, which will guarantee our victory." Another somewhat sarcastically observed, "In the morning a field chaplain encouraged us to hold out undaunted by death, in the afternoon he got drunk and was seen together with a French woman."[5]

From the outset it was hard to maintain the fiction propagated by the monarchy and the political elite that Germany was waging a defensive war against hostile neighbors. Germany may not have been solely responsible for starting the war, as the Allies would later claim, but German civilian and military leaders were eager for a war in order to gain territory on Germany's eastern and western borders, as well as new colonies, and needed only an opportunity. The assassination of Austrian archduke Franz Ferdinand in Sarajevo on June 28, 1914, by the Bosnian Serb Gavrilo Princip provided that opportunity by igniting a war between Austria, Germany's ally, and Serbia, which had close ties to France and Russia. It allowed Germany to implement its plan to win a two-front war against Russia and France, the so-called Schlieffen Plan. Named after its originator, General Alfred von Schlieffen, it called for a quick knockout blow against France and then moving troops to the eastern front to conquer Russia. Although Kaiser Wilhelm II maintained that Germany was defending itself, the Schlieffen Plan and the annexationist aims of Germany's leaders suggested a war of conquest.

Either way, Lieutenant Niemöller was absolutely committed to the effort. As he would later say, "If there is a war, a German doesn't ask is it just or unjust, but he feels bound to join the ranks." After two decades of a costly naval buildup, the war was also an opportunity for Niemöller

Lieutenant Niemöller (top, foreground) aboard a mine-laying ship shortly before the outbreak of the First World War. (United States Holocaust Memorial Museum)

and his fellow naval officers to finally prove their worth. The *Blauen Jungen* (bluejackets) couldn't wait to show off the firepower of their shiny new ships and to prove to their critics in the army that the navy was Germany's future.[6]

But as the German army advanced into France through neutral Belgium, the German navy dithered. The kaiser, his chancellor, and the chief of the High Seas Fleet felt that the timing was unpropitious for a decisive battle in the North Sea—England's Grand Fleet was too intimidating. While Germany's battleships remained in port, the British navy took immediate control of the North Sea through a blockade, which paralyzed Germany's surface fleet for the duration of the war; only submarines could subvert it. The ever-tightening blockade had devastating effects on Germany. Since Germany imported nearly half of its barley and meat and one-quarter of its milk products, food became scarce as early as June 1915, and bread rationing was instituted. The nation also imported all of its cotton, two-thirds of its copper, and three-fourths of its oil. Shortages of these materials as well as of tin, nickel, platinum, and rubber severely disrupted the war effort.[7]

With neither the Allies (France, Russia, and Great Britain) nor the Central Powers (Germany, Austria-Hungary, and the Ottoman Empire) able to score a decisive victory on the western front, the two sides dug in, building parallel trenches from the English Channel to Switzerland, and slogged it out for four long years. Despite the odds against Germany winning a war against three of Europe's great powers, the heirs of Friedrich the Great persevered. German hopes soon focused on the eastern front, where Generals Paul von Hindenburg and Erich Ludendorff successfully beat back the Russian invasion into East Prussia, earning a reputation as the invincible protectors of Germany's eastern border.

Pastors and theologians attributed Germany's survival in 1914 and 1915 to its distinctive Christian character and undying faith in God. Otto Dibelius, a pastor in Berlin, made this point in a sermon on the power of faith.

> According to mathematical necessity Germany should have been crushed in 1914 by superior power—and she is still alive. By mathematical necessity our munitions should have been exhausted by the beginning of 1915 for the lack of raw materials—and we are still shooting! By mathematical necessity we all should have starved in the summer of 1915—and we are still eating and drinking! There is a reality that evades sober calculations. And the strongest part of this reality is the power of faith.[8]

In view of the deadlock on the western front and Britain's blockade, the "U-Boat Party" in the navy advocated unrestricted submarine warfare. "We cannot allow our people to be starved out," Wilhelm II declared in February 1915 in defense of the idea. Despite the fact that the U-boat force was relatively small, German leaders decided to use it to attempt to cut off the British Isles from overseas trade. Declaring all the waters around England and Ireland to be a war zone, Admiral Hugo von Pohl, commander of the German High Seas Fleet, warned that enemy merchant ships bound for England or Ireland would be destroyed, even when it was not possible to ensure the safety of the passengers and crew. Although German U-boats would try to avoid sinking merchant ships navigated by neutral nations, it could not be guaranteed that they would not be mistaken as enemy ships, Pohl cautioned.[9]

The true danger in this new policy, some of his advisers warned, was that it might provoke the ire of the United States, which was neutral, but also an active trading partner with Britain. It did not take long for this prophecy to come true. The combined effect of sinking 787,120 tons of Allied merchant shipping in the seven-month campaign and torpedoing two British ocean liners, the *Lusitania* in May and the *Arabic* in August, resulting in the loss of over 2,000 passengers and crewmen, including 131 Americans, enraged President Woodrow Wilson. He condemned the use of submarines against merchant and civilian ships, stating that German submarine warfare violated "many sacred principles of justice and humanity." Berlin reluctantly called off unrestricted submarine warfare in September 1915—lest it incite the Americans to actively join the Allied powers. Admiral Tirpitz strenuously opposed this decision, to the point that he tendered his resignation.[10]

IT WAS AMID this confusion over naval policy that Niemöller reported in December 1915 for duty in Kiel. "I now left behind me the happiest days of my youth and the best friends of those days," he later wrote. "The serious purpose of life and the grim realities of war were to begin for me." In February 1916, when the German army launched its attack on Verdun, Niemöller was assigned to a large mine-laying submarine, the *U73*. It had the capacity to launch torpedoes, but because of its limited speed it was unlikely to ever have the opportunity. Heavily damaged by severe weather in the North Sea, it had been nicknamed the "floating coffin" because of its impairment and other shortcomings. Finally, at the end of March 1916, after weeks of repair, the *U73* was ready for its next mission: laying mines in hostile ports in the Mediterranean. Before it embarked,

Niemöller was promoted to senior lieutenant. On April 1, the *U73* made a nocturnal passage from the Baltic Sea to the North Sea through the Kiel Canal, stopped at Cuxhaven to take on thirty-four mines, and—avoiding the heavily protected English Channel—headed north past the Shetland Islands and into the Atlantic Ocean. "This was how our 'Christian cruise' began!" Niemöller would write in his memoir on the war.[11]

In April and May, the *U73*'s mines sank six ships, including the massive British warship *Russell*, killing 125 men. When the *U73* arrived at the Austro-Hungarian naval base at Cattaro (present-day Kotor, Montenegro) in the north Adriatic for repairs, the eighty-seven-year-old Austrian emperor Franz Joseph had the crew decorated for its exploits. "Our joy was real and very great," Niemöller later said.[12]

While at Cattaro, Niemöller's crew learned of the great Battle of Jutland off the coast of Denmark, where nearly 250 British and German ships, including dreadnoughts, fought what would turn out to be the largest naval encounter of World War I. In this old-style battle between surface ships, the Germans inflicted greater losses than they suffered, but it was in no way the decisive victory Tirpitz had striven for, and it did nothing to alter the balance of power at sea.[13]

When the new commander of the High Seas Fleet, Admiral Reinhard Sheer, submitted his report on the battle to the kaiser, he confessed that, despite the victory, the German navy could never hope to defeat the British navy or even bring the British blockade to an end. He concluded, "A victorious end to the war . . . can only be looked for by the crushing of English economic life through U-boat action against English commerce." The impotence of the surface fleet led to another year and a half of idleness for the big ships.[14]

The sheer brutality of the land war stands out when one considers that the Battle of Jutland resulted in "only" about 9,800 British and German casualties. By contrast, a month later, on the first day of the Battle of the Somme, combined British and German casualties exceeded 65,000. By the end of the war, the German armed forces had suffered approximately two million deaths, of which fewer than 35,000 were navy men. Whether these men died in the ground war or on the high seas,

Niemöller personally felt their deaths. Of the twenty-three classmates who passed final high school examinations with him in 1910, only five survived the war.[15]

In the summer and fall of 1916, the *U73* laid underwater mines in the Aegean. By Christmas the crew was celebrating the sinking of another nine ships. Three more managed to limp away after sustaining damage. "Revenge," the Protestant pastor's son said, "is sweet." Niemöller bragged in his memoirs that one of their mines near the Greek island of Kea "had bagged the British hospital ship *Britannic*," the sister of *Titanic*, taking thirty lives. It was at that time the largest Allied ship sunk in the war.[16]

In January 1917, Niemöller took a temporary commission on the *U39* as coxswain while the *U73* underwent extensive repairs. Unlike the *U73*, the *U39* was "a real submarine, with plenty of torpedoes," and she had a seasoned crew. Life aboard the *U39* was also more dangerous, for a torpedo boat seeks its prey, while a mine-layer need not be anywhere near the enemy. The experienced Captain Lieutenant Walter Forstmann, recipient of Prussia's highest military award, the *Pour le Mérite*, commanded it. By the end of the war, the *U39* was the second most successful U-boat in the German fleet, sinking a total of 153 ships.[17]

After sinking two British steamers in the eastern Mediterranean in January, the *U39* headed to the Ionian Sea. On January 28, the crew spied two French troop ships escorted by three destroyers. *What a chance for us!*, Niemöller thought. They immediately torpedoed the troop ship *Amiral Magon*, with 935 soldiers and 80 crew members on board. It sank in ten minutes. While one of the destroyers sought to rescue the men from the water, the other two sped off with the second troop ship. The *U39* stayed in the vicinity, attempting unsuccessfully to sink the remaining destroyer. "All we could do is put up our periscope here and there, to prevent the destroyer from picking up too many survivors," Niemöller later wrote. "War is war!" The entire crew of the *U39*, Captain Forstmann recalled, "was proud of its deed." The whole purpose of war, Forstmann asserted, was "to annihilate the enemy's armed forces." The people being picked up out of the water after all were soldiers bound for the front, soldiers who would not hesitate to kill Germans. After the *Amiral Magon* had slipped

A U-boat officer in His Majesty's Imperial Navy, Niemöller poses with his Iron Cross medal, 1917. (Zentralarchiv der EKHN, Darmstadt)

beneath the surface along with 203 French soldiers and crew members, the *U39* made for home, where Niemöller was awarded the Iron Cross First Class. "I wore my 'Iron Cross I' with a feeling that I had earned it."[18]

The crew could rest assured that, according to German Protestant war theology, their actions didn't make them bad Christians. One of the hallmarks of Protestant preaching during the Great War was a just-war theory holding that a soldier could kill to protect his family, home, and country—especially from enemies so treacherous as the British, French, and Russians—and still be a good Christian. To be sure, there were pacifists among the Protestant pastorate who preached that war ran counter to the Christian command to love one's neighbor, but they were few and far between. The clergy more often praised soldiers for their willingness to sacrifice for God and country. As one pastor put it, the German soldier was fighting to protect all that was sacred, "land and people, wife and child, *Volk* and fatherland." Walter Lehmann, the Holstein pastor, preached, "He who in these days sets forth to defend the German hearth, sets forth in a holy fight."[19]

According to Lehmann, the German soldier's purpose went beyond defending family and fatherland. God was using the Great War and German soldiers to accomplish his will. "Germany," he declared, "is the center of God's plans for the world." The object of the war, Pastor Johann Rump from Berlin asserted, "is to prepare the way for carrying the Gospel to the nations." In a sermon to soldiers, Rump assured them that "God in heaven looks down upon you German men and youths. You shall be his warriors, called to a costly crusade against barbarism and cunning, bestiality and fraud. . . . You are the armed priesthood of our German sanctuary. . . . You are not only fighting 'with God,' but also 'for God.'"[20]

Niemöller believed that the deaths of soldiers and civilians were an unpleasant but necessary consequence of the war. "I accepted all the horrors of the war as a matter of course and without being shaken to the depths of my soul," he said after the war. What did weigh on his mind was the fate of his fatherland: the war that was supposed to be over by Christmas 1914 showed no signs of abating after two and a half years.[21]

IT WAS TO Niemöller's chagrin that he spent the eventful spring of 1917 on dry land. He desperately wanted command of his own U-boat, but again he found himself landlocked, this time in a wireless-deciphering course in Tøndern, Denmark. This was all the more irritating because German leaders, realizing that morale was collapsing and casualties were mounting, had decided to strike a decisive blow against England by renewing unrestricted submarine warfare on February 1 and to prosecute it "with the utmost energy."[22]

The logic behind this decision was that, with Russia in disarray and France on the brink of collapse, the real power behind the Allied war effort was Britain. And along with that power came an obvious vulnerability: Britain's dependency on comestible imports, especially wheat. German naval commanders calculated that, as of December 1916, Britain had only fifteen weeks' worth of food left, and that they could sink enough merchant ships to starve England into submission in six months.

Advocates of this new campaign insisted that, unlike the previous unrestricted campaign, this one would need to be truly boundless—all ships, enemy or neutral, were to be sunk without warning. This campaign would last from February 1917 to November 1918.[23]

The decision had immediate repercussions. On February 3, the United States severed relations with Germany. Two months later, on April 6, 1917, after U-boats had sunk 1,140,000 tons of shipping, the United States declared war on Germany.[24]

Niemöller, meanwhile, had received orders to report to the admiralty in Berlin to temporarily replace a junior civil servant who was on sick leave. He did not take to office work. "I detested pen-pusher's work . . . and not unnaturally considered such an occupation below the dignity of a combatant naval officer fit for service in war time."[25]

One advantage of being in Berlin, however, was that he could court Else Bremer, the older sister of his good friend and former schoolmate Hermann Bremer. Else, the oldest daughter of a medical doctor, was born in Elberfeld in 1890. When Heinrich Niemöller moved his family to Elberfeld in 1900, Martin and Hermann became best friends, and the two families enjoyed socializing together. Hermann followed Martin into the navy, becoming an officer as well. In 1916, the two young officers took a leave together to visit their families in Elberfeld, during which Martin spent an evening enjoying Else's company. "Rarely have I been so happy as on this evening," she recorded in her diary. The mutual attraction grew during Niemöller's time at the admiralty in Berlin. On Sundays, when Else wasn't busy studying for a philosophy degree to prepare for a teaching job, they would see each other, often sailing on the Wannsee or the Havel. "This renewal of our friendship of our childhood days," Niemöller fondly remembered, "was followed by a regular exchange of letters and ended in our engagement a year later."[26]

During Niemöller's time away from the action, German U-boats ravaged Allied and neutral shipping. April 1917 saw the greatest losses of the war: 458 ships, with a combined weight of 841,118 tons.[27]

The success of German submarine warfare forced the British to develop increasingly sophisticated means to detect and destroy U-boats. "It must be admitted that the British have learned a thing or two by now," Niemöller noted. "They hunt us with hydrophones, which pick up the beat of our engines, and when they think themselves close enough they drop depth charges." Under these new conditions, it was a challenge for a U-boat commander to get close enough to a merchant steamer to torpedo it. They ran the risk of being detected and attacked by enemy warships patrolling the trade routes and escorting merchant ships. With the introduction of a convoy system by the British in late May, sinkings by U-boats fell off markedly. Moreover, the convoy system enabled the transportation of over two million American doughboys across the Atlantic and to the front in eighteen months, a feat German military leaders had believed would take twice as long.[28]

Niemöller did not have to stay ashore long. After a few months, he was assigned to the *U151*, which set sail for the Azores in the fall of 1917. "Our thoughts turn to our dear ones at home and then to the front where our brothers and friends are fighting and dying on the field of battle," he wrote. "O Germany, may your honor ever be maintained!" Between September and December, the *U151* damaged or sank seventeen ships, including the captured and then scuttled Norwegian steamer *Johan Mjelde*, from which the crew seized twenty-two tons of bar copper—exceedingly valuable and sorely needed in blockaded Germany. By the time the *U151* returned to its base in Kiel on Christmas Day 1917, it had completed the longest cruise of any German submarine in World War I: 114 days and nearly 12,000 miles. The kaiser himself awarded the commander the *Pour le Mérite* and invited all the officers of the *U151* to spend four weeks of R&R in Garmisch-Partenkirchen in Bavaria. "What a different world," marveled Niemöller.[29]

After so much time at sea, the crew was inundated with news on their return to shore. Niemöller was relieved to learn that brother Wilhelm, injured for the third time on the western front, was recuperating well. Also welcome was the news that Russia had withdrawn from the war after Lenin's Bolshevik revolution in October 1917. Germany's beleaguered army then redeployed thirty-three divisions to the western front, where the

Germans would now enjoy numerical superiority over the Allies. While victory over Russia was something to celebrate, the specter of Lenin and his Communist firebrands destroying a traditional monarchy must have been unsettling to a conservative such as Niemöller.

Indeed, this was an especially challenging time for German monarchists. The state's unprecedented mobilization of more than thirteen million men and the requisitioning of food, fuel, and other matériel for the war had left most Germans in a precarious position. Even before the "turnip winter" of 1916–1917, the German newspaper *Vorwärts* was reporting that "in Berlin, thousands of people battle daily for a tiny quantity of meat or lard." Women and children were forced to wait in food lines, grow their own food on scarce land, and scavenge in the countryside. In response to the cereal shortages caused by the blockade, Germans had been using potatoes, an indigenous German crop, to supplement grains in the making of bread. But that winter the potato famine of 1916 left turnips as the principal food. Prices of basic foods increased 800 percent, and many Germans were forced to live on less than a thousand calories a day. Soup kitchens did their best to feed the starving, but infant and female mortality rose by 50 percent. Collapsing from hunger or freezing to death waiting in a food line was "a prominent symbol of the time." People were slowly starving to death. In March 1917, working-class women in Berlin demonstrated under a bright banner reading, CURSE THE KING, THE KING OF THE RICH.[30]

When Martin Niemöller returned to port in December 1917, the reality that "dire want dominates every aspect of life at home" was appallingly apparent. The situation grew worse the following year when the Allied blockade tightened further. To make a deplorable situation even worse, the worldwide influenza pandemic of 1918 caused the mortality rate among women to double compared to 1913. By the end of the war, over seven hundred thousand German civilians had died of malnutrition and disease. Meanwhile, the mounting number of dead and disabled soldiers brought further hardship and disillusionment to the home front.[31]

For many among the hungry masses, the 1917 revolutions in Russia aroused hope that the war's end was in sight and that domestic reform was possible. Workers and activists were emboldened to take matters into their own hands. There were 240 worker strikes in 1916, and 562 in 1917. The fragile domestic unity of 1914 was unraveling amid increasingly radicalized worker opposition.[32]

A splinter faction of Socialists—frustrated by the failure of the moderate Socialists in the Social Democratic Party to unilaterally and unequivocally oppose the war—broke off from the SPD in 1917. They formed a new party, the Independent Social Democratic Party (USPD), which was less interested in bringing about reform through parliament than with mass action against the conservative monarchy. That these radical leftists greeted the revolutions in Russia enthusiastically was no surprise. "The revolution has triumphed in Russia," they exclaimed. "We too will gain victory when our turn comes!" The USPD leader Hugo Haase proclaimed, "The dawn of freedom shines across the Russian frontiers into this hall. We are full of admiration for our Russian brothers fighting for peace and freedom." Demonstrating the USPD's standing were the nearly one million industrial workers they turned out for a mass strike in the munitions and metal plants of Berlin between January 28 and February 4, 1918.[33]

The war had thoroughly divided the nation. To the distress of the monarchy and pro-war political parties, it wasn't just civilians turning against the war and the kaiser. After catastrophic losses at Verdun and the Somme in 1916—termed "idiotic reciprocal mass murder" by one German officer—morale in the army deteriorated precipitously. The miserable life in the trenches took its toll on soldiers, most of whom were working-class conscripts already lacking in patriotic ardor. Standing for hours, sometimes days, knee-deep in mud as barrage after barrage hit their trenches, and surrounded by stinking, decomposing corpses, all the while fighting off rats, fleas, and lice, many soldiers concluded that an immediate cessation to the war was preferable to the distant prospect of victory.[34]

Wilhelm II's notion of "we are all German brothers" died on the western front in 1916, if it ever existed in the first place. Another slogan, this one attached to a train carrying reinforcements to the western front, crystallized the spreading discontent: WE DO NOT FIGHT FOR GERMANY'S HONOR, WE FIGHT FOR THE MILLIONAIRES! Desertion had been minimal in the first two years of war but rose markedly in 1917 and 1918, eventually depriving the army of some 750,000 men.[35]

Morale in the Imperial Navy was no better. One sailor, Joachim Rigelnatz, pined in 1917, "Oh, how I wish the war were finally over! For my part I would not care if we suffered a great defeat if it would only help us to obtain a halfway acceptable peace." Idleness, war-weariness, abysmal food, gnawing hunger, horrible living conditions, draconian discipline, and resentment over the disparity between the conditions of officers and enlisted men resulted in conflict on a number of German ships.[36]

The British blockade and bad harvests had led to a drastic reduction in the bread ration for the common sailor, who then was expected to endure on a regular diet of turnips and rutabagas, which in turn led to pent-up resentment toward officers, who still enjoyed meat. The end result was that many crews went on strike for better food and treatment. Notably, submarines were free of such encounters, probably because they were so busy sinking enemy shipping.[37]

Collective resistance by these lower-level navy personnel did not always result in court-martials or the brig. Many officers, perhaps too ashamed to bring attention to the rebellion on their own ships, gave in to strikers' demands. When stokers, who toiled in grimy coal bunkers feeding blazing furnaces, refused to perform their duties on the battleship *Friedrich der Grosse* because their soap ration was severely reduced, the officers in charge were forced to give in. And when the cooks on the *Prinzregent Luitpold* served a particularly revolting meal, the crew went on a brief hunger strike demanding decent rations. The first officer on the ship tried to impose discipline, but he too relented and told the cooks to prepare something edible.[38]

When sailors mutinied, however, navy leaders sent an unequivocal message. In August, about six hundred sailors walked off the battleship *Prinzregent* for three hours to protest arbitrary punishments meted out to some of their comrades. The leader of the walkout, stoker Albin Köbis, gave a brief speech that concluded, "We are the true patriots! Down with the war! We no longer want to fight this war!" The navy handed down five death sentences, two of which were carried out on September 5. Köbis was one of the mutineers executed by firing squad. About seventy-five sailors were imprisoned, sentenced to a combined total of 360 years of penal servitude. Rather than attempt to understand the sources of rebellion among enlisted men, the navy blamed Socialist agitators, and the top brass clamped down even more on political activity among sailors.[39]

IT WAS IN this context that Niemöller finally took command of his own U-boat, the *U67*, in the summer of 1918. His orders were to lay a minefield off Marseilles and destroy enemy ships plying the Mediterranean. On July 6, the *U67* torpedoed the steamer *Bertrand* in the waters between Tunisia and Sicily. With his first mission as a U-boat commander a success, he returned the *U67* to Pola, at the tip of the Istrian peninsula, for repairs. Niemöller took this opportunity to travel to Berlin to propose to Else Bremer, or as he later put it, "to get the promised yes from the girl I loved." The wedding was set for Christmas 1918.[40]

On the western front, the German army had launched a series of aggressive maneuvers beginning in March. By July, when the spring offensive ended, the German army had suffered in the range of a million casualties without achieving a breakthrough. Kaiser Wilhelm II was still attempting to inspire the masses with talk of divine will; in June he declared the German Volk "the chosen people," and added, "The Jews who used to be are no longer." Reinforced by the arrival of American troops, the Allies counterattacked "the chosen people" on August 8. General Ludendorff dubbed it the German army's "Black Day." What later came to be known as the Hundred Days Offensive would culminate with Germany's surrender in November.[41]

Even as the reality of defeat set in, Niemöller burned passionately for the fatherland. "If there ever was heroism displayed in the war—apart from the contempt of death shown in its opening weeks—it was in the closing stages," he would write, "when it was no longer a question of victory or honor, but just the stern sense of a warrior's duty which prompted action. The mere fact that this sense of duty was still alive, after four dreary years of fighting, gave hope to many like myself for the future of our people." Niemöller carried out his duty well after German defeat was a foregone conclusion. On September 29, Ludendorff informed the kaiser that Germany could not win the war and asked that a new liberal government negotiate an armistice to prevent a disaster. Yet Niemöller and many other naval officers were keen "to stick it out" and "strive for conditions which might bring us bearable peace terms"—that is, to sink enough Allied ships to enter negotiations from a position of strength. Indeed, late that month, his U-boat sank two cargo ships, one British and one Greek, killing nineteen people in total.[42]

On September 30, under pressure to demonstrate a willingness to reform, the kaiser appointed the liberal prince Max von Baden as chancellor. For perhaps the first time during the war, Niemöller was at odds with the government. The Allies would soon break through the Hindenburg Line, forcing German troops to retreat to their nation's western border. Under such conditions, there was little reason to believe that torpedoing more Allied ships would ensure more "bearable" peace terms. The new reform-minded government, which included Social Democrats, believed that the Allies would be more lenient if the war was brought to an immediate conclusion and the conservative Prussian-German state replaced by a liberal democratic republic like the United States, Britain, and France.

Chancellor von Baden spent October asking US president Woodrow Wilson for a "restoration of peace." Von Baden also submitted to the Reichstag legislation that would reform Germany's autocratic monarchy into a democratic, parliamentary monarchy. This "revolution from above" was realized on October 26, when the Reichstag agreed to revise Bismarck's constitution. The hated three-tier voting system was abolished, ministers were made responsible to the parliament, and command over the army and navy was wrested from the kaiser and turned over to civilian authorities.

Though it was clear that the war was lost and that the democratic forces were now in charge, the commanders and officers of the *Blauen Jungen* weren't ready to give up their fight. The utter failure of the Imperial Navy throughout the war was more than the admirals could tolerate. Germany's Supreme Navy Command made the alarming decision, without government authorization, to launch a final "death sortie" against the combined British and American navies in the North Sea.

By launching the whole German navy in a final sortie against Britain's hated Grand Fleet, German naval leaders intended to offset their own humiliation by going down in battle. As one stoker observed, the officers preferred "a heroic defeat of the fleet to its surrender." If the navy did nothing, the reasoning went, it would have to suffer the greatest embarrassment of all: handing over its pristine fleet to the British as reparations. A navy "shackled by a humiliating peace," the chief of staff of the High Seas Fleet proclaimed, "shall have no future."[43]

In late October, the navy sent out secret orders "to get all seaworthy boats ready to return to Germany forthwith in order to make them available for a last stand." The rest were to be scuttled. Able ships were to assemble in the North Sea off Wilhelmshaven. Niemöller's U-boat was one of the half-dozen inoperative subs scheduled to be sunk in the Adriatic, but at the last moment he was able to return it to seaworthy status. On October 29, the same day Austria-Hungary requested an armistice, Niemöller steered the *U67* from its Adriatic port in Pola and prepared to sail for the North Sea.[44]

Niemöller was not opposed to the order, though he held little hope of it changing the course of the war. "The fact that this critical time was chosen by the German people to indulge in a suicidal orgy of internal strife was the great crime of the year 1918," Niemöller would later write. According to the conventional conservative line after the war, defeat was not the result of the Allies' superior armed forces but rather of the self-interest of German liberals and leftists, who placed their political victory over their nation's victory in the war. The legend that internal enemies "stabbed Germany in the back" holds little truth. Germany simply lacked the men and matériel, not to mention the desire, to keep fighting.[45]

The naval leadership's plans for a final sortie failed to account for the war-weariness of the enlisted men. On ship after ship in the ports of Wilhelmshaven and Kiel, sailors refused to leave their moorings. Naval command had no choice but to call off the sortie. Officers may have seen something heroic and honorable in going down with their ships, but most sailors just wanted to go home.

The naval mutiny turned into revolution on November 3, when military police trying to reestablish order in Kiel killed nine demonstrators and wounded twenty-nine others. Enraged sailors ripped the epaulettes off the uniforms of officers and took their swords away, symbolically stripping them of their authority. And they hoisted the red flag of the revolution over their ships. Within days the revolution spread through Germany via the nation's rail network. Red sailors, soldiers, and workers formed democratic councils and demanded peace, the abdication of Wilhelm II, a democratic republic, and freedom of the press. As the revolution moved south and east, the council movement took control of city after city, rapidly forcing the abdication of the twenty-two federal princes, beginning with the king of Bavaria on November 8. By the following day, when the revolution reached Berlin, Chancellor von Baden announced that Wilhelm II had abdicated under protest and handed over the chancellery's keys to the Social Democratic leader Friedrich Ebert. Germany was now a democratic republic with a socialist government. One of its first acts was to secure an armistice on "the eleventh hour of the eleventh day of the eleventh month."[46]

Niemöller was still navigating his U-boat through the Mediterranean on his way to the Atlantic when the kaiser abdicated and the republic was declared. Although the final suicide sortie would never happen, Niemöller took heart in the "extremely gallant attack" by his sister sub, the *U52*, on the British battleship *Britannia* that same day. *Britannia* was the last ship to be sunk in the war and took fifty men to the bottom of the sea with her.[47]

It wasn't until November 29 that Niemöller's U-boat and ten others arrived in Kiel, having made the long journey around the British Isles. In contrast to the docked ships and U-boats flying the red flag of the revolution, the eleven U-boats sailed into port flying the black-white-and-red ensign of the Imperial German Navy. Their commanders "paid off" (decommissioned their ships) immediately on arrival—the better, Niemöller wrote, "to avoid any risk of the red flags being hoisted on our boats."[48]

THREE

From U-Boat to Pulpit
(1918–1933)

I<small>N</small> S<small>EPTEMBER</small> 1918, <small>WHEN</small> N<small>IEMÖLLER'S</small> <small>SUBMARINE RETURNED TO</small> the port of Pola after its last mission in the Mediterranean, he learned that Hermann Bremer, his best friend and his fiancée's younger brother by one year, was missing in the Irish Sea. The confirmation of his death that autumn added to Niemöller's grim outlook. He and Else postponed their December wedding to mourn their loss.[1]

The reality of their defeat in the First World War was hard for most Germans to accept. Unable to admit that they had lost on the battle-field, the military and political leaders who had thrown caution to the wind in 1914 and aggressively pursued a war of annexation were now placing responsibility for the outcome on liberals, leftists, and Jews who had nothing to do with the war's design. The myth that Germany had been stabbed in the back by these elements shifted blame away from the real culprits—Kaiser Wilhelm II, his general staff, and the admiralty. Throughout the next fourteen years of Germany's "experiment" with democracy, German elites continued to refuse to take responsibility for the war and its devastating economic consequences.

Although it was officially still the German Empire (*Deutsches Reich*), the state that existed from 1919 to 1933 is commonly known as the Weimar Republic, or just Weimar, after the town 140 miles southwest of Berlin where the new democratic constitution was drafted. The authors of that constitution met in Weimar to avoid the revolutionary upheaval taking place in Berlin. Weimar was also Germany's cultural mecca, the town where eminent authors, composers, and artists including Bach, Goethe, and Schiller had lived and worked. As the spiritual and artistic opposite of militaristic Prussia, Weimar symbolized the new beginning of a liberal, democratic Germany.[2]

Martin Niemöller was not one of the conservatives persuaded to give Weimar a chance. For many committed Lutherans, the replacement of the monarchy with a government based on the will of the people was not just repugnant politically but also, and far worse, an affront to God. Government by the people ignored the most basic truth about mankind: the reality of human sin.

For Lutherans, life took place in two separate spheres or realms. One was spiritual, embodied in the church, and the other was temporal, the everyday world. In the sixteenth century, Luther had insisted that because the kingdom of God and the kingdom of this world had distinctive characteristics—the one eternal, spiritual, and heavenly; the other finite, secular, and fallen—they had to be to governed by different means. God was lord over both kingdoms, but His method of rule varied. In the spiritual kingdom, He ruled through the Gospel and the Holy Spirit; in the worldly kingdom, He ruled through divinely appointed human authorities who applied law and force to maintain order in a sinful world. After all, the Gospel alone could not hold lawlessness in check. That required the sword—though the sword could not teach people how to be God-fearing Christians. Though separate, the two kingdoms served each other. By maintaining law and order, temporal rulers provided a safe space in which to preach the Gospel. And by preaching the Gospel to all mankind, the church continually reminded temporal rulers and their subjects of God's kingdom and their higher Christian calling.

To pious Germans, the French, Russian, and German revolutions were rebellions against God and His sanctioned rulers on earth. Whether the new rulers were selected by political fiat or the ballot box, God's power was being usurped. Protestant Church leaders blamed thinkers like Karl Marx and Jean-Jacques Rousseau for propagating delusions about the nobility of man and the sovereignty of the people. Niemöller's sympathies lay unequivocally with the German monarchy. As a proud naval officer, he had sworn to God that he would loyally serve Kaiser Wilhelm II in war and in peace. Only with the exiled kaiser's death in 1941 did Niemöller feel free of his oath.[3]

In the aftermath of the socialist revolution, Niemöller allowed his conscience to guide him. In January 1919, for instance, he refused an order to tow two German submarines to England as reparations. Full of indignation, he recalled years later, he rushed to his superior's office and announced, "I have sailed in submarines for three years, fighting against England, sir; I have neither sought nor concluded this armistice. As far as I am concerned, the people who promised our submarines to England can take them over. I will not do it!" The armistice required that the boats be turned over, but since Niemöller's superior was of a similar mind, he was not docked for insubordination.[4]

Niemöller realized that this would not be the last order to conflict with his ideals of "truth and honor." The revolution and the new German republic filled him with bitterness and sorrow. "I could not reconcile myself to serving the new state as it was being constituted," he later wrote. "For the time being, I did not even wish to remain in Germany; my love for my country was temporarily shaken and obscured." He resigned his naval commission on March 27, 1919.[5]

Free corps recruiting poster: "Guard against the External and Internal Enemy!" (Poster Collection, GE 532, Hoover Institution Archives)

Twenty-seven years old and adrift, Niemöller began pondering his options. One that attracted him was to keep fighting as a member of the *Freikorps*, a volunteer right-wing paramilitary unit. The free corps was comprised of armed and demobilized officers and troops unified by shared hatred of the left-leaning Weimar Republic. Ernst von Salomon, a free corps fighter, recalled the group's mentality: "They had not yet got over the war. War had molded them; it had given a meaning to their lives and a reason for their existence. They were unruly and untamed, beings apart, who gathered themselves into little companies animated by a desire to fight." This mentality was in stark contrast to many troops who, after four years of hardship and bloodshed, sympathized with the workers' revolutionary platform.[6]

In a potent illustration of the axiom that the "enemy of my enemy is my friend," the free corps joined the Social Democratic chancellor and future president Friedrich Ebert in violently suppressing Communist uprisings, which sought to replace the moderate socialist government with one akin to the Bolshevik government in Russia. In mid-January 1919, the free corps brutally assassinated Rosa Luxemburg and Karl Liebknecht, the leaders of the Communist movement, known at the time as Spartacists. Later that spring they ruthlessly crushed the leftist republic founded by the Jewish independent socialist Kurt Eisner in Bavaria. An anti-Semitic Bavarian nobleman sympathetic to the free corps shot Eisner dead in the street. Although the army and the free corps were willing to align temporarily with the republican leaders, their ultimate goal was to overthrow the socialist republic and replace it with conservative rule.

By 1920, about 250,000 veterans had joined approximately 120 free corps. With ex-naval officers especially prominent in their ranks, the free corps offered Niemöller the camaraderie he so desired. He shared their virulent anti-Communism and belief in the stab-in-the-back myth. His former naval instructor, Admiral Löwenfeld, organized one of the largest free corps units, eventually reaching more than 6,000 strong, and invited Niemöller to join. The ultrareactionary nature of the free corps appealed to Niemöller, and he gave serious consideration to joining them. But he was engaged to be married, and the free corps didn't strike him as a career for a future husband and father.[7]

Another possibility he considered seriously was immigrating to Argentina and becoming a sheep farmer, a move many disenchanted German naval officers made after the Weimar revolution. "Overnight the Argentine seemed to be the promised land for some hundreds of us," he wrote. "I hastened to devote all my spare evenings to learning Spanish and to making inquiries about living conditions and prospects." However, the logistics of moving to South America proved too daunting.[8]

Moreover, leaving Germany would deny him any role in shaping the new Germany according to the Protestant national ideals he believed his country needed now more than ever. In his 1934 memoir of this period, he remembered wanting to influence his fatherland's "morality and manners."[9]

As Niemöller awaited an opportunity to put his idealism to work, he took a job as a farmhand in a small Westphalian village in the region of Tecklenburg, southwest of Wersen. He and Else married on Easter Sunday 1919; his father performed the service in Elberfeld. Since there was no room for Else in the farmhouse, she lived with relatives nearly five miles away in Westerkappeln and saw her husband only on weekends. "I had a married life like that of a naval officer," the new bridegroom explained. "On service during the week, at home from Friday to Monday."[10]

Soon after Martin married Else and took up farming, Germany's hopes of a peace treaty based on President Woodrow Wilson's conciliatory Fourteen Points were dashed. In June, the Allies forced the new government to accept the Versailles *Diktat*, as Germans called the treaty. Particularly loathsome was Article 231, which stipulated that Germany accept full responsibility for starting the war and thus for all losses suffered by the Allied powers. This amounted to 132 billion gold marks, or $31.4 billion, to be paid in several stages. The assignment of guilt, the enormous reparations bill, and the loss of significant territory to Poland outraged Germans, most of whom believed that they had fought a defensive war and were the true victims.

The Germans' righteous indignation knew no bounds of class, political party, or religious conviction. Socialist chancellor Philipp Scheidemann referred to the Versailles Treaty as "a murderous plan." "What hand would not wither" that signed such a document, he asked. He resigned in protest, leaving his successor, also a Social Democrat, to put his name to it. Protestant Church authorities spoke for many Germans when they declared, "The demand that we accept sole guilt for the war places a lie on our lips that shamelessly affronts our conscience. As Evangelical Christians we ceremoniously raise before God and men the holy protest against the attempt to press this scar on our nation."[11]

The Allies also demanded that the German army be reduced to a mere one hundred thousand lightly armed men, the navy to fifteen thousand sailors, and the free corps disbanded entirely. Many of the men who were dismissed as a result had no career to fall back on, adding to their misery. In all, Germany lost in the treaty 13 percent of its territory, 12 percent of its population, 48 percent of its iron industry, 16 percent of its coal production, 80 percent of its naval fleet, all of its colonies, and, as far as the people were concerned, all of its dignity.

Appalled by the election of the moderate socialist government in January, the signing of the Versailles Treaty in June, and the adoption of a progressive constitution in August, Niemöller focused on tilling, hoeing, and harvesting. While he took great pride in his profession—it had also been his great-grandfather's, in Wersen—he still felt the urge to serve his country. He considered a career as a teacher but worried that the socialist government would not allow him to speak his mind.

For reasons that are not clear, Niemöller did not give serious thought immediately after the war to following his father into the clergy. He certainly remained a loyal churchgoer. Martin and Else worshiped every Sunday at either the small village church in Wersen—where his father had been born and his grandfather had been schoolmaster and organist—or at the church in Westerkappeln, where Martin's mother had been baptized and confirmed. It was a chance evening encounter with one of the Westerkappeln pastors that sparked Niemöller's memory of a night, late in the war, aboard the *U67*, when he had mused with his comrades about a postwar career in the church. Although it had been nothing more than a passing thought at the time, by late 1919 it seemed clear that this was the solution.

By donning the collar, he thought, he could serve God and country with little worry about interference from the state. Although the November 1918 revolution had overthrown Kaiser Wilhelm II and replaced the monarchy with a democratic republic, it was only a partial revolution in that it did not attempt to dislodge the established elites. Instead, President Ebert's moderate socialist government sought a *modus vivendi* with the armed forces, business leaders, landowners, and churches. In regard to the churches, the Weimar constitution allowed them to retain their privileged position and guaranteed that the state would not interfere in their operations. "My boy, the freest profession in the whole world today," his father assured him at the time, "is that of Protestant pastor." In hindsight, this paternal optimism was laden with irony. The socialist republic, detested by clerics, kept its promise of non-interference in church affairs, while the subsequent Nazi government, eagerly awaited by many churchmen, did just the opposite.[12]

Niemöller freely admitted that it wasn't theology but the possibility of German renewal through Christianity that drew him to the clergy:

> I had no particular liking for theology as a science for the solution of problems. But I had, in my own life, seen cases where the hearing of the Word and the belief in Christ as our Lord and Savior had made men live anew and become free and strong. This teaching was one I took with me from the home of my childhood days and I had clung to it through all the vicissitudes of life. For that reason I felt I could serve my people with an honest and open heart, helping them better in their present hopeless state than I could by withdrawing to a farm and living the life I had intended to live there.

Recalling his ordination on June 29, 1924, in Münster's Church of the Redeemer, Niemöller wrote, "The journey from submarine to pulpit was completed and my service for my people and native country, in my new profession, was beginning." In short, he joined the ranks of the Lutheran Church for the same reason he had joined the Imperial German Navy: to advance the cause of the fatherland.[13]

Niemöller began his studies in January 1920 at the University of Münster. He did not find it easy to go back to studying, especially with Else pregnant and the prospect of a newborn in a few months. That year would be one of the most volatile for the young couple and for the young republic. Having suppressed Communist revolts in Berlin and Munich, the free corps now turned their guns on the moderate socialist government—the "November criminals" who had signed the despised *Diktat*. In February, General Walther von Lüttwitz, "father of the free corps," refused a state order to disband his troops as stipulated in the Versailles Treaty and prepared to march on Berlin with the Ehrhardt brigade. Headed up by a naval officer, the Ehrhardt brigade had its origins in the suppression of the Spartacist uprising in Wilhelmshaven and was considered the best-organized and -trained free corps in postwar Germany. The plan was to overthrow the government and establish a military dictatorship with the right-wing politician Wolfgang Kapp as head of state.[14]

On the morning of March 13, 1920, the Ehrhardt brigade entered Berlin unopposed to escort Kapp into the chancellery. The coup-makers found the building empty. The Social Democratic party leadership had fled Berlin and called a general strike to block the Kapp government. "Paralyze all economic activity! Proletarians unite! Down with the Counter-Revolution!" The strike was so thorough that it paralyzed not just Berlin but most of the nation. With no water, electricity, transportation, or garbage removal, the Kapp-Lüttwitz putsch withered in just five days.[15]

Those five days of turmoil proved advantageous for another group of disaffected partisans: the Communists. In Germany's industrial heartland, the Communists assembled a 50,000-strong "Red Army" prepared to fight for control of the Ruhr district. With the government in disarray, the Communists took over the local administration of one industrial city after another, including the Niemöllers' Elberfeld. "A 'Red Republic' was proclaimed in the industrial area and chaos reigned supreme," Niemöller remembered. Thousands of right-wing volunteers flooded the area to join free corps units countering the Communists. On the day of the Kapp putsch, Niemöller and some fellow seminary students had walked out of class to organize an Academic Defense Corps in support of the Kapp government. The next day, 750 strong, they joined the fight against "Spartacist terror" in the Ruhr, as Niemöller called it.[16]

Niemöller led one of the three Academic Defense Corps battalions. While fighting in the vicinity of the Lippe River, where he had played sailor as a child, his adjutant at battalion headquarters announced, "A personal call for the lieutenant commander!" It was Niemöller's mother on the phone. "God bless you, dear boy, you have got a little daughter," she said. "She has fair hair and blue eyes. And Else is doing well." He had hoped for a boy but kept that to himself. There was no question of going to see his wife and little Brigitte—his priorities lay elsewhere at the moment.[17]

In early April, under the command of General Oskar Freiherr von Watter, the free corps and its allies routed the Communists. The right had a policy of taking no prisoners. A student volunteer, Max Zeller, wrote his parents, "We shoot even the wounded. . . . Anyone who falls into our hands first gets the rifle butt and then is finished off with a bullet." Estimates vary, but approximately one thousand Communists were killed along with two hundred to three hundred rightists. "We were greeted as liberators from the hell of Bolshevism," Niemöller maintained, although few industrial workers in the Ruhr saw it that way.[18]

All across Germany the right was gaining ground as resentment directed at Versailles and Weimar grew. One beneficiary was a movement centered in Munich. It aimed to woo the working class away from leftist parties and toward the cause of *völkish* (racial) nationalism. Its chief proponents combined non-Marxist socialist rhetoric that appealed to workers—such as demands for higher wages—with the nationalist rhetoric of the right. To give organizational expression to these sentiments, its fiery leader, Adolf Hitler, founded the National Socialist German Workers' Party, or Nazi Party, that year. In short order, the party adopted the swastika as its symbol and founded a newspaper, *The National Observer* (*Völkischer Beobachter*). It also established a paramilitary squad, the Storm Detachment (*Sturm Abteilung*, or SA), to protect party leaders from attack by the left and to engage in street battles with its many enemies—trade unionists, Socialists, Communists, and Jews. The Nazis welcomed many former members of the free corps and other virulent antirepublicans.

Niemöller's role in the Academic Defense Corps did not go unnoticed by the republic's army leaders. In April 1920, he was invited to join the Reichswehr at the rank of captain. But he turned down the offer, determined as he now was to follow his father into the church.[19]

THE GERMAN PROTESTANT Church (*Deutsches Evangelische Kirche*, or DEK) was much changed by this point. The abdication of Germany's twenty-two federal princes, who had served as supreme bishops, and the flight of the kaiser deprived regional churches of political support, financial security, and legal foundation. Even more important, the church no longer had strong ties to the national government. The three-century-long alliance of throne and altar—from Martin Luther to Wilhelm II—had come to an end.

The twenty-eight regional churches that made up the German Protestant Church adjusted to the demise of the Christian state by gradually embracing their new autonomy. As frightening as the separation of church and state appeared to church leaders accustomed to a protective monarchy, it had its advantages. Otto Dibelius, a leader in the Prussian church, described the new situation as a "liberating storm" in his small book *The Century of the Church*. The state even allowed churchmen to levy their own taxes. By the late 1920s, "throne and altar" had been replaced by a slogan more appropriate to Protestantism's new allegiances: "church and volk." Once they grew accustomed to it, church leaders celebrated their independence. They protected their power too; Germany saw no devolution of ecclesiastical authority in the way of American or British Congregationalism. The regional churches were hierarchical institutions led by a supreme church council with minimal input from locally and regionally elected assemblies, known as synods. Reform-minded pastors and theologians called for more power for the parishes and synods—but to little effect.[20]

No doubt Niemöller was relieved that the churches survived—indeed, thrived—under the Social Democratic state. But that didn't diminish his hatred for the republic or his support for right-wing causes. While attending classes to prepare for the ministry, he maintained close ties with the members of the former Academic Defense Corps, participated in right-wing antirepublican organizations such as the National Union of German Officers, and attended addresses by nationalist professors. In the summer of 1921, he mourned the death of an old navy friend killed in violent clashes with Poles in the German-Polish border area.

Niemöller's return to school while supporting a growing family on a modest navy pension necessitated his taking various odd jobs, including railroad work. Money was so short that in the spring of 1922 the Niemöllers tried to sell their 1545 Luther Bible, a revised edition of Luther's translation of the Greek and Hebrew Bible. Fortunately, a loan from one of Else's brothers allowed them to keep their prized possession.

It did not help the young family that Germany was experiencing one of the worst inflationary episodes in economic history. Between December 1920 and December 1922, the price of a loaf of bread rose from about 2.5 marks to 163 marks. Workers demanded higher wages to make up for the price increases, driving prices up further. After French and Belgian troops invaded the Ruhr in January 1923 to extract reparations, inflation became hyper-inflation. By December, that same loaf of bread cost 3.99 *trillion* marks. Germans blamed their predicament on the Allies' reparation demands and also directed their anger at the "traitors" in the German government who insisted on fulfilling those demands. Right-wing thugs assassinated the Jewish foreign minister, Walter Rathenau, an advocate of fulfillment, in June 1922. Many on the right rejoiced; workers went on strike to protest.[21]

For the Niemöllers, the challenges went beyond the financial. In 1921, their second child was stillborn. Else was devastated. At the same time, Martin was struggling in his studies; he was no longer at the top of his class. That fall, in the chapel of the Münster clergy house, he preached his first sermon before a small group of theology students and the professor of homiletics. "After making a good start I got hopelessly stuck and had to consult my notes," he wrote. "I returned home that night with a sense of defeat." He begged his father to let him try again before the friendly audience in Elberfeld. That went much more to Martin's liking. It was the first step toward overcoming his initial fear of the pulpit.[22]

In the summer of 1922, Niemöller took a job as a plate-layer at the Münster railway yard. His first son, Hans Joachim (Jochen), was born in July, and he had another mouth to feed. The child was named for Hans Emsmann, a good friend of Niemöller's who died in the last submarine sunk in the war. With the birth of his second child and the value of money plummeting, Niemöller recalled, "I began to realize that I was up against the toughest years of my life."[23]

His working-class railway coworkers—Socialists through and through—liked to chide the Protestant college boy. One even picked a fight with him, but to everyone's surprise, the theology student got the better of the plate-layer. They invited him out for a beer one night, and he developed a better appreciation of the working-class plight. Months later, when Martin and Else encountered a repair crew on the tracks, she turned to him and asked, "Why are the men on the tracks waving?" "That's *my* gang!" he replied, smiling.[24]

Niemöller believed that getting to know these men, as well as experiencing poverty himself, furthered his preparation for the pastorate. "I discovered, and I still know, what it feels like to have no fixed employment or means of existence and sustenance," he wrote. But that newfound empathy did not alter his political views. In October, he took a week of leave to attend a conference in Bethel with his brother Wilhelm, who was also studying theology. They heard lectures by several of Germany's most prominent theologians, including two with strong racial-nationalist leanings, Adolf Schlatter and Paul Althaus. When Professor Samuel Jäger suggested in his lecture that Germany might bear some responsibility for the outbreak of World War I, the Niemöller brothers walked out in protest.[25]

Weekends were devoted to preparing for examinations and writing the equivalent of a master's thesis. Niemöller did this all the while smoking a churchwarden pipe and watching his infant son in the crib beside his desk. "Thus he was inured to a smoky study early in life," Niemöller joked. On the same day that French troops crossed the German border to occupy the Ruhr in January 1923, Niemöller handed in his thesis to the Münster Consistory Board.

The French invaded Germany's industrial heartland on the pretext that the Germans had defaulted on an agreement to deliver telegraph poles and timber as reparations. Those living in the Ruhr and Germans across the nation were further outraged when the French placed black colonial troops in positions of authority over white Germans. Right-wing propagandists proclaimed that the intention was to humiliate Germany, to inflict *Schwarze Schmach*—"black shame." As Niemöller recalled, "A wave of resentment and a growing spirit of opposition swept over the German people." It was a sentiment he certainly shared.[26]

Calls for a "war of liberation" rang out, and President Ebert once again turned to the disbanded free corps. Within a short time, nearly eighty thousand men had volunteered for the "Black Reichwehr" to disrupt the French occupation by sabotaging communication and transportation. The Niemöller brothers were pallbearers at the funeral service for the martyred saboteur and Nazi Albert Leo Schlageter. Trade unionists called on workers to resist by putting down their tools and refusing to follow French orders.[27]

In February and March 1923, ministry students Martin and Wilhelm drilled each other on the history of philosophy, an exam topic about which neither "knew the first thing." They had a primer that they tried to memorize by heart. Luckily for them, the author of the primer was also the professor who examined them in April. After passing his oral exams, Martin received his first position as a curate (assistant pastor or vicar) in Pastor Walter Kähler's parish in Münster. The young Niemöller family moved into Kähler's attic apartment above the rectory. As curate, he was responsible for holding Bible classes for confirmation candidates, conducting a weekly children's service, and visiting the sick and the aged of the parish.[28]

When Pastor Kähler was abruptly promoted to general superintendent of Stettin in eastern Germany, Niemöller's duties expanded considerably. He was now preaching to two congregations—and not the usual sort. The first was a community of refugees from Posen and west Prussia, territories Germany lost to Poland in the Versailles Treaty. The second was a small group that gathered at the house of the stationmaster of Telgte, a mostly Catholic town and pilgrimage site visited by thousands of Catholics every year. Niemöller was struck by the faithfulness of the embattled congregations, which he saw as greater than that of typical middle-class Protestant parishes. "My first love belongs to both of these congregations," he recorded in his autobiography.[29]

His new responsibilities did not come with a pay raise. The Niemöller family continued to live in the rectory attic on the salary of a curate.

Else picked the gold trim off her husband's naval uniforms and sold it to a jeweler. They were also forced to sell a chronometer Niemöller had taken from an Italian vessel as a souvenir. He briefly found work in the railway office and then a bank—all the while studying for a second set of oral exams, writing his second thesis, and performing parish duties. By October, inflation was so severe that Niemöller brought a haversack to work to bring home his wages in the form of bread, vegetables, and meat. "Money burned in people's hands and lost half its value in a day. . . . A terrible time!" Niemöller recalled.[30]

Across Germany, economic misery and political turmoil were the order of the day. The ongoing French occupation of the Ruhr buoyed the nationalist right's demands for revolution. By 1923, the Nazis were the strongest extreme-right party in Bavaria. The Munich police reported, "While other political events are poorly attended due to the enormous entry fees and beer prices, the halls are always full when the National Socialists put on one of their mass meetings." Between February and November 1923, thirty-five thousand Germans joined the Nazi Party. On November 8, Hitler told Nazi leaders, "The time to act has come." That evening, he and his followers stormed into one of Munich's largest beer halls, the Bürgerbraukeller, where a right-wing meeting was taking place, and declared to a stunned audience, "The national revolution is under way!" The next day—the fifth anniversary of the 1918 Weimar Revolution—Hitler's putschists, approximately two thousand strong, marched to the center of Munich, where they were met by a detachment of Bavarian state police. No one knows who fired the first shot, but the two sides exchanged heavy fire for thirty seconds, leaving fourteen Nazis and four policemen dead. Hitler was whisked away in the car of the SA's chief doctor.[31]

Two days later, he surrendered to police, and in April 1924 a Munich court sentenced him to a lenient five years' imprisonment for trying to overthrow the government. The conservative court went out of its way to praise the putschists, declaring that the accused had "acted in a purely patriotic spirit and according to the noblest and most selfless will." It was yet another example of how the Weimar Revolution had failed to dislodge conservative stalwarts from positions of power. The future führer served less than a year in the minimum-security prison of Landsberg, during which he wrote *Mein Kampf*. Although Niemöller had not yet read Hitler's political manifesto, he felt that he knew enough about the Nazis to vote for them in 1924 state assembly elections.[32]

A few days after the failed beer-hall putsch, Niemöller received a termination notice from the railway yard. He returned home distraught by his family's financial plight and worried about their future. After unburdening himself to Else, she casually replied, "By the way, the general superintendent sent a message asking you to come and see him after supper." The general superintendent in question was Dr. Wilhelm Zoellner, a friend of the Niemöller family. He offered Niemöller the prestigious position of manager of the Westphalian Inner Mission, the province's network of Protestant charities. It was a well-paying position, but not Niemöller's dream job. He wanted a quiet parish where he could shepherd his own flock, as his father did. To be sure, the Inner Mission improved people's lives, but as an administrator, Niemöller would mostly interact with business, civic, and church leaders—society's upper crust, not the needy. But this was no time to be finicky. Niemöller accepted the offer and began in the new position on December 1, 1923. "I can certainly say that I was thankful for this turn in our fortunes," Niemöller wrote, "but can scarcely pretend that it really made us happy."[33]

THE WESTPHALIAN INNER Mission was the model for Protestant charitable relief, primarily because the world-famous Bethel Institute fell within its remit. Founded by the social welfare pioneer Friedrich von Bodelschwingh in the late nineteenth century, Bethel was the largest caregiving facility in the German Protestant Church. Elderly people, orphans, the physically and mentally disabled, the homeless, and epileptics counted among the institute's charges. Bodelschwingh's son, Friedrich von Bodelschwingh Jr., took over the operation of Bethel after his father's death in 1910 and worked closely with Niemöller in his new job.[34]

Luckily for Niemöller, he started at the Westphalian Inner Mission just as the republic was emerging from the financial crisis. In the fall of 1923, the government issued a new currency, the Rentenmark, one of which could be exchanged for one trillion paper marks. The Rentenmark "miracle" and the 1924 Dawes Plan, which renegotiated reparations payments and secured US bank loans for the republic, set Germany on a path of economic stability that it would travel on until the 1929 crash. With economic stabilization came political moderation, as extreme left and right parties were immediately weakened. Historians call the period that followed the "golden twenties."[35]

Niemöller passed his second and final theology exams during his first few months at the Inner Mission. He was formally ordained a Lutheran pastor on June 29, 1924, in the Church of the Redeemer in Münster. That same day, he preached his first sermon as an ordained pastor and performed his first baptism on the newest Niemöller, Heinz Hermann, in the attic of the rectory. Niemöller later recalled the scene:

> My desk served for a baptismal altar and bore the crucifix, candlesticks and font, while the window behind it was draped with the ensign of submarine *U67*, which I had flown when entering Kiel on November 29, 1918. Hermann had been the name of my friend and brother-in-law who fell in *UB104*, and Heinz [Heinrich] was that of my father, rector of Elberfeld and servant of God. The journey from submarine to pulpit was completed and my service for my people and native country, in my new profession, was beginning.[36]

Niemöller's training in naval efficiency, his experience juggling jobs and school, and his obstinacy—Westphalians were said to have thick skulls—all came in handy as he strove to maintain and build up the Inner Mission. The purpose of the church's Inner Mission, much like its foreign missions in Africa and Asia, was to combine material relief with Christian edification. Socialist welfare could provide the former, but only the Inner Mission could provide both—that is, if it had the resources.

The war, revolution, and economic crisis had gravely hampered the Inner Mission. Its hospital buildings, youth centers, and old-age facilities were in disrepair, and the staff sorely needed modern training. All of this cost money. To this end, Niemöller founded the Westphalian Inner Mission Savings Bank in 1927. He registered the first savings book in his own name. During the seven years that he managed the Inner Mission, he often found the administrative, financial, and legal work challenging, but he also discovered he had an aptitude for it. By 1931, the bank had assets of 15 million marks; it would provide for the financial stability of the Inner Mission for years to come. The income was sufficient to repair old buildings, build new ones, and train nurses and caregivers. Among the new buildings Niemöller commissioned was a large sanatorium in his hometown of Lippstadt for the treatment of tuberculosis.[37]

While the Niemöllers were loath to partake in the new styles of Weimar music and dance or to adopt the relaxed social attitudes of the time, the golden twenties treated them well. They built a house in Münster to accommodate their growing family, bought a Hanomag car, went on vacations, and hired two maids. Else gave birth to a third boy, Jan, in 1925 and two girls, Hertha (named after her father's cadet training ship) and Jutta, in 1927 and 1928. The family now numbered eight.

When their oldest daughter, Brigitte, started school, Niemöller discovered what he considered the appalling state of Protestant education in Catholic Münster. He resolved to do something about it, through civic activism. By making common cause with the Catholics against the socialist leadership of the Prussian state and the federal government, he won election to the city council in 1929. In that position, he sought to improve Protestant life and schooling. Whenever he was accused of acting for political reasons, he would remind his adversary that he never joined a political party and that he was not a politician: *Ich bin kein Politiker.*[38] In fact, he had been a member of the German National People's Party (DNVP) as a student.

The problem with politics, as Niemöller understood it, was that it seemed to be all about enriching oneself or one's party or social class, not the well-being of the community, region, or nation. First as a naval officer and now as an ordained pastor, he considered party politics beneath him and preferred to leave matters of state to a trusted ruler, preferably a monarch or, if that wasn't possible, a charismatic leader who understood the symbiotic relationship between Germanism and Protestantism. Germanic Protestantism, he believed, was responsible for Germans' distinctive virtues—their perseverance, sense of duty, self-sacrifice, positive attitude toward work, piety, and honor. They were not crass materialists and individualists like the Americans, British, and French, or like German Socialists and republicans. It is no wonder that the renowned Swiss theologian Karl Barth, upon meeting the Münster pastor for the first time in 1925, remarked of Niemöller's attitude, "How Prussian!"[39]

Niemöller's claim to be above partisan politics was (and is) a tried and true method of political advancement. A variant of this appeal worked for the Nazis. In contrast to the worker-centered Communist and Socialist Parties, the Nazi Party portrayed itself as a *Volkspartei*, a people's party, innocent of class divisions. Thus, the Nazis molded their propaganda to reach whichever group they were addressing at any given moment. That Hitler's appeal to workers or the unemployed might contradict his appeal to businessmen or landowners did not seem to matter to his supporters. His message of national renewal and struggle against internal and external enemies attracted many anxious Germans, who saw their troubles as a consequence of the Versailles *Diktat* and the leftists who signed it. "I'm waging a ruthless war on Marxism using all the means—even the most extreme ones—that the law allows us," Hitler told a supporter, "including the right of self-defense, until this plague that is afflicting the German people has been fully and finally rooted out and exterminated." Later in life, Niemöller admitted that he had considered joining Hitler's party:

> I had come back from the war in 1918 and found everything changed.... And like many of the younger generation, I was rapidly becoming more and more disappointed with the Weimar Republic. But I was not sure of the advisability of a pastor joining any political party. I came to the conclusion that it was best not to be affiliated. I did vote for Hitler in 1924 and 1928.[40]

The good times could not go on forever, and when they stopped, Germany's deep well of political resentment overflowed. After the US stock market crashed in October 1929, American banks recalled the loans they had made under the Dawes Plan. The German economy went into a tailspin. The Weimar Republic's welfare state, which included benefits for war victims, unemployment insurance, sickness insurance, and many other costly programs, could not stay afloat. As unemployment skyrocketed—Berlin alone, with a population of 4 million, had 750,000 jobless—the hungry and desperate gravitated once again to the political extremes. The Nazis and the Communists flourished, while the moderate middle collapsed. In the 1930 parliamentary election, the Communists won 77 seats, up from 54, and the Nazis jumped from a mere 12 to an incredible 107 seats.

In December 1930, motivated by the success of the Nazi movement, Niemöller bought a copy of *Mein Kampf* and read it the following year. Public support for Hitler suggested that many were looking for a savior. Niemöller expressed this longing in a 1931 radio broadcast, "Call for the Führer"—one of several occasions when various media outlets asked him to speak on behalf of the disaffected right. "Where is the leader? When will he come?" he asked. "Our yearning and willing, our calling and striving fail to bring him. When he comes, he will come as a gift, as a gift of God. Our call for the leader, is a call for Mercy." Within the conservative nationalist milieu of the German Protestant Church, this type of public support for a charismatic leader with nationalist impulses would not have raised any concerns.[41]

Within the church, however, was a small minority who were more internationally minded and who sought better relations with Protestants in the United States and the rest of Europe. Among those in the burgeoning ecumenical movement was a young Lutheran theologian, Dietrich Bonhoeffer, a native of Berlin who had spent the 1930–1931 academic year studying in the United States at the Union Theological Seminary in upper Manhattan. In August 1931, the twenty-five-year-old Bonhoeffer attended a conference of the World Alliance for Promoting

International Friendship through the Churches in Cambridge, England, where he was elected one of three international youth secretaries. This would be the first of many such conferences for Bonhoeffer. Despite his youth, in the coming years Bonhoeffer became the leading German Protestant in the ecumenical movement. The contacts he made with other ecumenical pioneers—including George Bell, bishop of Chichester; Henry Smith Leiper of the United States; and the Dutch theologian Willem Visser't Hooft, the first general secretary of the World Council of Churches (WCC)—would prove very useful for German Protestants, including Martin Niemöller, during the Nazi era and postwar years.[42]

Niemöller's managerial zeal at the Inner Mission and entry into Münster's politics had come at some cost. For seven years he had put his dream of a "quiet and orderly" pastorate on hold, leaving his transition from U-boat to pulpit still incomplete. Moreover, he was on the road, crisscrossing Westphalia in his Hanomag, more often than he was with his family. When he was home, he was often entertaining overnight guests associated with his work or engaged in the affairs of the city council. By 1931, he had had enough. Satisfied with his many accomplishments at the Inner Mission, in January he gave six months' notice and began to look for a pastorate. With the world depression of the 1930s at hand and so many men out of work, his decision was a bold one; his father Heinrich had tried to change his mind.

There was no shortage of interest from parishes in Westphalia, where Niemöller was known and admired for his achievements at the Inner Mission. But an offer from a well-to-do parish in faraway Berlin came as a surprise. The peaceful, picturesque suburb of Berlin-Dahlem, southwest of the main city, with about twelve thousand residents, was home to some of the wealthiest and best-connected Berliners at the time. To be summoned to Dahlem was flattering, to say the least. Niemöller visited and liked what he saw. He got along well with the two other pastors there. In July 1931, the family bid farewell to the house they had built in Münster and moved into an apartment on a tree-lined street of Dahlem. Niemöller finally had his parish, but it would turn out to be neither quiet nor orderly.

The first thing he did was take his father's advice: "Junge. Mach Haus-
besuche!" ("Young man. Make house visits.") For Niemöller, the years
1931 and 1932 were the happiest of his life. As it would turn out, this was
the only period during which he could devote himself fully to his flock:
visiting homes, preaching the Word, administering the sacraments, holding confirmation classes, mingling with parishioners. Even after he had
earned more impressive titles later in his life, he remained proud into his
eighties to be known as Pastor Niemöller.[43]

FOUR

Trusting God and Hitler

(1933)

O N NEW YEAR'S DAY 1933, PASTOR MARTIN NIEMÖLLER MOUNTED THE pulpit in the nine-hundred-year-old church of St. Anne in Berlin-Dahlem and preached a fire-and-brimstone sermon on the topic of God's grace. In classic Lutheran terms, he began by acknowledging the anxiety that many Germans felt in their personal lives and even more so for their nation. "The year that lies before us," he preached, "is like an unknown country. . . . We are all stepping into the darkness."[1]

As the Great Depression continued its sweep through the industrialized world, nearly half the German workforce was either fully or partially unemployed by late 1932. Violent street fighting had broken out between the Nazis, Communists, and Socialists as they sought to protect their turf and project an image of strength and determination. In July 1932 alone, with the Reichstag election looming, police recorded dozens of deaths and hundreds of injuries as a result of political violence.[2]

When voting commenced on the last day of July, voters abandoned the traditional liberal and conservative parties in favor of the easy solutions offered by the far right and left. Coming out on top, the Nazis received 13.8 million votes and won 230 out of 608 seats in the Reichstag. Many of these votes came from Protestants, who were twice as likely as Catholics to support the Nazis. The next biggest blocs in the parliament were the Nazis' archenemies, the Social Democratic Party, with 133 seats, and the Communists with 89.[3]

In the wake of his impressive victory, Hitler demanded the keys to the chancellery, the highest seat of power in the German government. But he had to be appointed by the president, the World War I hero Paul von Hindenburg, who faced a dilemma. The conservative old field marshal didn't trust the zealous corporal whose party had just ridden a wave of violence to power. A government led by Hitler would "inevitably develop into a party dictatorship," Hindenburg believed. His conscience, his love for the fatherland, and his oath to the Weimar constitution could not countenance appointing Adolf Hitler to the chancellery. At most, Hindenburg quipped to a friend, the Nazi leader was qualified to head the postal ministry.[4]

Hindenburg and Germany's conservative elite—landed-estate owners, military officers, high-ranking civil servants, industrial barons, and church leaders—looked on with anxiety, and not a little admiration, as the Nazis flourished after 1930. These elites had opposed the left-wing revolution that gave birth to the Weimar Republic, and they had railed against the "November criminals" who agreed to the armistice in 1918, signed the Versailles Treaty in 1919, and passed social welfare legislation. They were no friends of democracy or the parliament, but neither were they enamored with Hitler. They shared the Nazi goal of overthrowing the Weimar Republic, but they wanted to replace it with a conservative authoritarian system, not with rule by rowdy, violent, brown-shirted thugs.[5]

Hindenburg and his advisers knew that they could not ignore the leader of the most popular party, the Nazi Party. Placating Hitler with an innocuous ministerial post in a conservative cabinet, they surmised, might allow them to tame and exploit his legions of supporters. But Hitler didn't want a subordinate role in the government—he wanted to run it. Reluctantly, Hindenburg tried to mollify the Nazis by dismissing Chancellor Franz von Papen after six months in office and replacing him with another staunch antirepublican. Hindenburg hoped that the former general Kurt von Schleicher would have better luck persuading Hitler to take a ministerial post. Meanwhile, the Nazis' 400,000-strong brown-shirted militia displayed their dissatisfaction with the establishment through further acts of terrorism.[6]

It was in this unsettled context that Niemöller preached his New Year's Day sermon. "What God's intentions may be with regard to our nation or to ourselves in the New Year, we do not and shall not know," he intoned. But he warned that, in these troubled times, God's grace is not just a source of relief or comfort. That is "easy Christianity" and "artificial grace." Rather, God offers us his grace so that we will put our whole trust in him and his son, Niemöller explained. "We are not God's generals but his soldiers. Ours is not to make the plans but to carry out the orders." The message was clear: only when we give ourselves over entirely to God through faith do we become strong and free.[7]

Making their way home after the service, some of Niemöller's parishioners most likely encountered an equally imposing demand for their trust—from the Nazi Party newspaper *Völkischer Beobachter* (*National Observer*). Emblazoned on the front page of the party's mouthpiece was Hitler's "Battle Message of 1933." Article after article underscored the Judeo-Bolshevik menace and called on Hitler's rank and file to reject power-sharing and to put their whole faith in *him*. "Any compromise," Hitler warned, "bears within it the seeds of destruction of the party and therefore of Germany's future." He declared himself "unalterably resolved not to purchase the thin gruel of participation in a [governmental] cabinet by selling out our movement's entitlement to power." He commanded his followers to reject half-measures and indecisiveness. "There will be no peace until we are in power," he wrote. "Victory must and will be ours."[8]

His loyalty to Wilhelm II allowed him to think this way.

Niemöller's parishioners must have wondered if it was possible to be a good Christian trusting both in God and in the Nazi leader. If they looked to their pastor for direction, the answer would have been clear. Niemöller made no secret of his support for the Nazis, although he never campaigned explicitly for Hitler from the pulpit. Niemöller saw no contradiction at this stage in calling on his flock to follow a merciful God while at the same time supporting the Nazi leader who demanded absolute political loyalty. German Protestants, Niemöller believed, could and should do both. After all, they had revered the alliance of throne and altar for centuries. It wasn't a great leap from there to the alliance of the Nazi Party and the Protestant Church.[9]

Chancellor von Schleicher proved unable to bring the intransigent Nazi Party into a coalition government and was dismissed after two months. Several of President Hindenburg's advisers believed that it was time to give Hitler a chance. Urged by his trusted friend von Papen, Hindenburg appointed Hitler to the chancellorship on January 30, 1933. The backroom intrigue that led to this decision is the subject of continuing debate among historians, but one thing is certain: the men around Hindenburg expected to use Hitler's chancellorship to reassert the conservative political traditions of the imperial era.[10]

Hindenburg and his circle felt certain that they could control the plebeian corporal and thereby rein in the SA, clobber the left, kill the democratic republic once and for all—and then kick Hitler to the curb. They "fenced in" the new chancellor with a cabinet of nine conservatives and three Nazis, with Vice Chancellor von Papen and President Hindenburg watching over. "Within two months," von Papen confidently told a friend, "we will have pushed Hitler so far into a corner that he'll squeak." No one expected Hitler to last through the year, to outmaneuver his conservative chaperones, or to turn on the conservatives after "exterminating" the left.[11]

Niemöller greeted Hitler's appointment with euphoria. For nationalists, it felt like August 1914 all over again—the crowds, parades, enthusiasm, and alleged unity of the nation behind a worthy cause. January 1933 wiped away the shame and betrayal of November 1918. Although nominally

Catholic, Hitler's charismatic, nationalistic, and anti-Communist rant-
ing were essential to Niemöller's support. And the new chancellor also
spoke frequently about the vital role the churches would play in the reborn Germany. The Nazi program committed to "positive Christianity"
and to battling "the Jewish materialistic spirit." After assuming power,
Hitler reassured the nation that the government would protect Christianity "as the basis of our entire morality" and "fill our culture again with
the Christian spirit." The Nazis claimed to stand for the freedom of all
religious denominations, "provided that they do not endanger the existence of the State or offend the concepts of decency and morality of the
Germanic race."[12]   *gave the Nazis leeway to persecute more*
heavily on rel.

All of this was most welcome to conservative Protestants. Hitler's appointment, they convinced themselves, would usher in the hour of the
church—God's hour. They anticipated that churches, which had been
gradually losing attendance for a century, would soon fill again. In the
first half of 1933, some 20 percent of the 550 or so pastors in Berlin
joined the Nazi Party, eager to participate in the movement for "one nation, one people, one church." Although Niemöller never became a Nazi
Party member himself, his young friend and colleague in Dahlem, Assistant Pastor Franz Hildebrandt, later described the Nazi program for na- *He was*
so swung
tional and racial revival, "with its vehement denial of all that was meant *by Nazi*
by individualism, parliamentarianism, pacifism, Marxism, and Judaism," *because*
he was
as fundamentally in keeping with Niemöller's ideology at the time.[13] *one. He*
believed all
His sermons during this period were rife with references to the *the*
dual awakenings of nation and church. Under the Weimar Republic, *same shit*
Niemöller believed, the nation had lost its way and the churches had lost
their public significance. The Nazi revolution would restore Christianity to its rightful place in the public life of the nation. Hopeful Protestants looked to Hitler to complete Luther's Reformation by replacing the
twenty-eight regional Protestant churches with one Reich Church. At
last, they believed, a hallmark of the Second Reich—the unity of church
and state—would be restored in the Third.

Hitler's Christian supporters remained loyal even as it became clear,
after assuming power, that he would not stop Nazi violence. Conveniently

for the Nazis, on the night of February 27 a fire gutted the Reichstag building; police arrested a disaffected, twenty-four-year-old Dutch Communist wandering amid the smoldering ashes and accused him of arson. (Recent research suggests that it was indeed the Dutchman, Marinus van der Lubbe, who started the blaze, although some historians believe it was the work of the Nazis.) Hitler seized the opportunity to accuse the German left of engaging in an international Communist conspiracy against the fatherland. President Hindenburg declared a state of emergency the following day, abolishing civil liberties. Hermann Göring, Hitler's right-hand man and minister of the interior for Prussia, announced that the war against the left would not be hamstrung by the law and that it wasn't his job to exercise justice but "only to destroy and exterminate." Nazi hooliganism offended men such as Otto Dibelius, a conservative church leader in Berlin, but he also acknowledged an upside to storm trooper tactics: "The signs of moral decadence which had been evident all over Germany toward the end of the Weimar Republic suddenly vanished."[14]

Niemöller took up the question of the proper role of Christians in the public life of the nation in a sermon. "The fact is," he preached, "it is simply impossible for us today to accept the comfortable formula that politics have no place in the church." The events of the last two months, he maintained, were of great importance "to our fate and to that of our nation," and he encouraged his parishioners to "take a conscientious stand . . . this very day." The date of the sermon, March 5, 1933, is particularly significant: that day saw another Reichstag election, the first and only election in Nazi Germany. Niemöller took his "conscientious stand" by voting for the Nazis. Despite all the advantages the Nazis enjoyed after driving vast numbers of their opponents from the streets, the party managed to secure only 44 percent of the vote.[15]

Niemöller's election-day sermon underscored the decisive role that Christianity should play in shaping German national identity. "When our German nation was born," he preached, "God gave it as soul the Christian faith. Our national development . . . has been inwardly based on Christianity, and from the Christianity of the national soul have come all the forces which made our nation develop and grow. . . . Our nation would not be our nation but for the Reformation." Germany "will either be Christian or it will cease to exist," he said. Christians therefore had an obligation to engage in the political sphere to ensure that the German-Protestant synthesis would continue to guide the people.[16]

Although the official stand of the Nazi Party was pro-church, during the first months of Hitler's chancellorship party members displayed a variety of religious orientations, raising some concerns among church leaders about the Nazis' commitment to the established church. The Nazis' program of "positive Christianity" was vague. For some Nazis, it meant a form of Christianity that emphasized Germany's special role in God's plan for establishing his kingdom on earth—something Niemöller welcomed. Others attacked traditional Christianity for its allegedly weak, crucified God and advocated in its place an Aryan Christianity that worshiped a powerful, manly Jesus. Still other Nazis identified as pagans who worshiped nature.[17]

[handwritten margin note: a clue that Hitler didn't care about religion. It was all just for support.]

This wide range of religious beliefs, as well as the Nazi desire to relegate religious faith to the private sphere and subordinate it to the nation, concerned Niemöller increasingly. He called on the new regime to take the vital interest of the Christian community into account and not be "deluded into thinking that the question of religion can ever be a private matter." If the anti-Christian Nazis succeeded in restricting Christianity to the private sphere or silencing it altogether, Niemöller warned his parishioners, they would be committing national suicide. It was the job of responsible German statesmen to protect and confirm "the alliance between the fate of the nation and the fate of the church." Niemöller earnestly believed that Hitler understood this, even if some of the party hotheads did not.[18]

THE NAZIS' VIOLENT tactics and ambiguity on religious matters left many conservatives—including President Hindenburg, who had the power to dismiss his chancellor—looking for some reassurance that the Nazis were more conservative than radical. To this end, the Nazi propaganda minister, Joseph Goebbels, staged a carefully choreographed ceremony intended to soothe the anxious elites and energize the Nazi base. With the Reichstag building in Berlin destroyed, Goebbels and Hitler chose to stage the reopening ceremony of the recently elected Reichstag on March 21, 1933, in nearby Potsdam, where the former Prussian and German monarchy had lived. The setting and the date were not arbitrary. No city was richer in the historical lore of the Hohenzollerns, and the date was the sixty-second anniversary of the inauguration of the first parliament of united Germany in 1871. The ceremony would underscore the continuity between the old Prussian-German monarchial and military traditions and the new Nazi government. The Nazis designated the Day of Potsdam an official holiday, and the events were broadcast on the radio across Germany.[19]

Participating in the ceremony were many Protestant dignitaries as well as President Hindenburg; the deposed kaiser's son, Crown Prince Wilhelm (wearing his death's-head hussar uniform with its high fur cap decorated with a skull and crossbones symbol); Chancellor Hitler; cabinet ministers; the diplomatic corps; and the Reichstag deputies. The Communists and Socialists were not welcome, and they were glad not to be there. Also in attendance were twenty-five thousand of Hitler's brownshirts, who marched beneath banners bearing the swastika; army generals and officers in their resplendent uniforms; soldiers, sailors, and a cavalry troop; veterans of the war; student fraternities in their colorful regalia; foreign ambassadors; the papal nuncio; and plenty of police as well as Nazi enthusiasts. All told, there were about one hundred thousand people in Potsdam for the ceremony. From early morning until late in the day, train after train arrived from Berlin unloading swarms of celebrants waving Nazi and imperial flags and wearing the Nazi insignia.[20]

The cold March morning began with Protestant and Catholic services. Hitler and Goebbels, both nominal Catholics, refused to attend the Catholic service because of anti-Nazi statements made by Catholic leaders. Instead, they honored martyrs of the Nazi movement by laying a wreath at the grave of Horst Wessel, a young SA member killed by Communists and the author of the Nazi Party anthem. Hindenburg and the Protestant

Newly appointed chancellor Adolf Hitler greeting Reich president Paul von Hindenburg, March 21, 1933. (akg-images)

members of the cabinet and Reichstag heard Bishop Otto Dibelius give the sermon in St. Nicholas's Church. It was a standard conservative Lutheran address. Dibelius defended the Nazi use of force to eliminate the nation's enemies as long as the SA refrained from arbitrariness and the state quickly reestablished law and order. "Once order has been restored, justice and love must reign once more, so that every man of good will may rejoice in his people," he announced.[21]

At the main ceremony in the Protestant Garrison Church, where the remains of Friedrich Wilhelm I and Friedrich the Great were interred, only Hindenburg and Hitler spoke. Each described the links between old Prussia and the new National Socialist Germany. The ceremony concluded with the laying of laurel wreaths on the tomb of Friedrich the Great, followed by a huge military parade that included thousands of storm troopers.

In an act of pure theater, Hitler, dressed like a conservative aristocrat in a dark morning suit with top hat in hand, met President Hindenburg in front of the church and bowed deeply. The chancellor firmly shook the hand of the president, who wore a *Pickelhaube* (spiked helmet) on his head and an imperial uniform glittering with decorations and insignia of various orders. The Nazi propaganda ministry soon reproduced millions of postcards and posters depicting Hitler's deferential gesture to old Prussia. No vestige of the Weimar Republic was to be found in the sea of swastika flags and the black, white, and red flags of the empire.[22]

Hitler followed the Day of Potsdam with a Reichstag speech on March 23 in which he declared that "the National Government regards the two Christian confessions as the most important factors for the preservation of our national culture. . . . Their rights will not be infringed." The very next day, Christian conservatives in the Reichstag joined with Nazis and other nationalist parties in voting to give Hitler powers to enact legislation by decree. The so-called Enabling Act allowed Hitler to erect his dictatorship unencumbered by the legislative branch.[23]

The Nazi appropriation of state power in March 1933 had its parallel in the Protestant churches. As the Nazis grew in popularity after the economic crash of 1929, a group of fervent Protestant supporters emerged in mid-1932 calling themselves the German Christian Movement. The German Christians (*Deutsche Christen*, or DC) believed that Nazism and Christianity were mutually reinforcing. As Nazi enthusiasts, the DC were anti-Semitic, but in a uniquely religious way: they denied the Jewish ancestry of Jesus and wanted to purge German Protestantism of everything associated with Judaism, including the Old Testament. Their goal was a racially pure church that excluded anyone with Jewish ancestry, even baptized Christians. As far as the DC were concerned, converts from Judaism to Christianity remained biologically non-Aryan and therefore were not welcome in the church. One particularly offensive DC slogan—"Baptism can't straighten out a hooked nose"—conveys the priority of race over God's grace. "If Christ were alive today," a DC district leader declared, "he would have been an SA man." These self-proclaimed "storm troopers of Christ" subscribed to a *völkisch* (racial) theology that viewed Jews and Judaism as alien to the German people and their norms, laws, and spirituality. The German Christians were the Nazi's fifth column in the German Protestant Church.[24]

German Christian leader Joachim Hossenfelder addressing the Nazi faithful at the Berlin Sports Palace rally, November 1933. (akg-images)

The German Christians loved spectacle more than Scripture. Pastors and parishioners, often dressed in SA uniforms with swastika armbands, would parade into churches carrying Nazi and DC flags, which were red with a large white circle and a black cross decorated with the initials "DC" and a swastika in the center. Once in the church, they would arrange the flags in the chancel, and on occasion they would consecrate a DC flag at the altar. Their services often portrayed Christ as a heroic Aryan warrior. At the end of the service, they would recess again with the flags, often accompanied by the organist playing the German national anthem or Luther's "A Mighty Fortress Is Our God." Other popular DC group rituals included group baptisms and weddings. In one instance, in August 1933, 147 couples were married—the grooms in SA or SS uniforms—in the Pankow district of Berlin, and in September 117 children were baptized together in the Neukölln district.[25]

When Niemöller first took up his pastorate in Dahlem in 1931, there were no German Christians on the parish council. But in the 1932 church elections, two were elected. That year the German Christians won one-third of the seats in the Prussian church's synod. After the Nazis took power, the number of pastors and parishioners identifying as DC increased dramatically. Although always a minority in Dahlem, they tried to rally supporters through propaganda such as inviting all of Berlin to a massive Sunday service in the Grunewald forest bordering Dahlem.[26]

Raised as a traditional Protestant, Martin Niemöller had strong reservations about the idea of Aryan Christianity and drew a thick line between his conservative-nationalist Protestantism and the DC's *völkisch* Protestantism. Although there was plenty of common ground between the two groups—they shared a commitment to conservatism, nationalism, anti-Communism, and anti-Semitism—there were significant differences as well. Traditional Protestants rejected a racial litmus test for membership in the church. They defended the Old Testament and the Jewish origins of Jesus. And they took offense at the blatant politicizing of Christianity. By twisting the cross to resemble a swastika, the DC won over many Nazis to the church but also alienated many conservatives, Martin Niemöller among them. Niemöller's disapproval of the German Christians was the starting point for his eventual opposition to Hitler's church policy, which favored the German Christians over the traditionalists.

In reaction to the German Christian's boisterous rallies and politicized church services, Niemöller preached that Christ "wants no frenzied enthusiasm." And in contradiction to the DC portrayal of Christ as an Aryan-Nordic warrior, Niemöller insisted that Jesus "treads the path that leads to suffering and to the cross." Bemoaning the DC's "large-scale propaganda scheme for Christianity" and the "sugary Christian confection" they concocted to entice the masses, Niemöller advocated the "unaffected message of Christ's word and work, of his life and suffering, of his death and resurrection—and nothing more."[27]

As the struggle for control of the churches intensified in the spring and summer of 1933, SA attacks on Jews rose steeply. Hermann Göring, the head of the Prussian police, declared that he was "unwilling to accept the notion that the police are a protection squad for Jewish shops." The literary scholar and baptized Jew Victor Klemperer described the atmosphere in Dresden as resembling the "mood as before a pogrom in the depths of the Middle Ages or in deepest Czarist Russia."[28]

The increasing number and ferocity of attacks on Jews were raising hackles internationally. During the first week of February 1933, rabbis across the United States railed against Hitler's appointment and the surge of anti-Jewish persecution it signaled. They pledged their support for their brethren in Germany and repeatedly called upon American political and religious leaders to denounce Nazi anti-Semitism. The Protestant Federal Council of Churches in America (FCC) followed with a strong condemnation of anti-Semitism and called on German Protestants to do the same. On March 27, anti-Nazi demonstrations took place across the United States. At the largest, in New York City's Madison Square Garden, prominent Jews, Christians, labor leaders, politicians, and a Supreme Court justice all denounced Nazi anti-Semitism.[29]

The FCC's faith in their German counterparts proved misguided. At no point during the twelve years of Nazi rule, much less in 1933, would German Protestants publicly condemn anti-Semitism in stark terms. It is telling that, while American liberal Protestants were planning demonstrations against Nazism, German Protestants were fighting over how much influence to give Hitler in church affairs. The schism that took place in German Protestantism was primarily over church autonomy— not Nazi politics and racial policy.

A few days after the massive demonstrations in New York, storm troopers participating in the Nazi-led boycott of Jewish-owned businesses marched through hundreds of towns and cities singing anti-Semitic songs, blocking shoppers, and smashing windows. The German Protestant Church was silent. Indeed, some clergy defended the boycott as a natural response to disproportionate Jewish influence in German society. The Nazis soon after passed the first major piece of anti-Jewish legislation, the April 7, 1933, Law for the Restoration of the Professional Civil Service. Its notorious "Aryan paragraph" banned Jews and baptized Jews from state employment. Although pastors and church officials were part of the civil service and paid by the state, the Nazi government did not include the churches in the April 7 legislation.[30]

The German Christians, however, wanted to pass a similar law that would ban "Jewish blood" from the pulpit and the pews. "Anyone of non-Aryan descent or married to a person of non-Aryan descent," the proposed church law read, "may not be called as a minister or official in the church." At their national convention in Berlin, the DC reiterated their call for the coordination of church and state and the creation of a united Evangelical Reich Church led by an all-powerful Reich bishop, similar to Hitler's role as head of state. One of their leaders, Joachim Hossenfelder, menacingly proclaimed, "The faithful have the right to revolt against a church government which does not totally affirm the victory of the national upheaval." In late April, Hitler appointed another DC leader, Ludwig Müller, a former naval chaplain virtually unknown in established church circles, as his representative to the German Protestant Church.[31]

THE SUDDEN ASCENDANCY of the German Christians, with the help of the Nazi state, alarmed traditional churchmen as well as a younger generation of pastors and theologians, who felt closed out of the church's governing bodies. They organized the Young Reformation Movement with the aim of blocking the DC and infusing the church leadership with new blood. At age forty-one, Martin Niemöller was among the three thousand pastors who joined the Young Reformers. His leadership and administrative skills, acquired first as a naval officer, honed as the manager of the Westphalian Inner Mission, and further refined as the lead pastor of the influential Dahlem parish, were sorely needed among the Young Reformers. In addition to his experience, his assertive temperament and confident nature catapulted him to the forefront of the Young Reformers within one month.

In addition to the Young Reformers' rejection of racial criteria for church membership, they clashed with the German Christians over who should assume the role of bishop in the emerging Reich Church. The Young Reformers wanted the highly respected director of the Bethel Institute, Friedrich von Bodelschwingh—Niemöller's good friend from the Westphalian Inner Mission. The DC threw their weight behind Ludwig Müller.

As impressive as the Young Reformation Movement appeared to be, with its august leadership and thousands of members, there was an incongruity at its core—the same that characterized Niemöller. Their "joyful affirmation" of the Nazi state and simultaneous demands for independence in church affairs and condemnation of the Aryan paragraph were incompatible. The Nazis weren't about to allow churches any more independence than they allowed political parties, trade unions, or courts. And could the Nazis really countenance a church that worshiped a Jew? The Young Reformers' contradictory position weakened their ability to oppose the regime and earned the derision of Karl Barth, a giant in the world of Protestant theology who was teaching in Bonn at the time.[32]

One Young Reformer who stood out for his anti-Nazi credentials was the now-twenty-seven-year-old Dietrich Bonhoeffer. Bonhoeffer joined the group because of its critique of the Aryan paragraph and the German Christians, but he vehemently disagreed with their support of the Nazis. He and his good friend Franz Hildebrandt, a Dahlem vicar and a colleague of Niemöller's, repeatedly pushed the church opposition to take a more radical stand against the Nazis, not just the Nazis' church policy. Still, Bonhoeffer and Hildebrandt were relatively inexperienced outsiders without much influence.

Bonhoeffer first met Niemöller in early summer 1933. Although they agreed about the need to fight the German Christian threat, they did not see eye to eye on much else. Their backgrounds could not have been more different. Bonhoeffer's family was liberal, cosmopolitan, academic, and unequivocally anti-Hitler. Niemöller—proud of his navy days and pleased with the rise of a strong, charismatic leader—was intent on demonstrating his national loyalty, even under Hitler. Just how different the two men were was evident after the state's passage of the anti-Semitic civil service law. Bonhoeffer published an article decrying the mistreatment of Jews and calling on the church to protect Jews and resist the Nazis. Niemöller was silent. He raised his voice only after the German Christians proposed a similar law that would ban baptized Jews from the pastorate.[33]

That few in the church, including Niemöller, were prepared to take up Bonhoeffer's radical call to action on behalf of German Jews did not go without comment in American Protestant circles. In May 1933, Samuel McCrea Cavert of the Federal Council of Churches wrote in the *Christian Century*, "The [German] churches have not, it has to be said regretfully, made any public protest against the injustice done to the Jews." Reinhold Niebuhr struck a similar tone in the same periodical the following month: "In dealing with anti-Semitism the [German] church has . . . been so busy preserving its own moral integrity that it has nothing to say to the state," he wrote. "In their very protest against anti-Semitism in the church they have by implication allowed it in the state. . . . Surely the church must know that a Christian attitude toward the very small groups of Jews who have become Christian has little influence upon the total tragic problem." Bonhoeffer was one of the scant few who agreed with this critique.[34]

In a letter to a friend, Bonhoeffer referred to Niemöller and his type as "naive, starry-eyed idealists" who thought that they were "the real National Socialists" because of their dual devotion to National Socialism and national Protestantism. This was nothing less than delusional, as far as Bonhoeffer was concerned. Nazism and Protestantism were inimical because the Nazis openly derided Christ's message of love and mercy. A good Christian, Bonhoeffer believed, could not be a good Nazi.[35]

In the coming months, Nazi church policy would prove Bonhoeffer right. Indeed, by that May even Niemöller was beginning to express concerns. While he did not explicitly critique Nazi attacks on Jews and leftists—of which there had already been many—he did respond to the increasing political and racial tensions in his May 21 sermon when he exhorted all Christians to follow the Gospel's call to "love our enemies" and "pray for all men." "Today," he said, "we like to talk optimistically of the new fellowship of the nation, but it is becoming more and more evident that even this new fellowship is such that it not only binds but at the same time divides." Should we really expect, he asked, a Nazi storm trooper to pray for a Socialist? A man dismissed from his job because of his race or politics to love the new government responsible for firing him? Niemöller insisted that the Bible demands as much, even if people are rarely so forgiving by nature. Christians, he added, could not be mere spectators to the events transpiring in their midst. They had a choice to make: either they could move toward God or they could turn away. Only by exercising love toward all men and women—"toward Christians and infidels and Jews"—could Christians do the former.[36]

The tensions between the Nazi-backed German Christians, on the one side, and the Young Reformers and the church establishment, on the other, escalated after the May 27, 1933, election of Bodelschwingh, the Younger Reformers' candidate, as Reich bishop. Once the new bishop took up his position in Berlin, he reached out to his friend Niemöller for assistance. From this point on, Niemöller was directly involved in the contest over church independence and bore witness to the German Christians' and Nazis' attempts to subordinate the church to their ideology. His simple pastor's life gave way to one of endless political rows. Legend has it that on Niemöller's office desk were two telephones and that he could frequently be heard carrying on two separate conversations simultaneously. Once his father said he overheard his son shouting "yes!" into one and "no!" into the other.[37]

Hitler was infuriated by Bodelschwingh's election. On June 24, 1933, in an effort to break the power of the establishment church, Hitler installed the Nazi jurist August Jäger as commissar of church affairs in Prussia. Jäger immediately suspended Prussia's established church leaders and appointed German Christians in their stead. Niemöller and his colleagues condemned the incursions into church affairs and accused the German Christians of falsifying the Gospel for political purposes. In a protest letter, they called on Prussian churches to observe a day of repentance and prayer the following Sunday, July 2, and to encourage their congregations to push back against the German Christians.[38]

The next day, at Niemöller's home, the Young Reformers made a momentous decision. They agreed to fight Jäger's appointments and pledged their "courage to confess and if necessary also to suffer." They were now challenging not only the Nazi-backed faction in the church but the state itself. When Dibelius, a superintendent-general in the Prussian church, declared, "I cannot allow myself to be suspended by any state commissioner," he was disobeying an official decree. Jäger's men in the church did not take defiance lightly. They responded by announcing that all ecclesiastical buildings must fly not only the church flag and the black-white-and-red imperial flag but also the Nazi swastika. In place of the Young Reformers' day of repentance, Jäger's minions decreed that Prussian churches were to celebrate a day of thanksgiving. The DC didn't expect the Young Reformers to follow this command, but they hoped to make an example of the noncompliant churches and to taint them as enemies of the state.[39]

July 2 became a litmus test, indicating where various parishes stood in the broader struggle. Dahlem's pastors defied church authorities by holding a service of repentance and sermonizing against state intervention in church affairs. Yet, at the same time, they preached that it was the duty of a Christian to obey the state, thereby limiting their critique to the church situation alone. This was typical of the opposition. The establishment could abide the Nazis—even celebrate them—as long as they were left in control of their separate spiritual universe.[40]

Believing that Jäger had successfully undermined his leadership, Reich bishop Bodelschwingh resigned after just four weeks. The state interference on behalf of the German Christians shocked and outraged Niemöller. But he was slow to appreciate Hitler's role in coordinating what was effectively a state takeover of the church. The signs were obvious, but Niemöller held tightly to his belief that Hitler would honor his promise to respect the rights of the church. Hitler then made his ambitions even clearer by ordering new church leadership elections for July 23, with an eye to securing DC majorities. Young Reformers and traditional church leaders would square off against the German Christians for the entire range of offices, from parish councils to the most senior governance positions.

Niemöller was instrumental in the Young Reformers' campaign, writing evocative brochures urging an independent, "confessing church"— one that based its proclamation on Scripture and the Reformation confessions, such as the Augsburg Confession from 1530, not the prerogatives of the Nazi state. "We struggle for a confessing church against false teaching in the church like that expressed daily by the leaders of German Christians," according to one such pamphlet. The Young Reformers summed up their appeal with the slogan, "Church must remain church." Meanwhile, the German Christians used the state's propaganda arm to disseminate the charge that the church opposition was "politically unreliable" and "enemies of the state." One German Christian campaign slogan declared, "The German Christians are the SA of Jesus Christ."[41]

Then the Gestapo stepped in. A week before the election, the secret police raided Niemöller's office, confiscating thousands of pieces of campaign literature. Bonhoeffer and an ally, Gerhard Jacobi of the Kaiser Wilhelm Memorial Church, marched to Gestapo headquarters to demand their right to campaign and the return of the leaflets. The head of the Gestapo eventually relented, but with the police, press, Nazi Party, and Hitler himself promoting the German Christians, the leaflets might not have mattered anyway. Dibelius recalled, "The whole party apparatus was placed at the service of the German Christians. SA men streamed from the party offices to register as voters and then to vote." The night before the election, Hitler took to the airwaves to promote the German Christian Movement, which has "consciously taken its stand on the ground of the National Socialist state."[42]

The German Christians won by a landslide, capturing nearly 70 percent of the vote, two-thirds of the seats in the church's governing bodies, and all but three of the twenty-eight church regions. The newly elected president of the provincial church of Brandenburg, Johannes Grell, could hardly control his excitement. In his view, German Protestants owed the complete reconstruction and reorientation of their church to "our wonderful National Socialist revolution, created through the dedication of a hundred thousand Brown Shirts ready to sacrifice their blood, and above all by the heaven-sent führer and savior of our Volk and fatherland, for whose sending our Protestant church cannot thank God enough." The German Christians soon moved to install the Aryan paragraph, leading Niemöller and his colleagues to protest that state laws had no place in the church. Their opposition was met with "gales of laughter" by the German Christian representatives, according to a Swedish journalist present at the Brandenburg provincial synod. The Aryan paragraph went through by a vote of 133 to 48. Most regions passed similar laws banning pastors of Jewish heritage. The journalist concluded, "The whole affair could only be characterized as religious barbarism."[43]

THE GERMAN CHRISTIANS were now in the position to control church affairs, and Niemöller could no longer sustain the belief that he was involved in merely a struggle between rival church factions. In the aftermath of the election, he openly criticized the state's intervention, particularly Hitler's speech the night before the vote. Though the election was lost and it was obvious there would be none to contest in years to come, Niemöller refused to stand down. He called on the Young Reformers to continue preaching the theology of a confessing church and to confront German Christian blasphemy.[44]

Niemöller barely managed to maintain local control in Dahlem, where two of five parish council seats up for election went to the German Christians. There were eight seats in all, but three were safely in the hands of Niemöller and his two fellow opposition ministers Eberhard Röhricht and Friedrich Müller. The vote over the remaining five was closer than Niemöller would have liked: 1,447 parishioners voted for candidates representing the church opposition and 1,046 for the German Christians. "Thanks be to God!" he recorded in his diary. He considered himself fortunate to share his parish with like-minded ministers. Most Berlin parishes had between two and four pastors, and most were divided, leading to considerable internal strife.[45]

The parish of Schöneberg in central Berlin was the site of one such duel. One Sunday a conflict arose between opposing pastors and their flocks over which group had the right to use the church. Both sides claimed possession by occupying strategic areas of the building. The German Christian pastor, Gerhard Peters, stood in front of the altar as his supporters arrayed themselves in the front pews. The opposition pastor, Eitel-Friedrich von Rabenau, held the pulpit while his followers piled into the rear pews. From the loft, a trombone choir accompanied opposition parishioners singing Advent hymns; from the same location, with gusto, the organist accompanied the German Christians singing "A Mighty Fortress Is Our God." When the musical confrontation died down, Rabenau tried to preach from the pulpit, while Peters recited the liturgy from the altar. Cries of "We want to hear Rabenau's sermon!" and "Peters is abusing the word of God!" were heard. The row lasted two long hours, with parishioners nearly coming to blows. Eventually Rabenau conceded the church to the German Christians and left the building with his following.[46]

At a Young Reformation meeting, Niemöller challenged his colleagues to clarify their position, asking rhetorically, "Is there theologically a fundamental difference between the teachings of the Reformation and those proclaimed by the German Christians?" He answered, "We fear: Yes!—They say: No!—This lack of clarity must be cleared up through a confession for our time." He ended by declaring that pastors should have to declare whether they backed such a confession or not.[47]

Bonhoeffer and a few other theologians took up this call and sequestered themselves at Bodelschwingh's Bethel Institute to write a confession of faith—a formal statement declaring to the world the church's faith, its deepest convictions, and what the pastorate should preach and teach. "The Holy Scriptures of the Old and New Testaments are the sole source and norm for the doctrine of the church," they began. By grounding the church in *both* Scripture and its interpretation in the Reformation confessions as formulated by Martin Luther and his followers, the authors explicitly rejected the German Christians' claim that National Socialist ideology had a place in church proclamation. Although the published version of the "Bethel Confession" lacked the teeth of Bonhoeffer's draft, especially on the Jewish question, it maintained that Jews alone could not be blamed for Christ's crucifixion. The document also defended baptized Jews. Niemöller may not have been as sophisticated theologically as the authors of this dense and lengthy document, but he nevertheless was convinced of its ultimate message.[48]

On a practical level, however, there wasn't much the confessing opposition could do against the numerically superior German Christians. Niemöller recommended boycotting the upcoming Prussian synod, but his colleagues overruled him, believing that they could negotiate with their adversaries. Their optimism proved unwarranted. On the morning of September 5, the confessing clergy arrived at the synod in their customary robes. The German Christians wore their brown SA uniforms and riding boots. To demonstrate his disdain for the whole farce, Niemöller wore a gray suit. There were so many attendees in SA uniforms that it was dubbed the "Brown Synod." In a span of just two hours, the DC passed twenty motions, including a motion banning anyone with a Jewish parent or grandparent from church employment. Niemöller asked to speak but was denied. When confessing church leader Karl Koch protested the lack of "brotherly collaboration," the brown block hissed and jeered. As the seventy-two robed clergymen, and the one in a gray suit, filed out in protest, the DC hurled invective at them, shouting, "Shame! Shut your mouth! Get out!"[49]

Incensed above all by the racial legislation, Bonhoeffer and Hildebrandt called for the opposition to completely break from the German Protestant Church and found an independent body. Only eleven pastors would have been dismissed had the law been implemented, but for these two theologians, a church that adopted the Aryan paragraph could no longer call itself Christian. The Aryan clause called into question the efficacy of the sacrament of baptism. The eleven Protestant pastors of Jewish descent were baptized Christians; their faith in Christ could not be overridden by their racial heritage.[50]

Bonhoeffer and Hildebrandt were willing to stake everything on this issue. They opposed it on moral and technical grounds—and because it was personal. Pastor Hildebrandt, who was raised Lutheran, had a Jewish mother and Bonhoeffer's brother-in-law, Göttingen University law professor Gerhard Leibholz, was at risk of losing his position due to his Jewish ancestry. But not everyone in the opposition felt so strongly. Niemöller, too, saw theological error in the Aryan paragraph, but the idea of leaving the official church was simply too radical a solution for conservative churchmen like him.[51]

Although the opposition agreed to remain within the official church, they did not end their protest. In the wake of the Brown Synod, Bonhoeffer and Niemöller drafted a four-part pledge and distributed it to pastors, asking them to affirm their commitment to the church's creed; to vigorously protest violations of that creed; to reject the Aryan paragraph; and to commit themselves to supporting non-Aryan colleagues. A letter from Niemöller accompanied the pledge, which was sent to Young Reformers and others likely to sign.

> Because of the distress [in the churches] we have called into being an "Emergency League" of pastors who have given one another their word in a written declaration that they will be bound in their preaching by Holy Scripture and Reformation confessions alone and that they will alleviate the distress of those brethren who have to suffer for this. . . . I am aware that this league cannot save the church and move the world; but I am equally aware that we owe it to the Lord of the Church and the brethren to do today what lies in our power, and that caution and restraint today already signify failure, because those in great distress lack proof of our fraternal solidarity. So let us act.[52]

Speed was of the essence because confessing churchmen were preparing for a showdown at the national synod scheduled for September 27 in Wittenberg. The opposition felt that arriving at the synod with a pledge signed by hundreds of pastors would make for a strong protest and bring public attention to the church schism. The early response to the pledge was encouraging. By the end of September, twenty-three hundred pastors had signed. By January of the following year, over seven thousand of the eighteen thousand pastors in the German Protestant Church had committed themselves to the pledge. Those who signed became members of the Pastors' Emergency League (PEL), the forerunner of the formal Confessing Church, founded in May 1934. Martin Niemöller was the PEL's leader.

Whereas the popularity of the pledge might have indicated a widespread rejection of Nazi ideology and policy, it did not. The authors of the pledge deliberately avoided political issues and said nothing about the persecution of unbaptized Jews. The pledge was concerned only with the Aryan paragraph as an infringement "in the area of the church of Christ." It is surely the document's apolitical quality that won over so many signatories. Where Bonhoeffer had hoped to make opposition to anti-Semitism, inside and outside the church, central to the fight against the Nazi regime, Niemöller's conservative path kept churchmen focused on the struggle within. That was as far as most were willing to go at the end of 1933.

FIVE

Fighting Pastor
(1934–1937)

W HATEVER HE SET HIMSELF TO, MARTIN NIEMÖLLER ALWAYS DIS-
played unusual determination, to the point that some have remarked that his autobiography, *From U-Boat to Pulpit*, should have been
titled *With U-Boat to Pulpit*. But despite his penchant for uncompromis-
ing positions, he rarely lost his sense of humor or his charm. "He was
like a man on fire," George Bell, the Anglican bishop of Chichester, observed after interviewing the Dahlem pastor in the midst of what came
to be known as the Church Struggle. Yet he was "smiling and friendly
all the time," Bell added, "and a man of very great faith." Bell left their
two-hour conversation captivated by Niemöller's "great vividness" and
inspired by his passion, piety, and sense of obligation to church and
country. "We could not have had a happier or more illuminating talk,"
Bell concluded.[1]

By outward appearances in the fall of 1933, Niemöller was indeed a happy man. The forty-one-year-old was the father of three sons and three daughters, with a fourth son, Martin (Tini), to arrive on August 11, 1935. He was the pastor of a historic church whose parishioners were among the richest and most influential people in Germany. His congregation valued and respected his guidance. After years of material hardship, he and Else were enjoying financial security. And the new nationalist government was ridding the country of internal enemies and defending itself in the international arena.

But the quick wit and broad smiles belied the troubles Niemöller faced. From the founding of the Pastors Emergency League in September 1933, his life was characterized by exhausting eighteen-hour days. He had little time with his family, and many of his friendships were ruined. The walls of his ultranationalist beliefs cracked—ever so slightly. The Nazis, he would come to realize, were not the partners he had hoped for in the nation's Christian and moral renewal.

NIEMÖLLER HAD HOPED that the PEL would at last give the church opposition some teeth in its struggle with the German Christians. The highly anticipated national synod, on September 27, 1933, in Wittenberg was the new opposition's first target. On a warm autumn morning, PEL leaders made their way from Berlin to Luther's city. They carried thousands of pamphlets entitled "To the National Synod" and bearing the signatures of twenty-two Berlin pastors who had signed in the name of the more than two thousand pastors. The text of the pamphlet defiantly declared that Hitler's German Christians had taken over the church and distorted the Gospel, rending the supposed church unity of previous years. Likening themselves to Luther, who had objected to the falsity of the church of Christ in his day, these modern-day dissidents proclaimed, "We will not stop protesting loudly and clearly, far and wide, against any violation of the church's confession."[2]

German Christian bishop Ludwig Müller leads a procession to
Castle Church, September 27, 1933. (Alamy)

Would the German Christians vote to implement the Aryan paragraph throughout the church? Would they elect Ludwig Müller, the
Nazi-backed German Christian leader, the new Reich bishop? Would the
opposition get to voice its disapproval of the nazification of the church
without being booed, heckled, and run out of the synod? These were
the questions pastors Dietrich Bonhoeffer, Franz Hildebrandt, Martin
Niemöller, and others faced as they distributed their pamphlet to the
throngs lining the street en route to Castle Church. Gertrud Staewen—a
twenty-four-year-old social worker, political radical, and parish assistant in Dahlem—helped pass out pamphlets and attach the protest statement to trees, telegraph poles, and building walls throughout the center

of Wittenberg. She would later join a resistance group that helped hide Berlin Jews and provided them with forged documents and food ration coupons.[3]

Meanwhile, both Castle Church (*Schlosskirche*), where the morning service was held, and City Church (*Stadtkirche*), where the synod proceedings would be held, were decorated lavishly in the black-white-and-red flags of the imperial era, the Nazi swastika flags, and the flag of the German Protestant Church, a purple cross on a white field. Following the church and political dignitaries was a detachment of "theological storm troopers": one hundred theology students organized into an SA contingent. Carrying trenching tools and heavy army packs, their field-gray uniforms adorned with the purple cross and the SS runes, the troopers settled into the church choir for the morning service. Swastika flags adorned the altar as Bishop Theophil Wurm of Württemberg delivered the opening address.[4]

For Niemöller, Bonhoeffer, and their group, the synod proved disappointing. The German Christian delegates neither acknowledged the PEL's protest nor addressed the controversy caused by the Aryan paragraph. The sixty delegates unanimously elected Ludwig Müller Reich bishop. In his acceptance speech, he proclaimed, "The Lord has called us into the breach as His warriors. We look upon the German movement for liberation and its leader, our chancellor, as a gift from God." Regarding the Aryan clause, he said, "Equality before God does not exclude inequality between men." He declared that "the political church struggle is over. The struggle for the soul of the people now begins."[5]

Within weeks of the synod, Bonhoeffer shocked his colleagues by abruptly leaving Germany. Accompanied by Hildebrandt, whose Jewish ancestry placed him in a risky position, Bonhoeffer accepted an offer to serve as the pastor of two German congregations in London. In a letter to Karl Barth, Bonhoeffer labored to explain his decision to leave. Bonhoeffer said that he wanted his own parish—which would have been difficult in DC-dominated Prussia—and a stronger connection with the burgeoning international ecumenical movement. He also expressed his disappointment over his isolation within the church opposition. "I thought it was about time to go into the wilderness for a spell, and simply work as a pastor, as unobtrusively as possible," he wrote, while the Nazis were taking over his church. "Perhaps this can also be a way of giving some real support to the German church." Barth wasn't convinced. "Get back to your post in Berlin straightaway!" he barked. "You need to be here with all guns blazing!"[6]

One reason he was needed in Berlin, Barth explained, was to counter the conservatives within the opposition, exemplified by bishops Hans Meiser of Bavaria and Theophil Wurm of Württemberg. But Bonhoeffer didn't heed Barth's counsel. He remained in London for seventeen months. He did, nevertheless, stay in contact with Niemöller, mostly to prod him to adopt a more radical line. Bonhoeffer did his best to contribute to the Church Struggle from afar, through his ecumenical work and frequent trips to Berlin.

Niemöller and many of his colleagues backed Hitler's foreign policy. In October 1933, he joined hundreds of PEL members in sending Hitler a congratulatory telegram after he withdrew from the League of Nations. The note gushed about the "manly deed" that supposedly preserved Germany's honor. "In the name of more than 2,500 Protestant pastors who do not belong to the Faith Movement of German Christians," the telegram read, "we pledge loyal adherence and prayerful support." Niemöller urged his parishioners to approve the action in a November 12, 1933, plebiscite. Ninety-six percent of Germans voted in favor of exiting the Geneva-based league, which they blamed for their homeland's many post–World War I humiliations.[7]

Not all the dissenting pastors felt as Niemöller did. An exasperated Hildebrandt wrote Niemöller from London, "I find it impossible to understand how you can joyfully welcome the political move in Geneva when you refuse to adopt an unequivocal attitude toward a church which persistently denies us [Christians of Jewish descent] equality of status." The rebuke was directed as much at Niemöller's nationalism as at his anti-Semitism.[8]

Indeed, although the PEL's pledge was unequivocal in its rejection of the Aryan clause, Niemöller's own position on Jewish-Christians in the church was less praiseworthy, and Hildebrandt knew it. In early November, Niemöller published a short essay in the opposition newspaper *Junge Kirche* (*Young Church*), reiterating that Christians were obliged to accept converted Jews into the church, though only at great sacrifice, given all that the church had "to bear under their influence." It was understandable, he argued, that Christians in Germany found the very idea of baptized Jews in the church disagreeable. But this was what Scripture demanded. He went on to suggest that pastors of Jewish descent should show self-restraint by not ministering in parishes where they might offend the congregation. Although Niemöller was a steadfast personal and professional supporter of Hildebrandt—and would choose the young firebrand, after his return to Germany with Bonhoeffer in 1935, for the critical position of PEL treasurer—Hildebrandt would have preferred that his movement's leaders preach genuine empathy rather than reluctant toleration.[9]

During Bonhoeffer's absence from Germany, it fell more and more to Barth to press confessing churchmen to stand firm against Müller's heretical and illegitimate church government. He warned that attempts to find common ground with the moderate wing of the German Christians—a goal of some conservative churchmen in the PEL—only muddied the issue. Ever difficult to pin down, Niemöller was not entirely aligned with either the radicals in Barth's circle or the conservative compromisers. He vacillated between the two wings, at times finding common cause with the radicals and at other times with the conservatives.

Not long after praising Hitler for leaving the disarmament talks, Niemöller preached a sermon on Reformation Sunday that took direct aim at the DC and their political theology of "German-Teutonic piety." He was especially offended by the uses to which the German Christians put Martin Luther. They did not care what Luther really stood for, he insisted; instead, they made Luther a "model prototype of the religious Christian hero." The temptation to worship Luther, Niemöller allowed, was great because "Luther as a German is nearer to us than the Jewish rabbi from Nazareth." But faith in Luther remained hollow and meaningless "if we do not join with Luther in confessing our faith in Christ and Christ alone."[10]

The typewriter that Pastor Niemöller used to compose sermons during the Nazi era and after. (US Holocaust Memorial Museum, gift of Sibylle Sarah Niemoeller)

On November 11, Joachim Hossenfelder, the German Christian bishop of Brandenburg and Niemöller's superior, finally had had enough of Niemöller's baiting and suspended him for insubordination. The official reason was Niemöller's appeal to ordination candidates to disregard the German Christian questionnaire asking about their racial heritage. But there was, of course, more to it than that. Through sermons, circular letters, articles in church periodicals, and protests, Niemöller and the PEL leadership—even as the nationalists among them fell into line with other aspects of the Nazi program—were mounting an organized resistance to the German Christian takeover. Niemöller's suspension was lifted the following day—but it was to be the first of many.[11]

In responding to these punishments, Niemöller followed a pattern: he would tell the Reich bishop that he intended to disregard his suspension and he would continue to preach. And he did so, to larger and larger crowds. On Sundays when the subway pulled into Thielplatz station in

Dahlem, the conductor would announce, "Thielplatz, anyone for Pastor Niemöller get off here." In addition to the Protestant faithful, among those getting off were Gestapo agents, foreign correspondents, and people who had never attended any church. Often Jesus Christ Church, which could accommodate 1,200—many more than historic St. Anne's—was full.[12]

Despite Niemöller's growing popularity, the German Christians appeared unassailable in the wake of the Prussian and national synods, the plebiscite victory, and the celebrations of Luther's 450th birthday. But the German Christians had a vulnerability: their own extremist wing. Flush with excitement at their newfound power, DC extremists held a giant rally in the massive Sports Palace in Berlin on November 13. Müller, Reich bishop and leader of the moderate wing, did not attend. German Christian extremists packed all twenty thousand seats in the arena. Amid the usual array of flags and martial music, Bishop Hossenfelder fired up the audience with talk of a great "*Volksmission*"—mission of the people— whereby *German* pastors would preach to *German* people in a *German* way about a *German* gospel.

Speaking for the Berlin German Christians was Reinhold Krause, a high school teacher and devoted Nazi. Krause began with a rousing call for the completion of Luther's Reformation in the Third Reich. Krause called Luther "the Nordic God-seeker" and said that only he could lead the way to "the German God and the German Church." A German church, he explained, was one rid of all Jewish elements, including the Old Testament with "its stories of cattle-dealers and pimps." Germans should worship a heroic Aryan Jesus—a fearless combatant, not the "crucified one." He insisted that only through a heroic Christianity could Germany bring about the spiritual awakening of its people. He proudly announced that the pure teaching of Jesus coincided perfectly with the demands of National Socialism. The DC audience repeatedly interrupted Krause's speech with extended applause and shouts of "bravo!" and "hear, hear."[13]

The next morning the Berlin papers carried articles describing the German Christians' neopagan and anti-Semitic assault on Scripture. Niemöller reacted immediately. He summoned Barth and Bodelschwingh to Berlin for discussions; then the three men, along with Niemöller's brother Wilhelm and Gerhard Jacobi, paid Reich Bishop Müller a visit. They presented him with a three-point ultimatum and an 8:00 p.m. deadline. They demanded that Müller condemn the extremist wing of the DC, suspend the offending church leaders present at the rally, and recommit himself and the Reich church leadership to their ordination vows. If these demands went unmet, the confessing church was prepared to officially split off and declare itself Germany's sole legitimate church. Hitler's reason for appointing Müller his church representative was for Müller to bring about a united Reich church, so the Reich bishop had little choice but to grudgingly comply.[14]

Niemöller and the opposition celebrated, but it was a temporary victory. For, like the German Christians, they were a house divided. After Müller's acquiescence, Barth and Niemöller argued over how to press their advantage. Niemöller saw an opportunity in the Sports Palace debacle to drive moderates such as Müller to break entirely with his extremist colleagues and to compromise with the church opposition. This would save the Protestant Church from a schism. Barth, ever the theologian, opposed all compromises on matters of faith and wanted to take the fight to Hitler himself, who had helped the German Christians come to power. To Barth's chagrin, Niemöller's position won out. PEL would reach out to Müller. A fuming Barth berated the "dictatorship of the U-boat commander Niemöller," who was turning the Sports Palace scandal into a victory for Müller. "All the trouble and anxiety that this year has cost will have been in vain," Barth vented, "if the only difference is that the future Reich bishop is—for example—called Niemöller." Lumping together the moderate wing of the DC with the conservative wing of the confessing clergy, in which he included Niemöller, was a common tactic of Barth's. To him, both were guilty of compromising the Gospel.[15]

Bonhoeffer and Hildebrandt sided with Barth and told Niemöller as much in emphatic letters and telegrams from London. They urged him to stand fast and cleanse "this entire plague . . . of old and new half-baked Christians from our ranks." "Now is the time," they exclaimed, "when we must be radical on all points, including the Aryan paragraph, without fear of the possible disagreeable consequences for ourselves."[16]

It is revealing that, even though Niemöller had spent his entire adult life within the military and church hierarchies, he did not dress down the London pastors, ten years his junior. He found their letters impetuous, but he knew that his two young friends meant well even if they added to his stress. He reassured the pair that he had no intention of taking a weak line with the German Christians, but that he was working to keep the broad opposition unified and therefore didn't want to entirely dismiss the possibility of winning over DC moderates.[17]

By the end of 1933, Niemöller had established himself as the leader of the resistance to nazification of the Protestant churches. But he was not ready yet to reject National Socialism itself. Nor did he have a vision for a new German Protestantism. Up to this juncture, Niemöller had demonstrated a talent for managing an opposition group, but not for imagining a reformation. He could only look back. What Niemöller really wanted, as Hildebrandt put it, "was nothing but the maintenance and confession of the old faith." Another colleague put the matter in more critical (and nautical) terms, describing Niemöller as a "good mariner" who lacked the qualifications for admiral.[18]

NIEMÖLLER WOULD CHANGE, however, during the second year of Hitler's dictatorship. His attempt to find common ground with the weakened Reich bishop in the aftermath of the Sports Palace fiasco went nowhere. Neither man was willing to compromise. When Müller sought to silence the opposition by forbidding church officials to criticize the Reich church government, Niemöller fired back with a declaration that he asked dissident clergy to read from the pulpit on Sunday, January 7, 1934. It ended with the refrain from the Augsburg Confession, "We must obey God rather than man." A few hundred pastors in Berlin read the declaration that Sunday; Müller suspended fifty of them and severely reprimanded Niemöller.[19]

Watching from the Reich chancellery, Hitler was vexed by the church question. His long-term goal was to see Christianity eliminated from

Germany. But for the moment he wanted a unified and orderly church under his sway. He seethed at daily accounts, especially those that appeared in the foreign press, of the bickering church factions. It gave the impression that the führer wasn't in control, that the German people weren't united behind him. What is more, the whole affair made little sense to the order- and hierarchy-obsessed Hitler. Why was the Reich bishop arguing with dissidents when he should be squelching their protest? And why was a former U-boat commander and current Nazi sympathizer leading the opposition? To end all of the vexations, he called a meeting for January 25 at the Reich chancellery with a dozen prominent church leaders, Niemöller among them, representing the various factions.[20]

Niemöller was thrilled that Hitler wanted to get involved, believing that the führer's support for the German Christians was due to a misunderstanding. Opposition leaders, or at least the conservatives, were certain that once Hitler understood Müller's heresies and the opposition's political loyalty, he would dismiss the Reich bishop and return the church to the old guard. They also knew that President Hindenburg sided with them and wanted to see Müller gone. So confident was Niemöller that he prepared a memorandum for Hitler explaining the Church Struggle and closing with a plea to the führer to entrust the opposition with the task of forming a new church government.[21]

At 1:00 p.m. on the twenty-fifth of January 1934, the dozen clerics filed into the reception room at the chancellery. Hitler, Göring, Müller, Minister of the Interior Wilhelm Frick, and others stood against the back wall waiting for them. Facing the government entourage, the clergymen aligned in a semicircle with the bishops in the front. Niemöller, the only pastor invited to the meeting, stood in the back with other lesser church officials. Frick introduced Hitler to each of them. Hitler then turned to Göring. The chief of the Prussian secret police reached into his red briefcase and produced a document. It was the transcript of a private phone conversation recorded that very morning between Niemöller and the theologian Walter Künneth. Göring read the transcript aloud, relishing the moment. Künneth had called to get Niemöller's impressions on the

forthcoming meeting with Hitler. Niemöller said that President Hindenburg had "summoned" the chancellor to a preliminary noontime meeting and would receive Hitler with the PEL memorandum in his hand.
Niemöller then joked that Hindenburg would administer the last rites to
Hitler before the meeting with the church leaders.[22]

When Göring finished, the room was silent. The clerics appeared
paralyzed. Göring described their reaction as "terrified to the point of
becoming dumb and invisible." Hitler later recalled, "The delegates of
the Protestant Church were so shriveled up with terror that they almost
disappeared." No one could have imagined a worse catastrophe for the
church opposition, and the meeting had not lasted five minutes. The
taped phone conversation convinced Hitler that the church opposition
was trying to drive a wedge between him and the Reich president, and
that the PEL had political, not just theological, goals. "This time the
U-boat commander has torpedoed not his opponents," Bishop Wurm
wrote a colleague afterwards, "but his friends and himself."[23]

When Hitler called his name, Niemöller stepped forward. The führer
asked him if the phone conversation had taken place. Niemöller admitted
that it had, but cautioned that it should not be misinterpreted. The goal
of the church opposition was to return the church to its confessions and
creeds. It did not reject the state. In fact, the church opposition was concerned not only with the well-being of the church, Niemöller explained,
but also that of the German people and the Third Reich.[24]

Hitler listened quietly, but this last remark clearly provoked him.
"Leave the care of the Third Reich to me," he said brusquely. "You take care
of the church." Hitler then complained about how tiresome the Church
Struggle had become. What most aggravated him, he said, was that pastors were inciting people against the government. On cue, Göring again
reached into his trusty briefcase to retrieve incriminating evidence. At
this point, the conservative bishops of Bavaria, Hanover, and Württemberg—who had retained control of their regional churches but refused
to side unequivocally with either the confessing church or the German
Christians—tried to assure Hitler of the church's political loyalty and return the discussion to the problematic Reich bishop.[25]

Hitler didn't care who was Reich bishop, as long as the church problem went away. He ended the hour-long meeting with a plea and an ultimatum. He appealed to the clerics to collaborate in a Christian and brotherly manner for the good of the nation. But if they couldn't bring the Church Struggle to a peaceful conclusion, then, he threatened, the state would cut off financial support and the church would wither on the vine. As the meeting ended, Hitler shook hands with each cleric.[26]

There are as many accounts of this famous meeting as there were men in the room. Niemöller himself offered various renditions at different points in his life. Some biographers have added their own embellishments. According to Niemöller, the reception ended not with a mere handshake but with the pastor refuting the führer. Niemöller maintained that, during the handshake, he told the chancellor, "You said leave the care of the German people to me. To that I must say that neither you nor any power in the world is in a position to take away the responsibility God entrusted in us to care for our people." Hitler— Niemöller recalled—was stone-faced, withdrew his hand, turned away, and left the room.[27]

Although the veracity of Niemöllller's account is doubtful, the purpose is transparent: to portray the devout pastor standing up to the diabolical dictator and even getting the better of him. Niemöller's account gained wide traction after 1945. In the aftermath of World War II and the Holocaust, German churchmen sought to burnish their reputations by exaggerating their resistance to Hitler and Nazism. Wilhelm Niemöller was particularly active in this endeavor, and Martin himself wasn't shy about self-aggrandizement. Church historian Klaus Scholder, however, disputes Niemöller's account, and the relevant documents—Niemöller's statements aside—bear no trace of Niemöller's final words to the führer.[28]

In any event, Niemöller remained a target of Göring's secret police. After the meeting, the Gestapo searched Niemöller's home for documents linking the PEL to foreign agents and hauled off all of his PEL files. Two days later Müller suspended Niemöller and over one hundred other PEL pastors. The day after that, the Gestapo arrested Niemöller at his home and brought him to Alexanderplatz headquarters for questioning. Only after a Reich cabinet member intervened on his behalf was Niemöller released, with the proviso that he report to the Gestapo periodically.

Exhausted by this series of events, Else and Martin decided to visit Martin's parents in Elberfeld, effectively accepting the suspension for the moment. He asked Hildebrandt, who had returned from London to Berlin in mid-January, to assume the position of PEL treasurer and preach in his place until his return. Disheartened Dahlem parishioners attended church that Sunday expecting to find a pro-Hitler DC replacement in the pulpit. Instead, they found Hildebrandt, who, by all reports, including one from Paula Bonhoeffer, Dietrich's mother, gave a rousing sermon calling on the faithful to put spiritual before temporal authority. During their absence, the Niemöllers also asked Hildebrandt, a bachelor, to stay in their home and care for their children. Hildebrandt readily agreed, but he got more than he bargained for. Early one morning, he was awakened when a homemade bomb exploded in the truss of the rectory, setting part of the roof on fire. Fortunately, no one was injured. Not surprisingly, the police never found the culprits.[29]

In the following months, Niemöller was constantly harassed and intimidated by the police. He was arrested and interrogated several times and repeatedly suspended from his pastorate. Many dissenting pastors received similar treatment. Fearful of creating martyrs, church authorities were loath to expel pastors outright, and some pastors continued to preach despite the ban. Usually, when a confessing pastor was suspended, the PEL would send a replacement. When the replacement was suspended or arrested, it would send another. The PEL salaries of suspended pastors came from member contributions, a service that fell under Hildebrandt's purview as treasurer. The confessing church increasingly functioned without much state support.

When Niemöller returned from Elberfeld to Dahlem and started preaching again, Müller summarily retired him. But Niemöller refused to obey the order, a decision his wealthy parishioners rallied behind. Soon after, in late February 1934, Associated Press Berlin bureau chief Louis Lochner attended a meeting in the Dahlem church basement, where Niemöller calmly presided. "The hall was jammed," Lochner reported.

"As the pastor entered, every man, woman and child rose to his feet, cheered, and finally broke into the strains of that old battle hymn of defiant Lutheranism, 'A Mighty Fortress is our God.'" Niemöller announced that he had disobeyed an order only twice in his life. "The first time came at the end of the world war, in 1918, when the captain in command of our U-boat unit ordered me to take my little submarine, with which I had sailed the seven seas, to Scapa Flow and sink it. 'Herr Kapitaen,' I said, 'I cannot do that; I refuse obedience.' Today the Reich bishop summoned me," Niemöller announced. "He informed me that I had been removed from my post; that I may no longer preach. 'Herr Reichsbischoff,' I said, 'I refuse obedience.'" He was only doing what any Christian would, he said. "The Bible says one must obey God more than man. I have a mandate from God, as an ordained minister of the Gospel, to preach. I shall continue to preach."

After that, Berliners from all over the city flocked in still greater numbers to hear the defiant pastor on Sundays. In March 1934, the American correspondent for the *Chicago Daily Tribune*, Sigrid Schultz, dubbed Niemöller "the fighting pastor."[30]

ALTHOUGH NIEMÖLLER'S RADICALISM dismayed his conservative colleagues, German Christian heresies and Müller's episcopal dictatorship compelled the two sides to seek common cause. Gathering in the Ulm Cathedral in southern Germany on April 22, representatives of both wings of the confessing church made a far-reaching declaration. With common purpose, they proclaimed theirs the "legitimate Evangelical Church of Germany." This was the first step in the founding of the official Confessing Church.[31]

This proclamation marked the beginning of the decisive break with the Reich church that young radicals such as Bonhoeffer and Hildebrandt had been calling for since the summer of 1933. From this point forward, the Confessing Church and the Reich Church each claimed to be the legitimate church. The Confessing Church established its own leadership body, known as the Reich Council of Brethren, and convened its own synods.

The second major step in the creation of the separate Confessing Church was the articulation of its theological foundation at the first national Confessing synod, held in Barmen from May 29 to 31, 1934. It was here that Karl Barth drafted the six theses known as the "Barmen Declaration of Faith," or "Barmen Confession," a masterpiece of clarity and concision. The first thesis set the tone for the whole declaration.

> Jesus Christ, as he is attested to us in Holy Scripture, is the one Word of God which we have to hear, and which we have to trust and obey in life and death. We reject the false doctrine that the church could and should recognize as a source of its proclamation, beyond and besides this one Word of God, yet other events, powers, historic figures, and truths as God's revelation.

National Socialism, Barmen made clear, had no place in the church's proclamation.[32]

When the delegates heard Barth's declaration read aloud, they rose to their feet and sang the hymn "All Praise and Thanks to God." Some postwar critics of Barmen point to a missing "seventh thesis," which they believe should have embraced Christians of Jewish descent and condemned anti-Semitism. But these issues were not foremost on the minds of churchmen in 1934. Had a seventh thesis been proposed, it probably would have resulted in an irreconcilable split; the Confessing Church was only recently unified and was undoubtedly fragile. Later that spring, Niemöller helped design a membership card for pastors and parishioners to sign, declaring their allegiance to the Confessing Church. By the early 1940s, millions of Germans possessed these red cards.[33]

The Barmen synod brought Barth and Niemöller closer. The respect between them grew day by day as they served together on the Council of Brethren. But the two men differed in many ways: politically, Barth hewed to the left, Niemöller to the right; Barth heralded from tiny, neutral Switzerland, Niemöller from imperialist, martial Prussia; Barth exuded cosmopolitanism, Niemöller provincialism; and Barth advanced an erudite Reformed theology, Niemöller a simple Lutheranism.

The two enjoyed kidding each other, especially over their respective approaches to theology. Barth once told a mutual friend that Niemöller should put his theology on a boat, sail it out to sea, and sink it. Niemöller gave as good as he got, telling a biographer, "I have never cherished theologians. Take Karl Barth, my dearest friend. All his volumes are standing there. I have never read any of them. I never heard a lecture by him. Theologians are here only to make incomprehensible what a child can understand." At Niemöller's sixtieth birthday celebration, after decades of friendship despite periods of great strife between them, Barth joked:

Not so long ago, a conversation between Martin Niemöller and myself went like this. "Martin, I'm surprised that you almost always get the point despite the *little* systematic theology that you've done!" "Karl, I'm surprised that you almost always get the point despite the *great deal* of systematic theology that you've done!"[34]

As unalike as the two men were, their talents were complementary. Niemöller ran the operations of the Confessing Church, while Barth took charge of theological matters. Together, they instilled in their church a resolute certainty in the correctness of their positions, a confidence that manifested itself in their determination to refuse all compromises with the German Christians. Niemöller's alliance with Barth in the spring of 1934 aligned him unequivocally with the radical wing of the Confessing Church.

Despite his many responsibilities, Niemöller would not have been a true German burgher if he had failed to take weeks-long summer vacations. In 1934, at the seaside resort of Zinnowitz on the Baltic, he relaxed by writing his autobiography *From U-Boat to Pulpit*. The first two-thirds narrated his submarine adventures and the last third his struggles against the democratic Weimar Republic. Anyone in the Nazi Party who questioned Niemöller's commitment to his nation need only have read this book to be convinced of his reactionary nationalism. In fact, this was a central reason he composed the memoir. Upon its publication, he sent a copy to the minister of propaganda, Joseph Goebbels, with a note explaining that it was written in the "spirit" of the Third Reich. Most likely because it was in line with the beliefs of the majority of Germans at the time, the book was wildly successful. By 1938, seventy-five thousand copies had been sold, and Niemöller used the profits to buy a new piano and a car.[35]

Niemöller's Prussian militarism and Protestant nationalism, proudly on display throughout the book, were the very principles that Hitler exploited in his rise to power. That Niemöller didn't play down these sentiments after a year and a half of Nazi terror and thuggery says a great deal about where his political sympathies lay in 1934. Just a month before Niemöller wrote his book, Hitler ordered the SS to murder nearly two hundred leading SA officials and conservative politicians he feared were undermining his authority.

After completing the book in the fall of 1934, Niemöller returned to the fight for church autonomy. At the Second Confessional Synod, in Niemöller's home parish of Dahlem, the Confessing Church took its final step away from the Reich Church. Niemöller helped push his colleagues to this radical decision: "We are at the twelfth hour," he declared. Worshiping alongside the German Christians was nothing less than "spiritual adultery," he declared. "Either we are a Christian church," he told a parishioner, "or a German Christian church, that is, a non-Christian church."[36]

The synod asserted that the Reich Church leadership had violated its own authority to such a degree that it could no longer claim to lead anyone. It was time for the Confessing Church to take its place and represent the entire German Protestant Church. One radical delegate declared, "We are not leaving this church, our church, to form a free church; we are the church."[37]

The Confessing Church set up illegal seminaries, where seminarians learned how to handle the turbulence and risk that came with shepherding a dissident flock. This was the work that coaxed Dietrich Bonhoeffer home. He left his post in London in 1935 to direct the Confessing Church seminary in Finkenwalde, in northeastern Germany. Of course

Müller and his deputies had no intention of handing over the reins to the likes of Bonhoeffer, Niemöller, and Barth. So the struggle went on.[38]

Increasingly, Barth and Niemöller were labeled enemies of the state. Niemöller bristled at the charge. As a devout German Lutheran, he found it preposterous that he or any of his Confessing Church colleagues could be regarded as anything other than patriots. A year earlier, Niemöller had even proposed that Confessing churchmen should join the Nazi Party en masse to counter accusations of disloyalty to the nation. When London's *Morning Post* published an article titled "Pastor Defies Hitler," Niemöller sent a copy to the Gestapo requesting that they let the foreign press know that the struggle he was waging was apolitical, confined to church matters alone. He used his sermon of February 3, 1935, to further clarify his position. Responding to the question of how a Christian should conduct himself or herself in relation to the state, Niemöller cited Paul's Epistle to the Romans, which begins:

> Let everyone be subject to the governing authorities, for there is no authority except that which God has established. The authorities that exist have been established by God. Consequently, whoever rebels against the authority is rebelling against what God has instituted, and those who do so will bring judgment on themselves.[39]

But such loyalty, in Niemöller's view, did not mean that secular authorities could encroach unchallenged on church autonomy. Nor could Christians be idle while the state undermined their religion. More and more, the Nazis propagated neopaganism through rituals glorifying Teutonic virtues and continued with their condemnations of the Old Testament. In a scorching indictment of the "new heathenism," Niemöller and his colleagues issued a manifesto attacking Alfred Rosenberg's *The Myth of the Twentieth Century*. By endowing blood, race, and nationality with divine qualities, the new heathenism endangered the German people by devaluing their Christian heritage, they argued. A plan to have pastors read the indictment from their pulpits one Sunday in March 1935 was temporarily thwarted when the Gestapo placed over five hundred

Pastor Martin Niemöller leading
confirmation candidates to
communion shortly before his
arrest in 1937. (United States
Holocaust Memorial Museum)

pastors under house arrest. Those who tried to leave their homes were
arrested and jailed. Other pastors did deliver the indictment that Sunday or the next, leading, eventually, to more than seven hundred arrests.
Niemöller's diary entry from Friday, March 17, 1935, reads, "Half past
ten at night arrested by Gestapo. Held at Alexanderplatz. 'Slept' [with
others] on six cots."[40]

When he returned to the pulpit, Niemöller lashed out at Nazi neopa-
gans repeatedly. "We are being drawn into a titanic battle," he preached,
"between heaven and hell, between God and the devil, between angels
and demons." There was no room for compromise because that would
amount to granting the pagan god of the Nazis a place alongside Jesus.
"Anyone in the Church," he told a fellow pastor, "who presents the German Christian heresy as having an equal status next to the message of
the Gospel, or quietly acquiesces to its presence in the church, is stab-
bing the community of Jesus Christ in the back."[41]

To clip the wings of the Confessing Church and curb any and all criticism of the state, Hitler created a Ministry of Church Affairs in July 1935 and placed the Nazi jurist Hans Kerrl in charge. Kerrl and Niemöller were immediately at one another's throats. Kerrl tried to govern the churches by establishing committees of German Christians and Confessing Church conservatives.

Niemöller's public criticism of the state's church policy became more strident. Through open meetings, catechism classes, and Sunday services, he kept his growing congregation informed and rallied them behind his cause. "God does not want us to await the end of his church in silent resignation," he proclaimed in August 1935. He often began or ended his sermons with prayers of intercession for those pastors who had been suspended, forced to retire, or arrested. At his Passion Sunday sermon, he announced, "Today all the bells of the German Protestant churches are silent, and in every divine service a prayer of intercession is being said for the five Protestant pastors from Hesse and Saxony who have been taken away from their congregations and put into concentration camps."[42]

THIS SAME CONCERN did not extend to other people in the camps. As he would famously confess after the war, he did not speak out on behalf of leftists and Jews when the Nazis arrested them. Niemöller's monarchism might explain his silence over the imprisonment of Communists and Socialists. But what of Jews?

Niemöller shared the anti-Judaic theology—sometimes called "Christian anti-Semitism," or "religious anti-Semitism"—prevalent in the Protestant Church at this time, as well as the everyday anti-Semitism of German society. Since most churchmen, Niemöller included, defined Jews by both race (bloodlines) and religion (Judaism), their anti-Semitism usually entailed both a racial and religious disdain for Jews. But as his (sometimes tepid) opposition to the Aryan paragraph suggests, he was not first and foremost racially anti-Semitic. The distinction between religious and racial anti-Semitism can be hard to grasp, in part because, though theoretically distinguishable, in reality they usually overlapped.[43]

Anti-Judaic theology was the core of Christian anti-Semitism. It lumped together all Jews across the world and throughout human history. It held that their obstinacy led them to reject Jesus's status as the Son of God and the messiah. By clinging to the fossilized religion of the Old Testament, by refusing to accept the word of God in the New Testament, and—most of all—by calling for the crucifixion of Christ, Jews had earned God's wrath and lost their place as his chosen people. This resulted, so the argument went, in Christians superseding Jews as His chosen people. Angry with the Jews, God destroyed their temple in Jerusalem, drove them out of the city, and forced them to wander the earth unwelcome and scorned by the nations of the world. God's eternal curse on the Jewish people would be lifted only when they accepted Jesus as the Son of God and when they abandoned their religion via conversion. All of this, Niemöller believed.

Christian anti-Semitism differed from racial anti-Semitism in that its adherents—at least theoretically—sought a religious solution to the "Jewish problem" through the conversion of Jews. Racial anti-Semites, on the other hand, believed that Jews were racially inferior and a plague on society. Because Jews could not change their race the way they could change their religion, racial anti-Semites wanted to eliminate all Jews, including those who had converted to Christianity, through expulsion or extermination. Niemöller would never go so far. His response to the Jewish question was steeped in the Christian practice of simultaneous disdain and love for this "pitiful" race that had yet to see the light of Christ.

Although Niemöller did not embrace the racial anti-Semitism of the Nazis, and though he opposed physical attacks on Jews, his anti-Semitism was not solely of a religious nature. Questioning the prevalent anti-Semitic mood in the 1920s and '30s would have been unusual. Like many Germans from his generation, Martin Niemöller grew to maturity during a period when anti-Semitism in its various manifestations—Christian, racial, economic, political—was respectable. He worshiped in a church where pastors preached contempt for Jews. He trained and served in a notoriously anti-Semitic branch of the armed forces from the age of eighteen to twenty-seven. And he spent the Weimar years in various right-wing and ultranationalist political movements that targeted Jews. He didn't like Jews because everything he had been taught and everything he had experienced suggested that they were a foreign presence in Germany who valued neither the nation nor the God that Niemöller so dearly loved.[44]

Protestant churchmen regularly articulated theological anti-Judaism in sermons, especially on the tenth Sunday after Trinity, known as Israel Sunday. On that day they were expected to reflect on the Roman destruction of Jerusalem in AD 70. Jewish history, Niemöller preached on Israel Sunday in 1935, was "dark and sinister" because the "eternal Jew" "lived under [God's] curse" and as a consequence was a "restless wanderer." He continued: "We see a highly gifted people which produces idea after idea for the benefit of the world, but whatever it takes up becomes poisoned, and all that it ever reaps is contempt and hatred because . . . the world notices the deception and avenges itself in its own way." Niemöller asked his congregation, why are Jews hated and why does God punish them? "Dear brethren, the reason is easily given: the Jews brought the Christ of God to the cross."[45]

This was a textbook, anti-Jewish Israel Sunday sermon, unremarkable in the annals of German Protestantism. But in the 1930s such sermons took on special meaning because they were seen to justify the state's persecution of Jews. Although Niemöller was not giving voice to Nazi racial anti-Semitism, his underlying scorn and lack of empathy for Jews was clear.

It is hard to believe that Niemöller's parishioners came away convinced that Nazi persecution of Jews was unjust or that their pastor truly wanted to solve the Jewish problem through conversion. It is unlikely, too, that his parishioners would have been moved by such a sermon to aid their Jewish countrymen or to welcome converts. And there can be no doubt that the thousands of sermons like Niemöller's, preached year after year on the tenth Sunday after Trinity in churches across Germany, helped to further establish a negative attitude toward Jews.

Still, Niemöller was seen by some Christians of Jewish descent as a champion of their cause. One young woman who was eagerly attending Niemöller's services was Senta-Maria Klatt, the daughter of a philosophy professor with nationalist sentiments and a Jewish mother. Her mother moved to the United States after the marriage fell apart, but Senta-Maria remained in Berlin. She wrote Niemöller in early 1936, explaining that "I have been attending your services regularly for months, and I have much to thank you for—strengthening my faith, answering many questions that have remained unclear to me, and learning the meaning of repentance. We conscious Christians in the Confessing Church thank the Lord for giving us men like you!" Dismissed from her job at a kindergarten in 1934 because of her Jewish heritage, she had taken a job as a secretary in the office of the Confessing Church of Berlin-Brandenburg, working closely with Confessing churchmen Otto Dibelius and Kurt Scharf. In this capacity, she acted as a trusted courier with confidential documents and was tasked with compiling and distributing "intercession lists" with the names of hundreds of persecuted pastors and parish members. She survived the war and came to Niemöller's defense in 1947 when he was accused of anti-Semitism.[46]

A month after Niemöller's Israel Sunday sermon, in Nuremberg on September 15, 1935, the Nazis instituted the infamous Law for the Protection of German Blood and German Honor, forbidding marriage and extramarital intercourse between Jews and German Gentiles, and the Reich Citizenship Law, restricting citizenship rights. Known as the Nuremberg Laws, they divided Jews into three categories: those with three or four Jewish grandparents were full Jews; those with two Jewish grandparents were "first-degree half-breeds"; and those with one Jewish grandparent were "second-degree half-breeds." All three groups now faced legal restrictions, although half-breeds had more rights than full Jews. Rooted in racial anti-Semitism, the laws did not take into account whether a Jew had converted to Christianity or not.

Confessing Church leaders were divided over how to respond. Some wanted to endorse the state's right to make such laws. Others, including Bonhoeffer and Hildebrandt, were forthright in their criticism and wanted the same from the church overall. Hildebrandt told Niemöller that if the Confessing Church endorsed the Nuremberg Laws, he would leave the church and resign his post in the PEL. In the end, delegates to the 1935 Confessing synod were so divided that they said nothing of substance. Bonhoeffer, Hildebrandt, and a few others were ashamed, disgusted by their conservative colleagues' timidity. Niemöller also considered the conservatives' silence unsatisfactory, though he did not force a confrontation over it.[47]

WITHIN A YEAR, as the Nazis ratcheted up their persecution of the Confessing Church, Niemöller began to rethink his position on resistance to the state. His optimism of three years prior had vanished. He no longer believed that the Protestant Church and the Nazi state would collaborate to re-Christianize and re-Germanize the nation in the aftermath of Weimar liberalism. But Niemöller had not simply discarded his naïveté; he had become an agent of church resistance.

In a November 1936 sermon in Dahlem's Jesus Christ Church, he expounded on the meaning of the Gospel passage "Render therefore unto Caesar the things that are Caesar's; and unto God the things that are God's." There could be no peace between the earthly kingdom of the Nazis and the spiritual kingdom of the church, Niemöller explained, if the Nazis did not render unto God what was God's. "For the temporal powers to make a claim to our whole being is to rob God. We cannot act as though Caesar has the power on earth and God the power in Heaven." For when Jesus said, "Render unto God what is God's," Niemöller argued, he meant that our whole being is God's. "What belongs to God? We ourselves belong to Him, we, totally and wholly!" We are willing, Niemöller acknowledged, to give the world—that is, the Nazi state— what belongs to it. If, however, the state demands what is God's, "then we must manfully resist."[48]

By urging Christians to "manfully resist," Niemöller was not advocating taking up arms or protesting in the streets. First and foremost, he was calling on Confessing pastors to continue to preach the Gospel, and parishioners to support and defend their pastors who disobeyed state ordinances that interfered with their freedom to preach. Confessing pastors also used sermons, Bible classes, and weekly church meetings to expose the laws and intimidation tactics used by the Nazi state to subvert the freedom to worship. And finally, Confessing Church leaders sought in various ways to remind the government of its duty to guarantee the church's independence and the right to worship.

The Confessing Church's July 1936 memorandum to Hitler, to which Niemöller offered minor edits, was an expression of this last form of church resistance. While showing due deference to the government and emphasizing their love for the German nation, the ten authors of the confidential memorandum accused members of the government of interfering in church affairs and attempting to de-Christianize the nation. They even reproached Hitler for soliciting "veneration in a form that is due only to God." They concluded by asking Hitler to ensure the freedom of the German people to worship "under the sign of the Cross of Christ."[49]

Although the memorandum focused on the government's obstruction of Christian teachings and its efforts to replace worship of Christ with glorification of German blood, the authors also took a forthright stand against Nazi anti-Semitism, which, they argued, was anti-Christian. Here, for the first time, we see Niemöller and the Confessing Church speaking explicitly against Nazi hatred of Jews.

> When the Aryan human being is glorified, God's Word is witness to the sinfulness of all humans; when anti-Semitism, which binds him to hatred of Jews, is imposed upon the Christian in the framework of the National Socialist worldview, then for him the Christian commandment to love one's fellow human stands opposed to it.[50]

These words are often taken as proof that Niemöller and the Confessing Church resisted the regime's racial policy. But the larger record of the Confessing Church cannot be ignored. A few exceptions aside—and Niemöller is not one of them—Confessing pastors responded to the persecution of Jews neither as humanitarians nor as religious brethren sharing a Judeo-Christian tradition. They remained concerned solely with the persecution of the churches. And while the memorandum called on Christians to counter Nazi hatred toward Jews by following the commandment to love one's neighbor, it had nothing to say about the theological anti-Judaism promoted by the churches. Only after 1945 did Niemöller and other radical members of the Confessing Church slowly come to see the error of their church-centered outlook. Nevertheless, the 1936 memorandum did break the church's silence on the persecution of Jews, and Niemöller continued to temper his defense of the Nazi state's right to do as it pleased in the secular world.[51]

When Reich Minister of Propaganda Goebbels suggested that churches stay out of politics and attend to the souls of the German people, Niemöller, who once would have agreed, responded that the churches would do so if the regime would let them preach the Gospel without interference. He even targeted Hitler himself, asking his congregation, "Does the führer's word still hold good?" In this case, the word in question was Hitler's 1933 promise to protect the church and its independence. Niemöller argued that as long as one man or woman remained in prison for defending the Gospel, Germans must say no—Hitler had not kept his word.[52]

For the Nazi authorities, Niemöller's preaching had stepped over a line, and his encouragement of others to follow his example was understood as nothing less than inciting resistance to the state. Niemöller's family and followers began to wonder how long the combative pastor would remain a free man. A family friend and prominent businessman, Kurt Schmitt, told Niemöller in a conversation in 1936, "You stand before the choice of clearly and single-mindedly carrying on the battle you've begun—if you do so you will definitely be put out of the way—or continuing to serve your church even beyond the present time by cautious self-restraint." Niemöller's response was that "this policy [of cautious self-restraint] might be correct for an economic enterprise but it is not applicable in questions of belief. Here there are no compromises. I must go my way."[53]

In a sermon in mid-June 1937, Niemöller read the names of seventy-two members of the Confessing Church either detained or otherwise silenced. What were these men and women guilty of? Niemöller asked. They refused to abandon their faith, he answered. Going against the German-Protestant creed by which he had been raised, he preached, in solidarity with the detainees, "We must not—for Heaven's sake—make a *German* Gospel out of the Gospel; we must not—for Heaven's sake—make a *German* Church out of Christ's Church; we must not—for God's sake—make *German* Christians out of Evangelical Christians!" Knowing full well that his name might soon be added to the intercession list, he told his parishioners, "I must speak thus once again today, for perhaps I will no longer be able to do so next Sunday. . . . Who knows what next Sunday will bring forth?"[54]

SIX

Hitler's Personal Prisoner
(1937–1945)

O N July 1, 1937, Martin Niemöller allowed himself to sleep in later than usual. It was a Thursday, and he had spent the previous three days traveling through western Germany preaching and attending meetings. Exhausted after taking the night train back to Dahlem, he took the unusual step of asking Assistant Pastor Franz Hildebrandt to teach the next day's confirmation class. "I told my friend Hildebrandt I was absolutely done for. I wanted to sleep and have a good morning's rest." His leisurely morning began with a hot bath and breakfast with his wife and two-year-old son Tini.[1]

The tranquil scene was interrupted by the ringing of the parsonage bell just before nine o'clock. Two Gestapo men had arrived. Would Pastor Niemöller come to headquarters for questioning? It wouldn't take long, they assured him.[2]

Niemöller had little cause to protest. By this point, a visit from the Gestapo was routine. He had been arrested five times already and was usually released within a few hours. He had never been held longer than a day. So neither family nor friends were greatly alarmed when, dressed in jacket and tie, he took his seat in the back of the Gestapo agents' black Mercedes. He could not have imagined that it would be eight years before he returned to his family and parishioners.[3]

At first, Niemöller was brought to the Gestapo's Alexanderplatz headquarters in central Berlin. After some time, he was loaded into a police car and taken to Moabit, the inner-city prison on Lehrter Street. The guards recorded his personal belongings and removed his valuables before locking him in cell 448. The 2.5-meter by 2.5-meter space contained a stool, table, mess tin, and bed made of wooden planks that folded down from the wall. There was a small window high up on another wall and a peephole in the door. A guard told Niemöller he was forbidden to unfold the bed except at night. Prisoner number 1325 lay down on the cell floor, still wearing his jacket and tie.[4]

Niemöller was not the only cleric in such a position. The government had given up on trying to peacefully incorporate the recalcitrant preachers into a nazified church and turned to outright repression. Eight hundred and five Confessing clergy had been arrested by the time Niemöller found himself on a damp cell floor, a figure that does not include those detained for less than a day, not to mention those suspended, retired, and harassed.[5]

The next day he wrote his wife. "My dear Else, I'm sorry that I did not at least say goodbye to you yesterday, but at that moment I thought of everything else but the possibility that I would not be back after a few hours. Despite the bustle, I would have talked over a few things with you that I'm thinking about now—especially concerning the children and the congregation's situation." It was the first of many letters Niemöller would write during eight months of solitary confinement at Moabit prison.[6]

Niemöller's imprisonment was a source of great satisfaction for Propaganda Minister Joseph Goebbels. "Pastor Niemöller finally arrested," he scribbled in his diary. "We have the swine now and we're not letting go of him. . . . The thing now is to break him so that he can't believe his eyes or ears. We must never let up." Hitler agreed, declaring of Niemöller, "He shall not be released until he's broken. Opposition against the state will not be tolerated."

The official arrest notice described Niemöller as a political rabble-rouser:

> Yesterday, the Gestapo arrested the Confessing pastor, Martin Niemöller of Berlin-Dahlem. . . . For a long time Niemöller has been giving inflammatory lectures and sermons disparaging leaders in the government and [Nazi] movement. With the intention of incensing the population he has spread untrue reports about measures taken by the Nazi authorities. Furthermore, he has incited resistance against governmental laws and decrees. His statements are part of the steady fare of the hostile foreign press.

In Bielefeld, the home of Wilhelm Niemöller's parish, a local newspaper printed the notice on its front page under the headline, "A Minister of the Devil."[7]

After the arrest, eight Gestapo agents returned to the parsonage to search Niemöller's study for incriminating evidence. Meanwhile, several Confessing clergy, including Hildebrandt and Bonhoeffer, arrived at the parsonage for a planned meeting and were immediately detained. No one was allowed to leave the building until the search was concluded. "Everyone was astounded at the meticulous tidiness of Niemöller's desk," Eberhard Bethge, one of the detained theologians, later wrote. "It was something no one expected of this spirited man." Word of the search and house arrests must have spread because soon Bonhoeffer's parents were driving by the rectory again and again, Mrs. Bonhoeffer peering anxiously out the car's window.[8]

After seven hours, the agents finished ransacking the place. They took bundles of Niemöller's correspondence, his diaries, Confessing Church materials, and 30,000 marks intended for the Pastors' Emergency League found in a wall safe behind a picture of St. Peter. That evening a group of girls from the parish gathered in front of the home and sang hymns to console Else.[9]

On the first Sunday after Niemöller's arrest, the Dahlem churches were swarming with Gestapo agents. Otto Dibelius preached in Niemöller's place but was soon arrested himself for mentioning the missing pastor in his final prayer. Dibelius was released quickly, but also prohibited from preaching again in the Third Reich. The Gestapo also detained and interrogated Wilhelm Niemöller for distributing Dibelius's sermon.[10]

Undeterred, Dahlem parishioners circulated a petition declaring that Niemöller had never misused his pulpit for political purposes. More than one thousand people signed the petition before it was sent to Reich Justice Minister Franz Gürtner, who lived in Dahlem on the same street as the Niemöllers.[11]

Beyond the petition, the Dahlem congregation held an intercession service every evening at six in St. Anne's Church. These prayer services asking God to intercede on behalf of St. Anne's imprisoned pastor and other jailed clergy took place without fail until April 1943, with as many as twenty-nine different Confessing pastors preaching at the nightly intercession between July and September 1937 alone. Niemöller's father Heinrich, brother Wilhelm, and son Jochen, a theology student, all took turns. On the fourth Sunday after Martin's arrest, Wilhelm held three successive services to accommodate all the parishioners. "Give Wilhelm a kiss from me; I'm so relieved when he is there," Martin wrote Else. After the war began in 1939 and many pastors were called up for military service, female vicars or (after 1942) newly ordained female pastors conducted services.[12]

With the arrest of his mentor, Hildebrandt understood that he could be next and made plans to immigrate to England. On Sunday, July 18, the day of his departure, he conducted a final service in Dahlem's Jesus Christ Church, ending with an illegal collection on behalf of the Confessing Church. The Gestapo's spies quickly moved in. Hildebrandt was arrested in the vestry as the outraged congregation looked on. Fortunately, he had left his passport at his parents' house. Had it been on his person, the Nazis would have confiscated it, making it impossible for him to leave

Germany. Concerned that Hildebrandt's status as a Jewish-Christian "half-breed" might doom him, the Bonhoeffer family worked tirelessly for his release, and after four weeks of solitary confinement, Hildebrandt was freed. He fled immediately to Switzerland and then London.[13]

The Confessing Church announced what turned out to be a huge intercession service for Niemöller on August 8, 1937, at Jesus Christ Church. All morning subway cars arrived in Dahlem discharging hundreds of Berliners, who made their way to the church only to find it cordoned off by the Gestapo. The wife of Dahlem pastor Eberhard Röhricht watched as the police ordered the crowd to disperse. The pilgrims marched to St. Anne's Church, but it too was blocked by the Gestapo. Finally they came to the rectory. Police met them there with vans ready to haul the protesters off to Gestapo headquarters. By the end of the day, 250 Niemöller devotees had been arrested, and the Röhricht telephone rang constantly with anxious inquiries about the whereabouts of friends and relatives. Pastor Röhricht spent the next day at Alexanderplatz negotiating the arrested pilgrims' release.[14]

Niemöller's arrest created an international uproar. The July 2 edition of the *Chicago Daily Tribune* announced on its front page, "Nazis Jail Leader of Church." The same day the *New York Times* carried on its front page the headline, "Nazis Finally Put Niemoeller in Jail." A July 3 *Times* editorial chided Hitler for making a martyr of the pastor.

> Such a leader is much more dangerous in prison than in the pulpit. The Nazis have done the one thing Dr. Niemoeller has practically asked them to do. They have made him a martyr, and as a result of this stupidity there is not the slightest doubt that hundreds of other pastors of the Confessional opposition will carry out their threat of forcing authorities to arrest them en masse. . . . More than any single act in this religious war, it tells the watching world how frightened the Hitler Government is of the opposition it has stirred up among the churches.

Anglican bishop George Bell wrote in the London *Times*, "I know Dr. Niemöller. He is a man whom any Christian might well be proud to count a friend. I have never seen a braver Christian nor a man in whom the lamp of faith burns more brightly."[15]

Bravery and faith, however, would not be enough to free him from a Nazi prison. Niemöller hired a high-profile legal team, led by his trusted friend Dr. Holst Holstein, with whom he met regularly to plan his defense.

Niemöller's ample correspondence is revealing about his daily routine and state of mind while in Moabit prison. Authorities allowed him to write letters to his wife, plus a dozen postcards, each day. Most of his correspondence was with Else and Wilhelm, but occasionally he wrote other pastors and members of the congregation. During his eight-month imprisonment, the "fighting pastor" received over ten thousand pieces of mail. He found it tiring to read and respond to it all, but he appreciated the support. "I want to tell you that brotherly love and intercession has constantly surrounded and strengthened me during these weeks," he wrote a fellow pastor in mid-August.[16]

For Niemöller, absence made the heart grow fonder. Save for a few reprimands, the letters to Else are loving and affectionate. Niemöller made frequent inquiries about the children—four teenagers, two preteens, and a toddler—and his wife's health and the heavy burden she faced in his absence. Else received generous assistance from relatives, parishioners, and the family's live-in maid, Dora Schulz. Still, the stress, anxiety, and exhaustion of caring for seven children, advocating for her husband's release, and dealing with parish affairs—all while under Gestapo surveillance—were overwhelming. Niemöller wrote his brother in late December, "Else has already suffered considerably and I notice it in the children, too. They should accept the fact that they will have to be without me for a long time and must be building anew."[17]

Trying to ease her concerns about his own plight, Niemöller reassured his wife time and again that he was strong and well. "I am in good spirits and have a lot of 'steam in the locomotive,'" he wrote her on December 24, after learning that his petition for a furlough to be with his family at Christmas was denied. He usually signed off his letters to Else with a tender good-bye: "In my thoughts I take you in my arms, dear, dear wife. Most intimately and truly, Your Martin," and "God send you great

Else Niemöller, 1938. (Zentralarchiv der EKHN, Darmstadt)

strength my love; my thoughts and prayers are like a wall around you. Intimately, Your Martin." After this last good-bye, he added the postscript, "I urgently need trousers, and money too."[18]

He often gave Else advice regarding congregational disputes, especially the schism that developed after his arrest. Although many in the Dahlem parish—including Olga Rigele, sister of the leading Nazi politician Hermann Göring—rallied behind the Niemöllers, others sided with Röhricht, who wanted to avoid further provocation. Niemöller bemoaned the parish "troubles" in his letters but urged Else and his supporters to hold firm to the Barmen-Dahlem line, refusing all compromises with the Reich Church and the German Christians.

Despite Goebbels's threat to break the dissident clergyman, international attention, especially among church leaders abroad, protected Niemöller from physical abuse at Moabit. Every ten days, Else was allowed to visit him for fifteen minutes in the presence of a warden. Sometimes one or two of their children, or another relative, joined her. During the first visit, Else was alarmed by how thin and pale her husband looked, so she arranged to pay five marks per day for better food rations for him.

By mid-October, Niemöller wrote her, "You'll have to accept the fact that I'm slowly losing my slender waistline; yesterday I had to re-sew a button on my vest."[19]

He always looked forward to the twenty minutes he had each day in the exercise yard, but it was not enough to offset the sedentary life in his cell, where he read, wrote, and prayed. A man accustomed to almost continuous human contact—except during prayer—Niemöller found himself confronting loneliness and torpor. "I've now had four and a half weeks of solitude," he wrote his pastor friend Ernst Koenigs.

> The first few days were not easy, but since I've acquired a Bible and a hymnal, I've been using my time to the fullest and am amazed how fast it passes. Initially I had a few worries remembering the "cabin fever" during my years as a cadet and lieutenant before the war. I'm now learning patience—late but thoroughly—and it isn't in vain: every day I learn a few hymns and read Scripture calmly, deliberately, and with the question, "Lord, what would you have me do?" Because of this I've come to see the value of my time under arrest as a basis of manifold thanks.[20]

Niemöller had his gripes—the bed was too hard, he had to scrub the cell floor, and he missed a good glass of wine—but despite the privations, he managed to keep his sense of humor. In late August, he wrote a church colleague:

> Fortunately I have not been thrown into a dark medieval dungeon, even though my view is restricted to a small piece of blue or overcast sky! And I don't have to subsist on bread and water, which would still be better than nothing, though I would rather eat my wife's cooking. And I don't have to sap my failing strength with forced labor, although given my old bones, scrubbing my cell on hands and knees is not the pure joy with which I would call down the blessings of heaven upon those who brought me here.[21]

He did what he could to remain engaged in the Church Struggle. In a show of support, the Pastors' Emergency League reelected the imprisoned Niemöller as its leader in October. "I want to convey my heartfelt thanks," he wrote a PEL colleague. In his letters, he continued to criticize bishops August Marahrens of Hanover, Hans Meiser of Bavaria, and Theophil Wurm of Württemberg, who were known for their willingness to compromise with the German Christians. State repression had created a degree of unity in the Confessing Church, which gave Niemöller some hope. Summoning naval imagery, he remarked to Else, "Somehow in these six months the church's ship has become buoyant again. The paint is chipped, the masts are broken, its whole appearance is not beautiful; but Christ will stand at the helm and the ship floats! Who would have dared hope it when Ludwig Müller thought he had pirated it."[22]

When Niemöller wasn't writing letters, worrying about church business, or preparing his defense for the upcoming trial, he took advantage of solitary confinement to read books, many in English, including Thomas Macaulay's multivolume *History of England*. He twice waded through the New Testament in Greek, perhaps reviving fond memories of his gymnasium days and reading Greek poetry for fun. He received a copy of Bonhoeffer's now-famous text *Discipleship* with an inscription from his colleague: "To Pastor Martin Niemöller at Advent 1937 in brotherly thanks. A book that he himself could have written better than the author." He enjoyed attending church services in prison but found that the preaching and singing left much to be desired. "The sermon was decent," he wrote his wife, "but what a sad thing the singing was, if one gets to comparing!" His spirits were lifted on January 14, 1938, his forty-sixth birthday, when more than four thousand cards arrived from around the world.[23]

Niemöller viewed his imprisonment as part of his fight to preserve the church's purity and autonomy. He saw himself as a symbol of all the less-known pastors and parishioners who were suffering for their faith and for the independence of the church. But he didn't want to be made a hero, he told Else, because that would bring attention to himself rather than the cause he represented. "Of all the masks, the 'heroic' is the least appealing to me."[24]

PATIENCE WAS NOT one of Niemöller's virtues, but he learned it in Moabit. He had no other choice. Originally his trial had been scheduled for mid-August 1937, but it was postponed first to October and finally to early February 1938—seven and a half months after his arrest. The delay was primarily due to the prosecution's difficulty in gathering convincing evidence of the pastor's alleged crimes. The official indictment accused him of misusing the pulpit for political ends, committing treason by besmirching the names of leading Nazi politicians and church officials, and illegally encouraging Confessing pastors to read aloud during services the names of parishioners who had resigned their membership, presumably to embarrass Nazis who left the church. Niemöller's lawyers responded with a simple plan: emphasize Niemöller's conservative, nationalist credentials to counter the treason charge, and his religious motivations to counter the charge of misusing the pulpit. His lawyers compiled a list of forty-two prominent defense witnesses, including an admiral, two generals, a former imperial ambassador, two senior members of the foreign office, a famous surgeon, and even Göring's sister. In addition, they also submitted a detailed and comprehensive written defense of their client.[25]

Before the trial began, Goebbels grumbled in his diary that "the Justice Ministry has prepared a fourteen day trial open to the public." He wanted an *in camera* trial, that is, one that would bar the public and the press from observing the trial. There should be no opportunity for agitation by Niemöller, he told the Ministry of Justice, and it should be over in a couple of days. "And then away with the chap!" "The Führer never wants him to be released again." The Third Reich, however, had not yet carried out a thorough nazification of the courts, and the presiding judge, Dr. Robert Hoepke, was a professional, not an ideologue. By most accounts, including Niemöller's, Hoepke conducted an impeccably fair trial.[26]

The judge did agree, after pressure from the Ministry of Justice, to the prosecution's request that the trial be conducted *in camera*, but he made few other concessions. Niemöller's attorneys protested vigorously that justice could not be served if the public was excluded, but the decision held. The hundreds of Niemöller well-wishers who had waited for hours to enter the court on the first day of the trial, including his wife and church representatives from abroad, were turned away. Niemöller wrote Else afterward, "Today I saw you only from a distance, but it was lovely anyway." Besides his attorneys, Niemöller's only allies allowed in court that first day were four members of the Confessing Church, including Superintendent Max Diestel, Niemöller's superior.[27]

Goebbels's hope for a brief trial with minimal input from Niemöller did not materialize. Instead, the trial lasted almost a month, and on the first day alone Niemöller spoke for more than three hours, detailing his decade of devoted military service to the kaiser, his refusal to turn over his U-boat to the British, his leadership of a *Freikorps* battalion against the Communist uprising in the Ruhr, his loathing of the Weimar Republic, and his long-standing support for National Socialism. The only reason he hadn't become a Nazi Party member, he explained, was that he believed it improper for a clergyman to join a political party. He declared that he found Jews unsympathetic and foreign, though as a Christian pastor, he could not allow bloodlines to overrule or negate baptism. After all, he noted, Jesus was a Jew, embarrassing though this fact was. Niemöller emphasized that his fight was not against the state but against the German Christians' attempts to impose Nazi ideology on the church's confessions and creeds. Later that day, in a letter to Else, he wrote, "I find speaking somewhat difficult after the long pause; I keep tripping over my own tongue. . . . In any case I look back on this first day with thanks to God." Goebbels was beside himself at the perceived ineptitude of the jurists, calling them derogatory names and threatening to put them before a firing squad once the trial was over. He would have done the same with Niemöller if he'd had his druthers. "I wish I could shoot Niemöller, that swine!" he vented after the first day. "The lawyers are all good-for-nothings!"[28]

On the second day, the prosecutors went on the offensive. Their goal was to undermine Niemöller's claim to be a model German conservative with impeccable nationalist credentials. The prosecutors accused him, his defense counsel, and the Confessing Church of colluding with the foreign press in a treasonous manner. The court, again under extreme pressure from the Ministry of Justice, now barred the four Confessing Church representatives from the courtroom. Outraged by the accusations of treason and the exclusion of his colleagues, Niemöller declared, "I will not say anything more and dismiss my defense council." For ten days the trial was suspended while the two sides tried to determine how to proceed. After the drama of the second day, Niemöller wrote Else, "Everything is lost, but not my honor. . . . It is reassuring to me that I will see you tomorrow; for my heart trembles at the thought that your strength may give out. . . . Give my greetings to the congregation and tell them that I place my entire confidence in God's mercy."[29]

The trial resumed on February 18, after the court agreed to allow Superintendent Diestel in the courtroom. Over the following week, it became clear that the prosecution had a weak case, especially on the charge of treason, which was eventually dropped for lack of evidence. The witnesses for the defense made quite an impression, speaking reverently about Niemöller's service to his country and church. On February 25, his three lawyers presented their final defense. The lead attorney, Dr. Horst Holstein, declared that Niemöller was "a completely unpolitical man" whose activity had been exclusively determined by the word of God. Two days later, Niemöller spoke in his own defense for the last time. He had, he said, no political quarrel with the state. He simply believed that there were limits to the state's authority—limits that stopped before the doors of the church. Goebbels scrawled in his diary, "The 'Holy' pastor becomes insolent and the court warmly encourages him. A real Scandal!"[30]

The trial concluded at 12:45 p.m. that day, but it would be another week before the verdict. Niemöller wrote his brother, "The days of waiting are nearing their end, and tomorrow at noon the judgment will be spoken. Everything else is uncertain, but I am happy and hopeful, whatever the judgment and whatever may happen to me afterwards. But let me give you my heartfelt love once more; it is good that I have you as my brother and that I know in any case someone will take care of my loved ones."[31]

On March 2, 1938, Else and eighteen-year-old Brigitte arrived in the courtroom and sat in the first row, while more than two hundred of Niemöller's supporters packed the rest of the seats in the chamber. Niemöller entered wearing a dark suit and a black tie. Judge Hoepke's verdict was as lenient as one could reasonably expect given the unrelenting demands from the Ministry of Justice. Niemöller was found guilty only of misusing the pulpit. He was sentenced to seven months and fined 1,500 marks. The prison sentence was waived because of the seven months he had already served. For all intents and purposes, it was an acquittal. In the aftermath, the Swiss newspaper *Basel News* celebrated the fairness of the verdict, writing, "There are still judges in Berlin."[32]

Relieved and joyful, Niemöller's family and friends congratulated him, then trooped over to the prison to wait for him as he retrieved his belongings. Meanwhile, the parish prepared a service of thanksgiving and Else looked forward to an extended vacation on the Baltic Sea.

But Hitler and Goebbels had other plans. Upon learning of the verdict, Hitler shouted that Niemöller should rot in a cell "until he's blue in the face." He ordered Niemöller placed in "protective custody" and sent to Sachsenhausen Konzentrationslager (concentration camp), twenty miles north of Berlin near the small town of Oranienburg. Goebbels recorded in his diary, "The foreign journalists are waiting for Niemöller outside the court, but he will be transported immediately to Oranienburg through a side door. There he can serve God through work and turning inward. He won't be turned loose to the people again." When it was pointed out that there was no legal basis to continue holding Niemöller, Hitler allegedly thundered, "Then he will be my personal prisoner." This time there would be no indictment, no assurance of a trial.[33]

The evening of the verdict, when Niemöller did not materialize in front of Moabit prison, his supporters feared that he had been secreted away to Sachsenhausen. Fellow pastor Kurt Scharf, whose rectory was a stone's throw from the concentration camp, was able to confirm what many suspected. Goebbels relished the victory: "Niemöller is in good hands in the concentration camp. He won't be released any time soon. This is how it will now be for all enemies of the state. Those who mistake the kind Hitler for a weakling, have to meet the hard Hitler."[34]

Sachsenhausen was not Moabit. Unlike the prison, which was run by the Justice Ministry, Sachsenhausen was under the purview of SS (*Schutzstaffel*, or protection squad) personnel, who were notorious for their brutal treatment of inmates. Opened in 1936, Sachsenhausen had begun as the detention site for political prisoners and social deviants—the real or perceived enemies of the Third Reich. During the period of Martin Niemöller's incarceration there, his fellow inmates included Polish prisoners and others from German-occupied territories, members of resistance groups, homosexuals, Jehovah's Witnesses, and those from groups deemed racially inferior, such as Jews and Roma (Gypsies). Between 1936 and 1945, more than two hundred thousand prisoners passed through Sachsenhausen, and nearly one-quarter of them died from exhaustion, starvation, exposure, abuse, or the withholding of medical care.[35]

Niemöller would spend from March 1938 until July 1941 in Sachsenhausen. Contrary to reports in the foreign press, he was not among the inmates who were organized into forced-labor units—some of whom were literally worked to death—or tortured. The primary source of the rumors that the Nazis tormented and abused Niemöller in Sachsenhausen was a series of articles and a book, *I Was in Hell with Niemöller* (1942), by Leo Stein. The book, articles, and even the author's name were fabrications by the author, who wanted to exploit Niemöller's growing fame. But the unsubstantiated stories of Niemöller's courage and determination while under conditions of torture captivated readers. The book is still cited today as proof of Niemöller's heroic resistance.[36]

Although he was Hitler's "personal prisoner" and as such spent his years in the camp in solitary confinement, Niemöller was aware to some degree of the conditions endured by others in the camp, including the sadistic beatings, hangings, and shooting of prisoners. In 1945, he said of his concentration camp experience, "When someone asks me: was it really so bad as the newspapers report? Then I always say, no, it was a hundred times worse."[37]

AFTER HIS LIBERATION, Niemöller would tell several stories about his confinement. While these convey some basic truths about his life in the camp, their purpose was less to establish an accurate historical record than to persuade his postwar audience that Christians in Germany stood up to Hitler and the Nazi regime. During a 1946–1947 lecture tour in the United States, he sought to convince Americans that his rubble-strewn country deserved their aid, and his own tale of suffering made for a persuasive argument.

The first of these stories described March 2, 1938, Niemöller's first day at Sachsenhausen. "We arrived in the dark of the night between twelve and one o'clock in the morning," he would recount. "I was brought into the Gestapo office and they robbed me of everything—my wristwatch, my wedding ring, the letters from my wife, and my Bible." Next he was led through a large barbed-wire gate into the interior of the camp. He was not placed with the rest of the prison population in one of the fifty-odd barracks but was instead put in the small auxiliary prison, in cell number one. "The next morning my door opened and the SS commander for the whole camp came in."

"You have been brought here as the personal prisoner of the führer," the SS man said. "We have never had such a prisoner before." Uncertain how to treat Niemöller given his special classification, the commandant asked, "Have you any complaints or wishes?"

"Yes, I have many complaints," Niemöller replied. "Your people stripped and robbed me last night of practically everything I had, of my wristwatch, my wedding ring, and my letters and Bible. I have many wishes, but mainly one. Let me have my Bible back, and that instantly!" The SS commandant had an orderly fetch the Bible. "And there I was, not yet half a day," Niemöller recalled, "not yet twelve hours in a concentration camp where 30,000 prisoners lived at that time without any

Bibles . . . and I had my Bible. Barbed wire and three iron doors could not keep the word of God from me."[38]

Niemöller's Bible was crucial to a second story with which he captivated his American audiences. He explained that, as the only man in the camp with a Bible, it was his duty to get the word of God to the other inmates, no matter the costs.

> I was in solitary confinement, I couldn't speak to anyone, but my cell had a window and the next morning outside this window I heard steps, more steps, and again steps. I put my table against the wall, and I put the footstool on the table, and I climbed up and peeped out. There I saw about fifteen people, one behind the other, walking around the lawn in the courtyard for their morning walk. Now I knew what to do. Beginning the next morning, and then every morning, if those steps passed below my window, I just pronounced a word of the Holy Scripture, a verse from the Old or New Testament, so the people outside could listen and hear.
>
> There it was the living voice of the living God in the midst of the gates of hell, and there was a Christian Church, even if we couldn't see each other, but were separated by the wall and the bars of the windows. They heard the voice of the Lord.[39]

There are no independent accounts of Niemöller's life in Sachsenhausen and thus no way to verify these stories. Whether he really demanded that the SS commander fetch his Bible "instantly," and whether he then read Bible verses through his cell window to other inmates, we cannot say. But concentration camp guards were not known for laxity, especially when Hitler, Himmler, and Goebbels took a personal interest in their prisoners. Yet tales of effrontery and moral fortitude have taken on legendary status and played a crucial role in establishing Niemöller's reputation as "the pastor who defied Hitler."

What do we know with certainty? We know that the pastor wore the prison uniform—black pants and a blue shirt jacket bearing the red cloth triangle of political prisoners. Above the triangle was the number 569, which may have previously belonged to another inmate. The numbers were recycled after inmates died, were moved to another camp, or were set free. Whereas at Moabit he was occasionally allowed contact with other prisoners, at Sachsenhausen Niemöller's solitary confinement was nearly total. He ate and exercised alone. According to Hans Ehrenberg, a Bochum pastor of Jewish ancestry and fellow inmate whose job at Sachsenhausen was to carry out the corpses, Niemöller would have heard guards berating and cursing prisoners in interrogation rooms. There would have been no escaping the screams of the tortured. For the first few months, Niemöller's diet consisted mostly of bread and potatoes, which took a toll on his health. His eyesight began to fail, his teeth were in bad shape, and his neuralgia flared up.[40]

Of more concern to his family than his physical health was his mental well-being. As he told Else in June, his body was holding together, but emotionally and psychologically he was up and down "like an anchored ship in a storm." Solitary confinement and infrequent contact with his family were Niemöller's torture. "No one ever raised a hand against me," he told journalist Dorothy Thompson in May 1945. "It is, however, suffering to be deprived of freedom for so many years."[41]

His contacts with the outside world were rare: medical and dental examinations in Berlin, meetings with an investigating magistrate, occasional visits from his parents and one from Wilhelm, and eventually twice-monthly visits with Else. The first letter Else received from Sachsenhausen was dated April 6, five weeks after her husband's transfer from Moabit. A month later, she was allowed to visit him at Gestapo headquarters in Berlin. Accompanied by an armed guard, Niemöller was brought to Alexanderplatz once a month, later every fourteen days, to spend thirty minutes with his wife and one of their children. Beginning in the spring of 1939, these visits ended, and Else had to go to Sachsenhausen, where children under seventeen were not allowed. They were forbidden to discuss taboo subjects, including politics, and to limit themselves to family matters. As Else later recalled, "I was only allowed to speak of the children, of the family, but having seven children there was enough material to speak about and the time went much too quickly." On November 15, 1938, when

Else arrived at Alexanderplatz to see her husband, she was told that a ban on letters had been imposed for eight weeks as punishment for an alleged breach of this rule by Niemöller. She wrote Heinrich Himmler, head of the SS, to protest but never received a response.[42]

When not banned from doing so, the imprisoned pastor was allowed to write and receive one letter every fourteen days. The permissible focus—as at Moabit—was his family and parish. Letter after letter demonstrated Niemöller's hunger for church news. "You haven't written anything about my parish!" he wrote anxiously in one early exchange. "Who's working with the confirmation candidates? Who's conducting the evening services?" With her husband imprisoned, one of Else's jobs was to check on the parish's sick and elderly. Niemöller frequently listed the names and ailments of the parishioners Else should visit and asked her to pass along a message: that he hadn't forgotten them. Nearly every letter contained birthday wishes, greetings, congratulations, and thanks for her to transmit to parishioners.[43]

The exchange of family news simultaneously lifted Niemöller's spirits and compounded his loneliness. "Please write me in detail about the children," he wrote on April 24, 1938. "Remember Mother's birthday on May 11. She'll be 70 years old, and you must write to her in my name that I think of her every day and I am full of love and gratitude."

"Give the children each individually a kiss from me" —May 3, 1938.

"I received the pictures of the children, but I can't look at them everyday" —May 26, 1938.

"I have a heavy heart because when we parted [after your visit] I forgot to have you greet the children, friends, and the parish" —August 19, 1938.

"My parents' visit was for me a refreshment"—October 18, 1938.

"I am now very curious how you will arrange the journey with all the children to Bielefeld to celebrate the golden wedding of my parents" —May 31, 1939.

"The fact that Jan is quite healthy again is a reason for my daily thanks" —February 2, 1940.

"That you should pray faithfully for me, I don't need to tell you, nor that I think of you and the children every day and hourly" —May 21, 1940.

"You can write Wilhelm that when I take my midday walk I smoke one of his cigars, not without thankfulness" —June 9, 1940.

"My dearest Else, Today is your 50th birthday and the fourth that I have missed" —July 20, 1940.

"Yesterday was the 5th birthday of our youngest. When I think about him I can't believe he's already five years old." And, "Tell the children how attached I am to them, and that I pray faithfully for each one of them. That's all I can do with my hands tied" —August 12, 1940.[44]

Niemöller's imprisonment wasn't hard just on Else and their children. His parents also suffered. "Yes, it is a terrible thing to have a son in a concentration camp," Heinrich told an American pastor visiting the Niemöllers' home in Elberfeld in August 1939. "But there would be something more terrible for us: if God had needed a faithful martyr and our Martin had been unwilling."[45]

Else Niemöller interceded where she could when Martin's health was at stake. During a regular medical examination, a Berlin doctor told him that he was in relatively good health but that he weighed just 136 pounds. Else was shocked and protested to Himmler that her husband's condition was deteriorating. She demanded that Martin be committed to the camp sanatorium, where he would receive better care. Himmler, responding personally to say that her husband was well looked after, denied her request. It is unclear if Else's entreaty was the cause, but over time Niemöller's rations improved. Himmler himself visited the pastor in the camp in January 1939 and reported to Hitler on his condition.[46]

NIEMÖLLER MAY NOT have known the full extent of the media attention, but his acquittal, re-arrest, and incarceration in Sachsenhausen had resulted in another international scandal. The archbishop of Canterbury, the primate of the Church of Sweden, the archbishop of Thyateire in the Greek Orthodox Church, the president of the Protestant Federation of France, and the chairman of the Foreign Affairs Department of the American Federal Council of Churches sent a telegraph to Hitler expressing their "deep concern about the further detention of Pastor Niemöller by the secret police in disregard of the verdict of the Court."[47]

US Protestants saw Niemöller as a hero of the faith. The Federal Council of Churches reacted to Niemöller's imprisonment by calling on American churches to hold prayer vigils for him. Throughout his three years plus in Sachsenhausen, Protestants were urged to commemorate various Niemöller anniversaries: his birthday, the date of his July 1937 arrest, the date of his re-arrest, and so on. For instance, Henry Smith Leiper, executive secretary for church relations in the FCC and one of the founders of the World Council of Churches, arranged to have the bell of New York's prestigious Riverside Church toll on July 2, 1939, the second anniversary of Niemöller's arrest, and to have the church's pastor mention Niemöller in his final prayer. At another point, Leiper exhorted Protestant ministers to "preach sermons on the modern Luther" to mark Niemöller's martyrdom in Nazi prisons and concentration camps.[48]

Some American pastors went even further. On Sunday, March 5, 1939, Reverend John Paul Jones of Union Church in the Bay Ridge neighborhood of Brooklyn performed a reenactment of Niemöller's imprisonment in Sachsenhausen. When Reverend Jones mounted his pulpit, he was seized and dragged away by two men wearing Nazi uniforms. He then gave his sermon from behind a replica of a prison door with a barred window and SACHSENHAUSEN inscribed over it.[49]

And it wasn't just clerics riding the Niemöller wave. In July 1939, *The Nation* described Niemöller as the symbol of the struggle against Nazism and urged antifascist forces in the United States to honor his resistance. Dorothy Thompson, who covered Niemöller's trial for the *New York Herald Tribune*, also considered Niemöller a hero. Thompson wrote that Martin Niemöller had risked his life for his nation as a submarine captain and now was risking it again for his faith. The Nazis, she asserted, believed that they were producing a race of heroes by educating Germans to march in goose-step, but little did they know that they were also "breeding, if not a race, at least a distinguished company of heroes, whose number Pastor Niemoeller has now joined. They are in the concentration camps and prisons."[50]

In spite of Niemöller's theological anti-Semitism, American Jewish opinion was mostly behind him. In 1938, the Chicago Rabbinical Association distributed to its members a special prayer:

> At this very moment, the lash is falling upon one who has had the courage and the character to rebel and to fight for that which is symbolic of the freedom of this day. Pastor Martin Niemoeller is fighting civilization's cause. It is not what he believes himself that counts so much. Niemoeller is the symbol of religious freedom as against pagan reactionaryism [*sic*], and his is the battle of all of us to whom liberty is dear, and who consider the right to live as our conscience dictates, as one of our most prized rights.

RABBI WILLIAM S. Maley, of the Jamaica Jewish Center in Brooklyn, placed Niemöller alongside Franklin D. Roosevelt, Albert Einstein, and Winston Churchill on his list of the ten "righteous men whose virtue will save the world." Addressing his congregation, Rabbi Edgar Siskin of New Haven, Connecticut, described Niemöller as a modern Christian hero whose "fearless sermons . . . have dared to defy truculent tyranny." Siskin concluded, "In a day of darkness, that is a glorious shaft of light. May we all be bathed in its refulgence and thereby become strengthened for the struggle of human freedom!"[51]

Niemöller also had Jewish critics in the United States. Samuel Volkman, a rabbi in Chicago, took aim at Niemöller's anti-Semitism, which was rarely discussed in the American press. Not that Niemöller's views were unknown; the pastor's sermons, including his 1935 Israel Sunday sermon, had been collected and translated into English in the 1937 book *Here Stand I!* In a letter to the *Christian Century*, Rabbi Volkman said, in reference to Niemöller's comments about "the eternal Jew," that "it is hoped that when the churches of America unite to do honor to the spirit of Niemöller, they will dissociate themselves from what can be regarded as nothing less than a particularly obnoxious kind of sanctimonious froth."[52]

Others found even more distressing Niemöller's militant nationalism. Some pointed to his enthusiastic participation in the unrestricted submarine warfare in World War I recounted in *From U-Boat to Pulpit*. Further evidence of Niemöller's militarism came at the outbreak of the Second World War, when he volunteered his services to the German navy while he languished in solitary confinement. A week after Hitler ordered the invasion of Poland on September 1, 1939, Niemöller wrote Admiral Erich Raeder, offering to serve his country in any capacity as a reserve officer. Raeder never responded to Niemöller's letter, but three weeks later Niemöller received a response from Field Marshall Wilhelm Keitel, chief of Supreme Command of the Armed Forces, who respectfully declined his offer.[53]

Many of Niemöller's friends and supporters in Germany and abroad couldn't believe it. At first they thought Niemöller's offer to fight was Nazi propaganda. How could the leader of the church's struggle against the Nazis propose to serve on their behalf—from a cell in Sachsenhausen no less? Anglican bishop George Bell—one of Niemöller's most high-profile and vocal supporters, whose own country declared war against Germany on September 3, 1939—was understandably one of those seeking answers.

Grasping for a reassuring explanation, Niemöller's allies maintained that he must have been trying to join the clandestine resistance against Hitler in the armed forces—something Niemöller himself suggested at times after the war. Another claim he made in December 1945 was that his three sons "were being drafted into the Army and I felt that the place of a father is by the side of his sons." Both explanations are problematic—the first because there was hardly any resistance in the armed forces in 1939, and the second because when the war broke out his sons, ranging from thirteen to seventeen years old, were too young to be drafted. In truth, his friends and family, in their limited and highly censored communiqués, had been able to advise him to volunteer in the hope that the authorities would accept and set him free. Yet there was more to the offer than even self-preservation. He still wanted to serve Germany, even under Hitler. "I was thinking only of my people and my country," he *also* said after the war, contradicting his own statements.[54]

Some of Niemöller's friends understood this. Karl Barth appreciated that two years of solitary confinement was a factor, but more significant were Niemöller's fervent allegiances to nationalism and Lutheranism. Barth knew that Niemöller would have been moved by the scraps of news he received in prison—disseminated by Goebbels's propaganda ministry—that Germany invaded Poland to put an end to Polish atrocities against Germans, including Protestant clergy. "Do not forget," Barth told Bell, "Niemöller has always been and certainly remains today a good—a too good—*German* . . . and do not forget, Niemöller is a very good—a too good—*Lutheran*."[55]

The adulated, imprisoned pastor was not, as many people thought, an out-and-out anti-Nazi. He was a critic of Hitler's church policy. Niemöller's offer to enlist in the navy exposed his broader sympathies. The American Protestant leader of the Federal Council of Churches, Henry Smith Leiper, came to a conclusion similar to Barth's. "The fact that he is against Hitler would not cause him to sit back and let anything happen to his country," Leiper wrote in *The Churchman*. "Martin Niemoeller is what he always was—one of God's choicest warriors, plagued by the blind spots common to historic Christianity, but according to his light a defender of the faith."[56]

If Niemöller's "latest adventure," as Barth called it, troubled some close observers, the American public on the whole was not especially perturbed. On December 23, 1940, Niemöller's image appeared on the cover of *Time* magazine with the headline: "Martyr of 1940: In Germany Only the Cross Has Not Bowed to the Swastika." Predictably, the accompanying article recycled Niemöller's supposed challenge, "Not you, Herr Hitler, but God is my Führer."[57]

As pleasing as such tributes were to Niemöller's supporters, they only infuriated Hitler and brought Niemöller no closer to freedom. And the years of solitary confinement were taking their toll. Midway through 1939, Niemöller entered a particularly difficult emotional period from which he did not recover for another two years. In June 1939, his spirits plummeted when the Prussian Church consistory announced his forced retirement. Niemöller was greatly wounded by this unexpected betrayal. He admitted to his wife a growing sense of "futility and hopelessness." "My existence," he wrote Else in October 1940, "is not much more than the life of an ape in the zoo, perhaps even less; because I am indeed completely isolated now." In February 1941, he wrote, "I'm swimming in a sea of apathy and must force myself to take a book in hand. It all seems so stupid and pointless." When his eighty-year-old father visited around this time, he tried to lift his son's spirits by stressing that the whole world was entreating God on his behalf. "My boy," he said, "the Eskimos in northern Canada and the Batiks in Sumatra are praying for you." In fact, the Nazis sought to turn the global attention to their advantage. "Niemöller is asking for leniency," Goebbels noted. "No question of it. Let him eat well, get fat, so that no one can mistake him for a martyr."[58]

Niemöller's despair was amplified by spiritual doubts. His admiration for the Protestant Church, which appeared to have abandoned him, began to falter. In 1940, he seriously considered converting to Catholicism. A few months after his arrival in Sachsenhausen, he wrote Else, "Who, by the way, came up with the good idea of sending me the Catholic missal? I read the Mass every morning . . . I'm amazed at the richness of the prayers and biblical lessons." The following year he wrote, "There flows through the Lutheran desert here and there a brook of living water, so that we do not need to be thirsty"; however, he observed, Protestantism seemed "sterile" next to the Catholic prayers and hymns. At Easter time, he told Else that the Roman breviary she sent him was, "next to the Bible and the hymnbook, my favorite and most read book."[59]

Reading the Mass, he explained, was "so refreshing . . . everything is so unambiguously focused on . . . the Lord Jesus Christ." In contrast to Protestantism's pious impulses, in Catholicism he found "the living, incarnate Word of God." As the Protestant Church remained hopelessly divided, the Catholic Church in Germany appeared united, furthering his disillusionment. Else pushed back in her letters, enlisting several

Confessing Church members to offer counterarguments. Even Catholic Bishop Clemens August von Galen of Münster, whom Else visited in February 1941, enjoined Niemöller to stay true to his own church.[60]

Rumors of his alleged conversion spread, sending shock waves through the Protestant world. In his own parish, there were intense discussions over whether to follow his example or remain in the Protestant Church. American theologian Reinhold Niebuhr struggled to understand Niemöller's motives. In Britain, Bishop Bell sought confirmation that Niemöller had, in fact, converted.[61]

As the concern of friends and family grew, Niemöller backed away from the possibility of conversion. "I seem to have missed the right moment for a decision," he wrote Else in February 1941, although he said that this was not his final word on the matter. Still, he admitted that lethargy had set in, making conversion unlikely. Else did her best to quash the rumors of her husband "going over."[62]

Adding to Niemöller's morose state, his father suffered a stroke in March 1941. To everyone's grateful surprise, Himmler granted permission for Hitler's personal prisoner to visit his father on his deathbed in Elberfeld. Under Gestapo guard, Niemöller was driven nearly four hundred miles across Germany to his parents' home. Two of his sons had accompanied Else to Elberfeld, but Martin was not allowed to see them, just his wife, mother, and father. The Gestapo were everywhere, including in his father's bedroom, where they sat behind a screen during the visit. Seeking to ease the tension, Heinrich called to his wife, "Mother, give the Gestapo a cigar, but please, not my best ones."[63]

Martin would have just thirty minutes with Heinrich. He came to his father at dusk. "Overwhelmed, I could hardly speak," Niemöller recalled, "and my dying father spoke with difficulty." The two men held hands, and the son mostly listened while his father recalled fond memories of his family and parish. Calm and composed, without a trace of fear, Heinrich expressed gratitude for the fullness of his life and for the love and devotion of his wife and children. "Then I kissed him for the last time in his life and heard his final words as if from afar, 'Behold, I am about to die, but God will be with you.'"[64]

Heinrich succumbed a week later. Niemöller took his father's death hard. "I think a lot about father," he wrote Else, "and I'm thankful that I was able to visit him on his deathbed, although since then everything has become doubly and triply as difficult." Another father figure of sorts, Kaiser Wilhelm II, who was born the same year as Heinrich, in 1859, died one month after Heinrich.[65]

SOON AFTERWARD, NIEMÖLLER's life took an ironic turn. Just as he had all but given up on the idea of conversion, the Nazi leadership moved him, on July 11, 1941, from Sachsenhausen in the Protestant north to the Dachau concentration camp in the Catholic south, where he was housed with three Catholic priests: Johannes Neuhäusler, Nikolaus Jansen, and Michael Höck. Neuhäusler and Höck were both in Sachsenhausen in 1941 and accompanied Niemöller to Dachau. They were given consecutive prison numbers: 26678 for Höck, 26679 for Niemöller, and 26680 for Neuhäusler. The relocation was part of the Nazi leadership's larger effort to assemble Christian clergymen and other prominent prisoners at Dachau. By the end of the war, 2,762 clergymen from all over Europe—approximately two-thirds came from Poland—had been imprisoned in Dachau. More than one-third of them died in the camp.[66]

The same month of Niemöller's transfer to Dachau marked a major turning point in the Nazis' efforts to solve the so-called "Jewish problem"—how to rid the Third Reich's expanding territory of Jews. Until the invasion of Poland on September 1, 1939, Nazi Jewish policy had focused necessarily on German Jews and then on Austrian Jews as well after the 1938 annexation of Austria. During these early years, Hitler had no single racial policy. German Jews, numbering approximately 550,000, or 0.7 percent of the German population, were subject to everything from boycotts and book burnings to legal discrimination and Aryanization (German expropriation) of their businesses. The jockeying for control over Jewish policy by various high-ranking Nazis resulted in multiple overlapping and contradictory policies. Despite the disagreements, the overall intention was to make Germany Jew-free (*Judenrein*) by making Jewish life in Germany so unbearable that Jews would emigrate. The persecution of German Jews reached an unprecedented level during the horrific Night of Broken Glass (*Kristallnacht*) on November 9–10, 1938. *Kristallnacht* was a Nazi-orchestrated pogrom; storm troopers beat, murdered, and harassed Jews across Germany and Austria. In addition to burning down hundreds of synagogues and smashing the windows of thousands of Jewish-owned shops, the Nazi radicals killed more than one hundred Jews and sent twenty-six thousand to concentration camps. Although there was no general outcry by Germans and Austrians over this public assault on Jews, the Nazi leadership was aware that conservative Germans did not approve of mob violence and disorder, even if they were not particularly concerned about the welfare of Jews. The Nazis determined that in the future, violence against Jews should be hidden from the public, preferably in some place outside Germany.[67]

Germany's *Blitzkrieg* (lightning war) victory against Poland provided the Nazis with both the impetus and the opportunity to implement a more lethal racial policy, unfettered by German qualms. The more territory Germany conquered in Europe, especially in eastern Europe, the greater the "Jewish problem" and the need for a more comprehensive solution became. Poland's population was one-tenth Jewish. When the Germans and Soviets divided Poland according to the Hitler-Stalin Pact of August 1939, Poland's three and a half million Jews found themselves living perilous lives under two very anti-Semitic regimes. In German-occupied Poland, the Nazis annexed the territory closest to Germany, killing and expelling tens of thousands of Poles and Jews in an effort to Aryanize the territory. They also established ghettos, like Lodz, to concentrate and isolate Polish Jews. Between 1939 and 1941, half a million Polish Jews died in these ghettos. In central Poland, the Nazis created an area called the General Government, administered by a notorious anti-Polish and anti-Semitic German, Hans Frank. The Nazis used this territory as a racial dumping ground for Jews and Poles until the Nazi leadership decided what to do with them.[68]

The war of annihilation against eastern European Jews entered a new and even deadlier phase when German armies invaded the Soviet Union in June 1941 in what they called Operation Barbarossa. As the German armies raced across eastern Poland and western Russia in pursuit of the fleeing Red Army in the summer of 1941, they encountered hundreds of thousands more Polish and Russian Jews. The German war against Communist Russia and its Jews was fought with ruthless severity.[69]

Following the German armies into the Soviet Union were mobile killing squads (*Einsatzgruppen*), whose orders were to murder Jews, Roma, and Soviet officials. By the spring of 1943, they had massacred approximately 2 million people, including 1.3 million Jews, 650,000 Roma, and thousands of Soviet officials. But shooting Jews one by one was inefficient and psychologically difficult for some of the killers. An alternative was sought. On Hitler's command, Hermann Göring authorized Reinhard Heydrich on July 31, 1941, to prepare "a master plan for carrying out the final solution of the Jewish problem." His plan, worked out with other Nazi leaders, was to build special killing camps equipped with gas chambers and crematoria for the extermination of Jews. In October 1941, signaling a change in policy, the Nazis banned Jewish emigration. The same month they began the construction of extermination camps in central Poland and deported the first contingent of German Jews to ghettos in Poland. The mass killing of European Jews began at Chelmno, the first extermination camp to begin operation, in December 1941; Nazi leaders met at Wannsee outside Berlin a month later to work out the details of the final solution. In the six extermination camps in central Poland, the Nazis gassed or worked to death approximately three million Jews.[70]

Dachau was a concentration camp, not an extermination camp. Although it had a gas chamber for the mass murder of prisoners, it was never used for that purpose because the SS preferred to exploit Dachau prisoners for their labor. Nevertheless, the mention of Dachau rightly brings to mind horrors and atrocities. It was the only camp in existence for the full twelve years of Nazi rule, and the composition of its prisoner population changed dramatically over those years. The first prisoners were political opponents of the regime, including some Jews in the

Communist and Socialist Parties. Some of these prisoners were tortured to death or driven to commit suicide. Soon after, Jehovah's Witnesses, criminals, Romas, "asocials," and homosexuals arrived. Prisoners wore striped uniforms affixed with a number and a colored triangle: political prisoners wore a red triangle, Roma black, Jews yellow, criminals green, Jehovah's Witnesses purple, and homosexuals pink. Austrian prisoners arrived in 1938 after the German annexation, including some prominent political prisoners from the former Austrian government. After *Kristallnacht*, eleven thousand German Jews were housed in Dachau; most of them were released after a few weeks. From its inception to the outbreak of the war, about five hundred prisoners died in Dachau.[71]

With the beginning of the Second World War and the arrival of foreign nationals, the treatment of Dachau prisoners worsened. Food rations deteriorated in 1941 and 1942 and epidemics broke out, causing the death rate to increase rapidly. Polish and Soviet POWS became the largest groups in the camp. Between August 1941 and June 1942, four thousand Soviet prisoners were shot to death. In November 1941, all Jewish prisoners were deported to Auschwitz. Nazi doctors conducted medical experiments on prisoners, killing hundreds. Crematoria were used to dispose of the mounting dead. In the last months of the camp's existence, Dachau became "catastrophically overcrowded" as transports of prisoners arrived from other camps that had been evacuated ahead of advancing Allied troops. A typhus epidemic broke out in November 1944, eventually taking the lives of 15,000 inmates. In April 1945, Himmler ordered the evacuation of the camp. The number of prisoners killed at Dachau is believed to be 42,359.[72]

Niemöller's arrival in July 1941 coincided with the deterioration of living conditions at Dachau. But in comparison with the existence of most Dachau inmates and with his time at Sachsenhausen, life for Niemöller and his Catholic companions was comfortable. Niemöller recalled after his release, "We were treated with rather more respect than the other inmates. There were eight cells, a chapel, and a sitting room, completely isolated from the other inmates, and a small court where we could walk around." No longer held in solitary confinement and free to communicate with a wide range of special prisoners, Niemöller would have been aware of the dominant conditions in Dachau and other concentration camps. We do not know whether Niemöller heard from other special prisoners about the mass killings of Jews by the mobile killing units in the east or the use of extermination camps in Poland.[73]

Among the Protestants in Dachau was Niemöller's colleague Heinrich Grüber, founder and head of the Relief Center for Protestant Non-Aryans, known as the Grüber Office. Initially, the center helped Christians of Jewish descent and their families emigrate and provided material aid to those who lost their jobs. After *Kristallnacht*, Grüber extended assistance to all Jews. On December 19, 1940, the Nazis arrested Grüber and put him in Sachsenhausen before transferring him to Dachau the following year. He survived and was widely honored after the war. A forest in Jerusalem is named for him, and he received an honorary degree of humane letters from Hebrew Union College in New York City. Several courageous members in the radical wing of the Confessing Church supported the Grüber Office until the Nazis shuttered it in 1941. The conservatives in the Confessing Church, for the most part, did not.[74]

Special prisoners had many unexpected privileges: they were allowed to meet in common areas, share meals together, read materials from the library, and receive visitors, who could bring food and other items. The Catholic priests were even permitted to convert a spacious room into a chapel. Else noticed her husband's improved disposition after a few weeks. In this new atmosphere, the old Niemöller with his sense of humor and fighting spirit reemerged. Bonhoeffer, who was in regular contact with Else, reported to Bishop Bell, "He is feeling considerably better since he is enjoying the company of two colleagues. There is no reason to worry about his physical and spiritual state of health."[75]

Bonhoeffer had isolated the principal change. More than anything else, daily contact and conversation with other men revivified Niemöller. In the morning he and his Catholic companions would read and discuss the Catholic missal, and in the afternoon Niemöller would lead a discussion about passages of Scripture. In the evening they would play cards. The four men grew to respect each other immensely and to relish their theological discussions. Through these exchanges, Niemöller developed a better appreciation for Catholicism, including, he explained after the war, various inadequacies he had not perceived during his crisis of faith. Just as the Protestant Church had its shortcomings, so too did the Catholic Church, he concluded. As Bonhoeffer told a colleague in April 1942, Niemöller was declaring "with new certainty the proclamation of the pure gospel in the Reformation."[76]

Many other high-profile prisoners were sent to Dachau during Niemöller's imprisonment. They included the kaiser's nephew, Prince Friedrich Leopold of Prussia; the former Austrian chancellor, Kurt von Schuschnigg; and the former premier of France, Léon Blum. Niemöller struck up a friendship with a colonel from the British army, Richard Stevens, who had endured two years of solitary confinement in Sachsenhausen before being transferred. On Niemöller's fiftieth birthday in 1942, Stevens brushed past Niemöller in the shower and told him he had been listening to the BBC on his clandestine radio. "I have direct news and greetings for you. Last night they had a service in St. Martin-in-the-Fields, on the occasion of your fiftieth birthday: the service was conducted by the Archbishop of Canterbury, and your friend the Bishop of Chichester preached the sermon."[77]

The move to Dachau only increased Niemöller's popularity abroad. A flurry of books on Niemöller appeared in the United States in the early 1940s. Popular biographies such as Basil Miller's *Martin Niemoeller: Hero of the Concentration Camp* (1942) exalted his piety and courage. "Hitler may break his body, but never his soul," Miller proclaimed to enthusiastic readers. Newspaper advertisements celebrating Niemöller's mettle blared, "He Wouldn't 'Heil Hitler' so Rev. Martin Niemoeller Begins His 7th Year in a German Prison Camp—Remember Martin Niemoeller!!" The film *Pastor Hall* and play *God Is My Führer* depicted Niemöller's heroic struggle. Goebbels followed these developments with contempt. Of the "rabble-rousing American film, *Pastor Hall,*" he wrote, "the supposed fate of Niemöller. A moronic piece of rubbish. Not worth the time spent watching it." In his 1943 autobiography, Pastor Hans Ehrenberg remarked on Niemöller's "canonization throughout Christendom."[78]

Niemöller's physical and mental well-being may have improved at Dachau, but he was still behind barbed wire, away from his family. And all was not well with them. Dahlem is about 350 miles north of Dachau, a ten-hour train ride. Sachsenhausen, by contrast, was less than an hour from the Niemöller home. Else's fortnightly visits to Dachau were time-consuming and exhausting. Meanwhile, the war had come home to Berlin, terrifying the population. Bombing raids by the British and Soviets began in 1940–1941. Göring had assured Berliners that enemy bombers could never reach the capital; suddenly it became apparent that no one was safe from the dangers of total war.

In the spring of 1942, Else spent two weeks hospitalized with an intestinal illness and could not visit her husband for three months. Friends and supporters did what they could to help, but by this point every family had its own troubles. Assistance did come from Maria Lempp, the widow of Barth's publisher, who offered her Leoni summer cottage near Munich to Else and the children, so that they could be closer to Martin in Dachau. She moved there with teenage daughters Hertha and Jutta, eight-year-old Tini, and their housekeeper Dora in the late summer of 1943. The three older boys, Jochen, Hermann, and Jan, were by then serving on the Eastern Front. Brigitte, their firstborn, had married a young patent attorney, a Nazi, in November 1941. Neither parent approved, and the relationship between Brigitte and her father was particularly strained for a time.

As the war neared its end, two personal tragedies struck. On December 30, 1944, sixteen-year-old Jutta died suddenly a day after contracting diphtheria. Niemöller had not even known she was ill when he received the news of her death from a camp guard. In the weeks prior to her death, she had accompanied her mother every other Thursday to Dachau to visit with her father, even though the guards did not allow her to see him. He was not allowed to attend her funeral. Then, on February 28, 1945, their oldest son, twenty-two-year-old Jochen, died in combat with the Russians in northern Germany. Else delivered the news herself. Jochen, who wanted to be a pastor like his father and grandfather, had been studying theology at Marburg University when he was called up. One month before his death, Jochen was given a four-day leave from his unit to visit his mother and his siblings in Leoni after his sister's death. Just before he returned to the front, he slipped Hertha an envelope. "Don't tell Mother, but if I don't come back, here is my letter." Martin was fully aware that one or more of his sons in uniform might not return, but to lose his oldest son, the son who had chosen his profession, was a hard blow. In his final letter to Jochen, Niemöller had shared his belief that after the war Germany would need compassionate pastors like Jochen to lead the German people out of the abyss.[79]

A small victory may have been Niemöller's only solace in these grim times. While the imprisoned Catholic clergy had been allowed to consecrate cell 34 as a chapel for their monthly worship, Protestants were denied the same privilege, apparently because their sermons were too unpredictable and might veer into politics. But in December 1944, Dr. Jannes van Dijk, the seventy-two-year-old Dutch former minister of defense, complained that during his four years in Dachau he had never been allowed to formally worship. Camp officials relented, allowing the Protestants to hold a Christmas service. Niemöller sat down to prepare a sermon, but he was apprehensive. The Protestant special prisoners in his cell wing included a Dutch Calvinist, an English Anglican, an Orthodox Serb, two Norwegian Lutherans, and a Macedonian of no particular denomination. All hailed from countries either at war with Germany or under Axis rule. How would they respond to a German clergyman preaching and dispensing the Holy Supper? Niemöller asked each individually, "Do you want me, a German Lutheran, to conduct Christmas Eve service and administer Holy Communion?" The six men confirmed that they did. So Niemöller preached on Christmas Eve 1944 in Dachau's chapel. For the next four months, he preached every few weeks to this unique congregation. After the war, he told American audiences that "those six people, being Christian people, believing in Christ, had overcome all enmity and hatred against a German, and longed for a world community in the Holy Communion."[80]

The story of the Dachau congregation became an important touchstone in Niemöller's postwar effort to recruit international Christian sympathy for German brothers and sisters in Christ. It was not a cynical ploy. Niemöller's thinking evolved during his eight years of incarceration, building on sentiments he had voiced before the war. In contrast to many of his Lutheran colleagues, Niemöller had always been relatively unconcerned about the confessional differences between the German Lutheran, Reformed, and United Churches. During the Church Struggle, it seemed to Niemöller that these divisions only served to weaken the church opposition's fight against the German Christians. He repeatedly argued that petty theological differences between the different Protestant traditions should not prevent a united front. In Dachau, he took this position a step further. He extended his openness to foreign Protestant denominations, foreshadowing his later work with the ecumenical movement in the World Council of Churches.

The international and multidenominational friendships he developed in Dachau turned Niemöller toward the possibility of a world Protestantism, not just a German Protestantism. During his Maundy Thursday sermon at the Dachau chapel on March 29, 1945, he poked fun at the disputes between various Protestant denominations. "At present these theological differences have become so subtle that one must be a philosopher with a better-than-average education to recognize them," he said. "If our salvation depended on such recognition, then the Kingdom of Heaven would be accessible only to learned thinkers—which is obviously contrary to the conception held by Jesus himself, and to his own words." Niemöller suggested that, just as denominational differences are insignificant for Christian worship, so are national borders. "We know only one comfort and one assurance," he told his multinational congregation in Dachau. "Jesus Christ the crucified."[81]

SEVEN

Guilt, Repentance, Renewal
(1945–1946)

I N MAY 1945, PROTESTANTS ACROSS THE WORLD LEARNED THAT PASTOR
Martin Niemöller had been liberated and was in the hands of American troops in Italy. Few of his followers had expected him to survive the
final months of Hitler's regime. Between July 20, 1944, when the resistance within the German army tried unsuccessfully to assassinate Hitler,
and the end of the war, Hitler ordered the execution of over eleven thousand Germans considered "enemies of the Reich." Among the dead were
Colonel Claus von Stauffenberg, Hitler's would-be assassin, and Dietrich
Bonhoeffer, hanged by the Nazis in Flossenbürg concentration camp on
April 9—two weeks before the Americans liberated the camp. The murder
of Niemöller's friend and the deaths of so many young Confessing pastors
and theology students on the Eastern Front severely depleted the ranks of
the Confessing Church in the immediate postwar years.[1]

By killing resistance leaders, the Nazis sought not only to send a message that opposition would not be tolerated but also to limit the role of their opponents in a postwar government. For years, rumors in the US press claimed that Niemöller had been selected by the German military and conservative resistance to head the postwar government. Although American newspapers exaggerated the support for a Niemöller-led postwar government, Adam von Trott zu Solz, a diplomat in the German Foreign Office and member of the Kreisau Circle planning to overthrow Hitler, had proposed Niemöller in 1941 because he was "the strongest internationally known exponent of anti-Hitlerism" and also popular at home.[2]

The Nazis, however, had no intention of allowing Niemöller to survive the war. To ensure that this would never happen, on April 25, 1945, a special detachment of guards set out from Dachau under the command of SS Obersturmführer Edgar Stiller, with "special prisoners" in tow. Hoping to stay ahead of advancing US troops, they bused and trucked Niemöller and about 150 other high-profile prisoners and family members on a southern route toward Italy. There were men, women, and children, ranging in age from four to seventy-three, who belonged to seventeen different nationalities. As the convoy dodged Allied air raids, it navigated the heavily bombed streets of Munich heading toward the Brenner Pass. One of the prisoners, the British captain Sigismund Payne Best, described the route: "At that time all roads leading to passes through the Alps were being regularly and badly shot up by our planes in order to prevent any large scale movement of [German] troops and munitions to the Southern Redoubt."[3]

After traveling all night, the convoy passed through Innsbruck in eastern Austria in the early hours of April 26 and arrived at Reichenau, a concentration camp outside the city, where it met another group of special prisoners who had been transported from Flossenbürg. During their night at Reichenau, many of the special prisoners saw for the first time the conditions most other camp inmates had experienced. The skeletal prisoners, lice-infested cells, and open cesspools that served as latrines shocked Niemöller after his relatively comfortable accommodations in

Dachau's bunker. Even at Reichenau, though, the special prisoners continued to be treated well, receiving tobacco and plenty of food. But there were ominous signs. An execution squad led by SS Untersturmführer Ernst Bader was also part of the convoy, as was a crate of hand grenades.[4]

The following evening, the special prisoners were reloaded on buses, but progress was halting, as the convoy made frequent stops to fix flat tires and fill empty gas tanks. The buses stopped for over an hour, exposed, at the top of the snowy Brenner Pass; some prisoners speculated that the guards were hoping that an Allied bombing raid would do their work for them. Eventually the convoy made it into northern Italy, where many of the prisoners were billeted in a hotel in the German-speaking village of Niederdorf (Villabassa). The weary prisoners contrasted starkly with their cheerful, brightly dressed Tyrolean hosts.[5]

This might have been Niemöller's final stop had it not been for Captain Best and some of the other special prisoners. During a bountiful dinner, drunken SS guards revealed to the captain their orders to kill Niemöller and others before US troops could liberate them. But the guards hesitated, hoping they could use their valuable cargo to negotiate their own survival. Meanwhile, the prisoners outwitted the guards. Bogislav von Bonin, an imprisoned colonel still in Wehrmacht uniform, made secret contact with regular German troops also stationed in the area and explained that SS guards had been ordered to kill him and other prisoners. Aware of Germany's imminent defeat and genuinely concerned about the fate of the prisoners, many of whom were former Wehrmacht officers, the German regulars came to their rescue. The SS, although heavily armed with machine guns and hand grenades, allowed the troops to take custody of their prisoners. Some SS men fled into the hilly terrain and were probably killed by Italian partisans. Others gave up their arms and chose to stay and face arrest by the Americans. A Wehrmacht platoon left a few men behind to ensure the prisoners' safety.[6]

On April 30—the same day as Hitler's suicide in his Berlin bunker—the former prisoners were bused from Niederdorf to the Hotel Pragser Wildsee, a chalet on a picturesque lake high up in the Dolomite Mountains. It was snowing. Although the hotel's two hundred rooms were unheated,

Niemöller with American troops in the Dolomite Mountains. (Critical Past)

there were enough blankets, not to mention abundant food and wine. One of the Englishmen in the group recalled, "After many years of viewing barbed wire, guard towers and cell walls, it seemed like a wonderful dream." Half a week later, on May 4, American troops liberated the prisoners for a second time, without incident. The accompanying Wehrmacht soldiers and SS surrendered, becoming prisoners of war.[7]

In short order, the Americans were sharing their rations of chocolate and cigarettes, a mobile laundry was set up on the lawn, and nets were erected for handball and other games. Rations were supplemented by long-forgotten luxuries such as waffles and syrup, eggs, and bacon. The international press soon descended on the hotel, jostling for photographs with the newly freed inmates, especially the anti-Vichy French politician Léon Blum, former Austrian chancellor Kurt Schuschnigg, and Niemöller, who struck various poses with and without his Bible. The evening before their departure, looking out over the snow-clad Dolomites as the sun was setting, Niemöller conducted a small service. The next day, May 8, he and his companions were taken to Allied headquarters at Caserta, Italy, just north of Naples. While they were en route, Germany's defeated military leaders surrendered unconditionally to the Allies. The war in Europe was over.[8]

"WHEN AMERICANS READ that their own troops . . . had found the celebrated Pastor Martin Niemöller," the *Washington Post* reported, "it was as though a grave had opened." The *Post* predicted that Niemöller would become "the advocate of his people in their hour of disillusion and despair, a witness to the world that, if German human nature is capable of the most bestial evil, it is also capable of great moral heroism." Dorothy Thompson, who interviewed Niemöller in mid-May at his hotel in Naples, declared, "He is a man from whom fear forever has flown." The faith that sustained him during his years of captivity "gives him now a spiritual authority possessed perhaps by no other individual in Protestant Christendom," she concluded. Dewitt McKenzie, an Associated Press correspondent and seasoned war journalist, exclaimed, "It's to stalwarts like Niemöller to whom we must look for help on the monumental task of remolding the character of the German nation." And the *Christian Science Monitor* gushed, "Pastor Martin Niemoeller, the fire of his defiance unquenched by eight years in a Nazi concentration camp, stands as a symbol of hope that German leadership will be found for the eventual building of a new Germany."[9]

And there were everyday Americans who shared the enthusiasm of their foreign correspondents. A widow from White Plains, New York, wrote, "I do thank God that you are a free man and can return to your family. You have shown wonderful Christian faith and endurance. . . . I hope you will come to America and tell your story. I would go miles to hear it."[10]

He would take up the invitation to visit the United States, but for the moment, he was stuck in Naples. As a German national in the custody of the US Army, he was not free to join his wife and children, who were waiting for him at Leoni on Lake Starnberg, near Munich. American army officials and political advisers in Europe were as yet uncertain whether Niemöller might play a leading political role in postwar Germany. Still, US authorities extended him many courtesies. General Harold Alexander, commander in chief of the Allied armies in Italy, entertained him at dinner. He was given a room in Naples's Parco Hotel and an official document allowing him a measure of freedom: "Pastor Martin Niemöller, age 53 years, height five feet, eight inches, dark hair, brown eyes, born at Littstadt [sic], Westphalia, has the permission of this head-quarters to circulate freely in the city of Naples." He was also allowed to ride in US military vehicles and to travel to Rome. During his eight weeks in Naples, he made friends with several Americans, including Lutheran chaplain David Ostergren and Jewish chaplain Samuel Teitelbaum, who later would describe Niemöller as a "refined Nazi" because he had all of the attitudes of a Nazi, except for his opposition to torture and violence. He attended performances of *La Bohème*, *Tosca*, and *La Traviata* at the local opera house, bathed in mineral springs, and visited Solfatara, a volcanic site north of Naples.[11]

Throughout, however, he was deeply frustrated. What he wanted was to hug his wife and children. In mid-May, when Bishop Garfield Bromley Oxnam, president of the Federal Council of Churches, visited Niemöller in Naples, the pastor described himself as a "prisoner." Later that summer, after his return to Germany, he complained that during his two-month deterrence by the Americans, his opponents in the church were able to regroup and rebuild their base of power.[12]

The American infatuation with Pastor Martin Niemöller was severely tested on June 5, 1945, when he granted an interview to dozens of British and American war correspondents gathered at his Naples hotel. In his first public appearance, he was clearly missing the oversight of a good public relations agent. Many of the journalists were hardened war correspondents who had covered German war atrocities and the liberation of the concentration and extermination camps. They expected some sign of contrition from this famous German, but instead, angry that his American captors were so slow in authorizing his return to his family, Niemöller gave voice to a mood that could only be called belligerent. In inexpert English, he responded impulsively to rapid-fire questions from reporters. Words spoken heedlessly that day would haunt Niemöller for years to come.

He acknowledged that, prior to the Nazis' rise to power, he "had nourished the hope that National Socialism, if it had gone the right way, might have developed into a system for creating good for the German people." His objections to Nazism were religious and not political, which explained why from his cell in Sachsenhausen he had offered his services to the German navy when World War II broke out. "If there is a war," Niemöller could defiantly declare in June 1945, "a German doesn't ask is it just or unjust, but he feels bound to join the ranks. I think the German people will be a little more cautious in the future, but more than this I cannot promise."[13]

Insisting that most Germans were ignorant of the scale of Nazi atrocities and shocked by what they saw when the Allies liberated the concentration and extermination camps, he asserted, "You are mistaken if you think any honest person in Germany will feel personally responsible for things like Dachau, Belsen, and Buchenwald. He will feel only misled into believing in a regime that was led by criminals and murderers."[14]

The German people were ill suited, he went on, to live under a Western form of democracy; indeed, in many ways Germans preferred authoritarian rule. "The German people are different . . . they like to be governed; they like to feel authority." What Germans needed now was not punishment but help. By way of conclusion, he said that he hoped to visit England and the United States to enlist Americans and British in his efforts to secure food and clothing for Germans. "The world will be astonished when it sees how many good people are left in Germany."[15]

Reaction in the US press was scathing. Reflecting on the Naples interview, the *New York Times* concluded that the pastor once celebrated as the champion of the resistance was not suited "to be a leader in the moral reconstruction of his country." Niemöller's assertion that Germany was unsuited for democracy was a particular source of concern. "If a democratic system cannot be erected in Germany, Europe will be right back where it started from, and Germany must be continuously policed or periodically chastened by war." Niemöller was, the *Times* continued, "a hero with limitations." And *Time* magazine, which had named Niemöller "Martyr of 1940," chimed in on the interview's broad impact: "Pastor Martin Niemöller, the one German whom Christians everywhere *had* respected, shocked a lot of people last week."[16]

Fearing that Niemöller's pugnacity and ill choice of words would do his cause and his reputation grievous harm, Swiss theologian Karl Barth telegrammed Protestant leaders in New York to see if they could help get his friend out of Naples and reunited with his family.

AMERICANS REFUSING RETURN TO GERMANY PROVOKED CRISIS. MARTIN NEEDS REST CARE PROTECTION AND PRESENCE OF FAMILY AND CLOSE FRIENDS. TAKE RAPID EFFECTIVE STEPS WITH WASHINGTON TO CHANGE SITUATION.[17]

Sam Cavert, general secretary of the Federal Council of Churches, swung into action, writing to President Harry Truman: "Pastor Niemöller is of so much potential value in our relations with the German people that we should like to raise the question in the right quarters whether prompt steps could not be taken to permit his return to his family without further delay." Truman's secretary responded that the supreme Allied commander in the Mediterranean Theater of Operations had been advised to grant Niemöller "preferential treatment" and that the War Department was giving Niemöller's case "the most careful thought and consideration."[18]

American Lutherans showed the least concern with the views that Niemöller articulated in Naples and invited him to the United States immediately after the interview. On June 8, the National Lutheran Council sent a cable to Niemöller at the Naples hotel, conveying their "earnest request that he visit the United States at his earliest convenience as guest

of the American Lutherans for purpose of conferring on postwar rehabilitation of European churches and other mutual problems." Niemöller
was grateful but would need to wait for US government approval, which,
given his recent comments, was not likely to come anytime soon.[19]

Not everyone, however, agreed that Niemöller could serve as a useful liaison between the United States and Germany. Marshall Knappen,
director of the education and religious affairs branch of the US occupation forces in Germany, argued, "Niemöller, the religious leader and
Confessional martyr is to be clearly distinguished from Niemöller the
politically-minded retired naval officer. The one is to be accorded the
freedom and respect which is due. The other . . . is to be watched carefully." After the infamous Naples interview, Knappen canceled a lecture
Niemöller was to give for American troops and reported to his superiors
that the pastor's "known political opinions are such as to raise a question
as to the advisability of any chaplain sponsoring his appearance before
an army audience." He was, Knappen decided, "potentially dangerous as
a political leader."[20]

Niemöller was bound to butt heads with American officials. At the
outset, the Americans hoped that he and other religious leaders would
set aside politics and focus on the moral rehabilitation of the nation. But
German church leaders believed that, if Nazism proved anything, it was
that the churches needed to hold more sway in public life. Niemöller
voiced this idea frequently; indeed, it was the philosophy he lived by from
1945 until his death in 1984. No longer was he content to live within the
constraints of the doctrine of two kingdoms, whereby matters of state
were left outside the church door.

He told a Swiss newspaper in September 1945, "The German Church
must act as custodian of German national policy so that the human
rights of the population might be continually protected." Niemöller had
come to believe that it was his duty as a church leader to weigh in on
almost every aspect of the Allied occupation and on the emerging Cold
War. He proved a constant thorn in the side of the US military government in Germany, fuming about everything from travel restrictions
and inadequate food to aggressive denazification procedures and the

Americans' brief nonfraternization policy. US military leaders quickly learned to keep him at arm's length.[21]

Niemöller's animosity toward the Allied occupation forces—the Americans, the British, the French, and the Russians—stemmed from the widely held German belief that the Allies intended to impose victor's justice on the German nation and that an occupation marked by revenge and retribution was in store. The tens of thousands of German women and girls raped by Soviet soldiers when they entered Berlin in April and May of 1945 confirmed Germans' worst fears about the Russians. And rumors that the Americans had decided to impose the harsh occupation policies recommended by the American secretary of the Treasury, Henry Morgenthau Jr., spread fear and resentment. The Morgenthau Plan, articulated in 1944, called for the destruction of German industry, the transformation of the country into an agricultural state made up of farmers, and the permanent division of Germany, among other things. It seemed calculated to create the most suffering possible. The rumors, however, were false: the American government had rejected most of Morgenthau's plan in favor of an Allied plan to demilitarize, denazify, democratize, and reeducate the German people. By no means did this mean a soft or friendly occupation, especially in the Russian zone, but the intention was not to cause suffering. The American nonfraternization policy, strictly enforced at first, was abandoned in September because it was both difficult to enforce and contradicted the goal of teaching good citizenship.[22]

The Allied policy of demilitarization was the least controversial and met little resistance by Germans. But the policies of denazification, democratization, and reeducation were more intrusive and consequently more resented. Since many Germans, Niemöller included, did not believe that the German population in general had been nazified, they did not agree with the need for denazification. With the Nazi leadership either dead—Hitler, Goebbels, and Himmler had committed suicide in April and May—or captured by the Allies, there was little need, many believed, to bother with small-time Nazis who had joined the movement out of opportunism and now regretted it. And democratization and reeducation seemed to suggest that the occupiers knew what was best

for Germans, which many Germans perceived as arrogant and presump-
tuous. Niemöller believed that the devastation of the war and publication of the atrocities committed in the camps were enough to make most
Germans despise Nazism. Whatever reeducation was still needed, he
maintained, should be done by German nationals, like himself and other
churchmen who had allegedly opposed Nazism.[23]

Although there were significant differences in the manner in which
the four occupation powers' implemented these policies, it quickly became clear that the Soviet decision to enforce communism in their zone
was creating an unbridgeable divide between the three Western zones
and the Eastern zone. In 1949, the split was solidified with the creation
of the Federal Republic of Germany, or West Germany, and the German
Democratic Republic, or East Germany.

ON JUNE 12, 1945, US authorities told Niemöller that he was going to
be interrogated at the Supreme Headquarters Allied Expeditionary Force
(SHAEF) at Versailles. After two days at Versailles and no interrogation,
he was moved to a detention center in Wiesbaden near the SHAEF's new
headquarters in Frankfurt. For two weeks he was interrogated without
being allowed to communicate with his family. At this point, his frustra-
tions with the Americans boiled over. "I'd had enough," he fumed and
went on a hunger strike. Fearing negative media, the Americans granted
Niemöller his freedom on June 21. With the necessary travel documents
in hand, he and fellow Confessing churchman Hans Asmussen made
their way to southern Bavaria in a borrowed car.[24]

"In the morning at six o'clock, I stood under my wife's window and
found her with Hertha, Martin [Tini], and Dora." It was June 24, 1945,
nearly eight years to the day since his July 1, 1937, arrest. "I shall never
forget that day," Else recalled. "It was in the morning, quarter to six,
that I heard a voice under my window and there he was. Oh, we were so
glad, my daughter and I! Then we went to the bed of our little Martin
and I said, 'Look who's here.' And he saw it was his father and embraced

him, and oh, the joy!" Else told Martin that the eight weeks between his liberation and their reunion, during which she waited every hour for his return, were "worse than the whole eight years before." Having left most of his possessions in his Naples hotel room, he wrote the American authorities: "My petition is that things might be forwarded if possible, because my few bits of linen are outworn and I have no clothing for the winter left; besides I left at Naples my best shoes, some books and documents of importance and several pieces of toilet-soap, things I can't spare just now."[25]

Niemöller was conflicted about what to do next. After recuperating in Switzerland, he wanted to return to his beloved Dahlem congregation, which had stood by him throughout his imprisonment. But the situation in Berlin, now located in the center of the Russian occupation zone and jointly administered by all four former Allies, was chaotic and uncertain. Not only was his parish under new leadership, but managing a war-ravaged pastorate in Berlin would leave him little time to address the two most urgent tasks facing the church: first, the re-Christianization and reconstruction of Germany, and second, the overhaul of the church's leadership, organization, and mind-set. In the meantime, he was stuck in Leoni—a tiny, isolated village. He had neither an office nor a secretary and had little capacity to communicate with church leaders across Germany, which was now firmly under four-power occupation.

And there were larger questions too. Many had pegged Niemöller as the German Protestant Church's next chairman. But, despite his great admiration for Niemöller's leadership of the church opposition, Willem Visser't Hooft, the Dutch general secretary of the provisional World Council of Churches, recommended to occupation authorities that the elderly bishop Theophil Wurm would make a better choice. Niemöller, Visser't Hooft said, was not sufficiently statesmanlike. Sylvester C. Michelfelder, president of the US Council of Lutheran Churches, acknowledged in his diary that "Niemöller has come into disfavor pretty much because of his unfortunate interview with the Press in Italy. There he said, 'My Soul belongs to God but my body to the State.' This in America and Britain has caused much offense."[26]

As for the possibility of Niemöller playing a leading political role in postwar Germany, Anglican bishop George Bell called the idea "inexpressibly mad." Bell, who was in close contact with Niemöller prior to his arrest and remained one of the pastor's most ardent supporters during his time in the camps, shared Visser't Hooft's misgivings. "He is a keen spiritual personality, but he would never make a statesman." After eight years in prison, with little access to unfiltered news, "there is a lot he does not know." The bishop was sympathetic to Niemöller's interest in traveling abroad and currying support for Germany's rebuilding effort. Even so, discussing Niemöller's proposal to go to the United States and England, Bell was terse: "I hope he doesn't."[27]

The fallout from the Naples interview was proving to be a serious obstacle to Niemöller's effort to help his people. There was much debate at the time, and still today, whether his comments, spoken extemporaneously in front of the Parco Hotel, represented his true feelings. One place to look for clues was in the transcript from Niemöller's interrogation in Wiesbaden. American officials asked for his opinions on some twenty-three questions regarding German responsibility for Nazism and Germany's political future. His written responses were long and detailed, clearly the result of considered reflection. Question 9 asked about the readiness of "German church people" to accept general responsibility for the crimes of the Nazi regime. Niemöller answered along the same lines as he had in Naples. The German Protestant Church, he asserted, never agreed with the terror exercised by Hitler and his party; it opposed right from the beginning his plans and measures to put an end to spiritual freedom. "It is scarcely to be expected that those persons—to whom I belong myself—are inclined to take responsibility for things they fought against and had to endure themselves against their will." As to the slaughter of Jews, Niemöller said, "I myself, after nearly 8 years arrest in concentration camps, was stunned when I learned by American papers what really happened. Such as things are, I must deny that not only the church but the far greater part of the German people in general could regard themselves responsible for those crimes as were performed by the Nazi regimes and their hangmen, whoever they may have been."[28]

But in a departure from the defiant, unrepentant tone he struck in Naples, Niemöller recognized that "there can only be disgust, abhorrence and shame that such crimes could happen, and that they really happened in the midst of the German people." The Christian people of Germany, he went on, "certainly will not consider themselves free of every responsibility for the fact that such things came to pass." He admitted that the German people did not stand up to the signs of Nazi terror in 1933 and 1934. And he regarded all the German suffering under Nazi rule and during the war "as a hard, though well earned, punishment from heaven." He expressed the hope that, after the Allies punished Nazi criminals, there would be no new wave of hatred against the Germans. It was God's right to punish the German people, but this right did not extend to the victors of the war.[29]

Although the interrogation transcript indicates that Niemöller retained a nationalist outlook toward the foreign occupiers, it also suggests that the reality of the extermination camps and the moral vapidity of the Nazi regime had expunged any remaining allegiance he might have had to Nazism and right-wing authoritarianism. And most important, he seemed to warm to the idea that Germans, even those who were not Nazis, were not free of responsibility. Regarding the future German government, he told his interrogators that since a return to a constitutional monarchy was unlikely—the German populace would have an aversion, he believed, to another person holding office for life—"a democratic republic with a strong position of its president will prove the best." Niemöller was not a democrat at heart in 1945 and still preferred a strong conservative leader, but his politics had evolved. His recent experiences—leading the Church Struggle, surviving the Nazi camps, living under foreign occupation, and absorbing the realities of the Holocaust—had changed him. To what degree remained to be seen.[30]

ALTHOUGH NIEMÖLLER'S FOREIGN friends had come to his defense after the Naples interview, they wished that he and other leading churchmen would admit publicly that they had failed as the shepherds of the

German nation by not condemning the Nazi project, root and branch, from the start. Karl Barth, Willem Visser't Hooft, and the American Federal Council of Churches were urging him during the summer of 1945 to lead his nation in repentance. If only all German clergymen would acknowledge their failure publicly, repenting and demanding the same from their countrymen, it would be a helpful step toward reestablishing German Protestantism's reputation.

For Niemöller, though, the challenges facing his family, his church, and his nation were so staggering and demoralizing that he could barely comprehend how to move forward. The elation of liberation and reunion with his family had long since dissipated. Else told a family friend, "He sees everything black." About a month after his return home, Niemöller confided in his close colleague Hans Böhm, "Nowhere do I see anything resembling hope." There were plenty of reasons to be despondent. Of the seven Niemöller children, two, a son and a daughter, had died during the war, and two other sons were Russian prisoners of war. Eight years of imprisonment, as well as the tense months following his release, had taken a toll on both Else and Martin. Their temporary housing in Leoni was cramped, and the cupboards were bare. A long, cold winter would soon set in. Niemöller still received a small salary from the Dahlem parish, but it wasn't enough. His beloved fatherland lay in ruins, occupied by Allied troops who seemed intent on exacting victor's justice. Horrific images of the Holocaust, perpetrated by his countrymen, haunted him.[31]

Equally as bleak as his personal situation was the state of the Protestant churches themselves. Scores of church buildings had been reduced to rubble, but they could be rebuilt. More important, the gospel of repentance, forgiveness, and love seemed to have been forgotten. In particular, the church leadership showed little interest in atoning for their complacency toward and complicity in the Third Reich. The self-righteous tone of his colleagues, especially those who had risked the least in the Church Struggle, and his contact with foreign churchmen prompted a new outlook in Niemöller.

Because Niemöller had been locked up for nearly a decade, and because many of his young Confessing colleagues had been killed in battle or taken as prisoners of war by the Russians, power had shifted back to the older bishops, who had joined neither the Nazi-backed German Christians nor the Niemöller wing of the Confessing Church. "This group of neutrals represents the leading group" in the postwar church, Niemöller lamented in July 1945. "And here lies the real church problem. Nothing can be achieved by neutrals. . . . They will evade all real decisions and will hinder all real activity in the Church." The same churchmen who had avoided direct confrontation with the Nazis were now avoiding confronting their own people with their complicity in Hitler's regime.[32]

Niemöller worried that his colleagues' stubbornness would inspire similar feelings among parishioners, jeopardizing the reformation of the church and undermining chances for reconciliation between Germany and her former enemies. For the moment at least, German survival depended on food, fuel, and housing provided by the Allies. More assistance would be forthcoming, Niemöller believed, if Germans genuinely repented for Nazism. And that burden fell largely on the church because it was among the very few German institutions that outlasted Hitler's onslaught. Political parties, universities, trade unions, corporations, courts of law, and cultural organizations had been either co-opted or crushed by the Nazis. Although the Protestant and Catholic churches had had no easy time during the Nazi period, they at least survived. It was thus left to the churches to repent publicly on everyone's behalf.

But Protestant Church leaders, like Bishops Wurm and Meiser, understood all too well that their parishioners wanted no such thing. In the wake of the unconditional surrender, they did not want to hear about German guilt. A scarred and war-weary population looked to their church leaders to relieve their misery and address their grievances with the occupying powers. Meiser and Wurm were happy to oblige. Even as they (dubiously) claimed to have resisted Hitler, they tended to speak of the "guilt of the other," by which they meant the Allies. An example of this mentality was Bishop Wurm's open letter to the English in December 1945. His denunciation of the expulsion of Germans from the eastern territories, the dismantling of German factories, and the supposedly indiscriminate internment of former Nazi Party members earned him the respect and gratitude of many Germans.[33]

Niemöller was appalled by his conservative colleagues' attitude. He wanted to see the church reborn, in the mold of the Confessing Church and with the Barmen Declaration of Faith at its foundation, not a return to the pre-Hitler status quo. In July 1945, with American approval, he convened a meeting of the surviving Confessing churchmen in Frankfurt. At the meeting, they discussed how important it was for the church to acknowledge the guilt of the German people as well as that of the churches. But a week later, at another gathering of German church leaders—this one overseen by conservative churchmen in the medieval Hessian town of Treysa—Niemöller found a contrary tone. Church leaders at Treysa expressed satisfaction with the response of the established church to Nazism and believed that church leaders had earned the right to lead the reconstruction and re-Christianization of their nation. "You should have seen this self-satisfied church," Niemöller barked. He wanted real change; instead, the outcome of the Treysa gathering was stasis. The conservative neutrals had replaced the German Christians in successfully opposing meaningful reform.[34]

Some foreign observers shared Niemöller's concerns. Robert Murphy, a political adviser to the American Office of Military Government, reported to US Secretary of State James F. Byrnes that the Treysa conference provided "little evidence that the German Protestant Church repented Germany's war of aggression or the cruelties visited upon other peoples and countries." Stewart Herman, who had replaced Ewart Turner as pastor of the American Church in Berlin and who also maintained close ties to the Confessing Church, concluded after the conference, "It cannot be said that the attitude of the church toward its political responsibility is as yet satisfactory, let alone clear."[35]

The German Protestant Church's survival, Niemöller pointed out to his colleagues at Treysa, was due to their accommodation of Hitler, not, as they liked to claim, to their resistance to Nazism. Of all the churchmen to address the German people after the war—Bonhoeffer might have rivaled him had he not been murdered—Niemöller made the strongest emotional appeal to Christians to take seriously their obligation to confess and repent.

Niemöller's position did not make him popular with either his church colleagues, who thought he was too critical, or the American military government in Germany, which thought he wasn't critical enough. The Naples interview remained a point of reference for the Americans. Eleanor Roosevelt addressed the controversy of Niemöller's role in postwar Germany on August 7 in her widely read column "My Day." She described his Naples interview as sounding "almost like a speech by Mr. Hitler." The former first lady went on: "Pastor Niemöller sounds to me like a gentleman who believes in the German doctrine of the superiority of race." She believed that his statements made him "unfit to establish any kind of government which would train the German people in democracy."[36]

General Lucius Clay, the American military governor, shared Roosevelt's misgivings. Various reports and an interview with Niemöller led Clay to the conclusion that, "while permitting Niemöller to take active leadership in religious affairs, we have not felt it is advisable to utilize his services in other fields as yet. While his anti-Nazi stand was demonstrated fully by his own actions, it is still too early to predict as to his wholehearted rejection of the militaristic and nationalistic concepts of the former German state."[37]

But Niemöller never thought of himself as a political leader. He certainly wanted to steer the political course of the occupation in a German-friendly direction, but he was never interested in a political career. His commitment was to reforming the German Protestant Church.

BEFORE HIS ARREST, Niemöller had tried to reform the church from within, and now he continued that effort. Despite his disappointment with his colleagues, at Treysa he accepted a leadership role as vice chairman of the newly formed Protestant Church in Germany (EKD) and head of the church's foreign bureau. This position gave him the opportunity to influence the church's restoration at home and to use his status as Hitler's former prisoner to encourage reconciliation and ecumenical fellowship between the German church and churches elsewhere. As the liaison to foreign churches, he would have the opportunity to travel and speak directly to the people who were most likely to listen and help: American Protestants. Nazi aggression had left deep scars in Britain, France, and Russia; these nations, especially the French and Russians, were not keen to offer assistance. Americans, whose war experience had been very different, had abundant resources and a powerful Protestant organization, the Federal Council of Churches, which had developed a strong relationship with the German churches during the interwar period and had rallied behind Niemöller and the Confessing Church during the Church Struggle. Although Niemöller certainly had critics in the American churches—some fellow Protestants questioned the sincerity of his new outlook—American churchmen played a significant role in encouraging, promoting, and applauding his postwar transformation.

Ewart Turner was a particularly enthusiastic ally. Turner, a Methodist who had been pastor of the American Church in Berlin from 1930 to 1934 and a correspondent for the Religious News Service from 1934 to 1945, counted himself a friend of the Niemöllers. When he arrived in Leoni in October 1945, Turner—who affectionately called Else "Mutti"—told her that now more than ever the church and nation needed her husband's passion, his faith, and, above all, his leadership. Turner reported back home, "The Niemoellers show signs of the strain they have been under, both are nervous and not well at all." It helped that Turner brought the news that the Niemöllers' son Hermann, who had been captured by the Soviets on the Eastern Front, had escaped a POW camp in Czechoslovakia and was making his way to Berlin. And it was no small matter that he brought food he had "liberated" from a nearby American air force base.[38]

Turner and Niemöller took long walks in the Bavarian countryside and talked late into the night about the future of Germany and German Protestantism. Over three days, Turner interpreted for him the mood in the United States and England. He told the "fighting pastor" that if the German church took the initiative in confessing the guilt of the German nation, it could begin the process of establishing a genuine fraternity between Germans and Christians abroad. "We had some tense moments together," Turner recalled, "but Frau N. was magnificent and Martin soberly considered my arguments."[39]

Indeed, time was of the essence. Soon Protestant leaders from the United States, Britain, France, Holland, Norway, and Sweden were scheduled to descend on Stuttgart to meet with their German counterparts. The speed with which the foreign churches reached out to the German churches was unprecedented. After the First World War, it was four years before the German churches were invited to participate in an ecumenical gathering. This time it took a mere four months—a sure sign that the interwar ecumenical movement was bearing fruit. Barth, among others, wrote Niemöller saying that the foreign delegates coming to Stuttgart expected the Germans to provide a declaration of guilt and signs of repentance. Niemöller was one of the few respected German church leaders expected to respond, making his presence at Stuttgart all the more important. Here was an opportunity to demonstrate the church's repentance to forward the cause of reconciliation between nations and churches.[40]

Driving a borrowed US Army car, Martin, Else, and Ewart set out for Stuttgart on October 17. They carried a document, acquired by Turner from his friends at the air force base, certifying that Pastor Niemöller was traveling on an official mission attached to the US High Command in Frankfurt and that every courtesy was to be extended him along the way. "Any discourtesies," the document concluded, "are to be reported immediately to American High Command and forwarded to General EISENHOWER."[41]

At six o'clock that evening, they arrived on the outskirts of Stuttgart, stopping at the home of Pastor Wilfried Lempp. To Niemöller's great surprise, Lempp announced that Martin was scheduled that very night to give the opening sermon for the conference at St. Mark's Church in the presence of world church leaders. The speech would be broadcast

Martin Niemöller with Anglican bishop George Bell and Lutheran bishop Otto Dibelius, October 1945. (Ewart E. Turner Papers, Special Collections Research Center, Temple University Libraries, Philadelphia, PA)

internationally. While Martin mulled over what to say at such a historic moment, Else chose for him a Bible passage, Jeremiah 14: 17–21. "We acknowledge our wickedness, O Lord, and the iniquity of our fathers," reads one part. "For we have sinned against thee."[42]

Amid the bombed-out ruins of Stuttgart, Niemöller rose to the occasion. Outmaneuvering his more conservative colleagues, he atoned for German crimes, specifically those of German Protestants. "Our guilt as Christians is much greater than the guilt of the Nazis, the German people, and the military," he declared in his sermon, "because we knew which way was false and which was right. . . . We are guilty of having been silent when we should have spoken." The vast audience hushed at his words. It was a stunning display of contrition, all the more so since it came from a man who had himself spent eight years imprisoned by Hitler. Until this point, church leaders had only spoken about guilt in general terms, in the sense that all people are guilty before God. With the encouragement from his international colleagues, Niemöller expressed German guilt in the most concrete terms.[43]

Two days later, October 19, the gathering issued the famous "Stuttgart Declaration of Guilt," drafted by German church leaders and toughened by Niemöller. "By our passivity," the German Protestant Church affirmed, "infinite suffering was experienced by many peoples and countries." The statement acknowledged that church officials, as the moral leaders of the nation, were especially negligent: "We accuse ourselves for not witnessing more courageously, for not praying more faithfully, for not believing more joyously, and for not loving more ardently."

The statement was by no means perfect. No one was asked to rethink or repudiate the conservative worldview that had fostered the conditions enabling Nazism in the first place, counseling obedience to authoritarian rule no matter its horrifying consequences. It did not mention Jews; what it did say about the Holocaust was expressed in vague terms. But given the sharp disagreements within German church leadership, the declaration was probably as complete and contrite as one could have reasonably hoped for. The Federal Council of Churches' Sam Cavert, the American delegate at Stuttgart, recognized Niemöller's crucial role in bringing about the declaration of guilt with his unflinching sermon. "If Christians the world over could achieve such humility and repentance," Cavert extolled, "a new world would be born."[44]

By confessing that the church was in "a solidarity of guilt with the German people," church leaders satisfied foreign demands for a confession. It was a turning point in relations with the Western churches. Cavert was relieved that Niemöller seemed to have left his Naples interview behind. "I am completely re-established in my confidence in Niemoeller," he wrote his FCC colleague Henry Smith Leiper, "and have told him that he has a standing invitation to come to America as soon as his responsibilities in Germany permit." For Niemöller, too, Stuttgart was a turning point. The outpouring of warmth, compassion, and Christian fellowship from the foreign delegates offered him the hope that he had been struggling to find.[45]

IN DECEMBER 1945, the Niemöllers moved from Leoni in southern Germany to Büdingen in central Germany, near Frankfurt, in the state of Hesse. The summer cottage in Leoni that had served as his home for five months was too small and isolated, and he did not feel welcome by his old nemesis from the Church Struggle, Bishop Meiser, the leader of the Bavarian Lutheran church. When the prince and princess of Isenburg-Büdingen, whom Niemöller had married in 1936 and defended after the war, offered the Niemöller family a roomy apartment in their magnificent castle in the small town of Büdingen, they were eager to accept.[46]

Over the next year, Niemöller crisscrossed Germany preaching and expanding the message he had delivered at Stuttgart. It was a message that his countrymen still did not want to hear. Many parishioners remained convinced that the main duty of church leaders was to intervene with the Allies on their behalf—to lessen the hardship brought about by occupation policies they saw as harsh, impractical, even vengeful. By contrast, Niemöller spoke openly about Germans' collective responsibility for Nazi evils. Protests erupted in the middle of his talks. A flood of letters excoriated Niemöller for playing into the hands of the Allies. Didn't he know that he was simply providing the occupation powers with further justification for their harmful policies? But that was not how Niemöller saw it. For him there were two reasons to confess—the first spiritual and the second practical. To find peace with God, he told his audiences, we must "confess our guilt to people who suffered because of it." And second, a confession of guilt would have positive political consequences. "Christians in foreign countries listen today to the voice of the Confessing Church because [at Stuttgart we] recognized the guilt."[47]

Where the Stuttgart Declaration had been vague, Niemöller became more specific by naming the groups and people the Nazis had persecuted and taking personal responsibility for remaining complacent. The origin of the "Niemöller confession" ("First they came for the Communists . . .") lies in these 1946 speeches. There is no hint of the poetic and rhythmical recitation of groups and actions that makes the famous confession so captivating, but its basic structure is apparent. In a January address in Frankfurt, for example, he lists Communists, the incurably ill, and Jews as groups the Nazis assailed while he and other Germans passively watched with disinterest, if not silent approval. In another speech from this period, he added to his list Jehovah's Witnesses, who had been attacked by the Nazis because of their international connections, their refusal to serve in the military, and their emphasis on the Old Testament. Although the poetic confession makes no mention of the Nazis' atrocities abroad, Niemöller also frequently condemned in these speeches the atrocities committed by Germany's invading armies in Greece, Poland, Czechoslovakia, the Netherlands, and elsewhere.[48]

All Germans, whether they actually committed a crime or not, had to take responsibility for what took place in their country at the hands of their countrymen, Niemöller insisted. He included himself and other Confessing churchmen. "I think we Christians belonging to the Confessional Church," he said in Frankfurt, "have all the reasons for saying: 'My fault, my fault, my most grievous fault.'" *Mea culpa, mea culpa, mea maxima culpa.*[49]

A January 22, 1946, visit to Erlangen University demonstrated the opposition that Niemöller faced—and the confrontational style he cultivated in the aftermath of the war. Invited by a campus Protestant group, the pastor spoke to some 1,200 students at Neustädter Church. A number of them booed, hissed, and stomped their feet in protest when he mentioned German guilt and the Protestant Church's complicity. Under fire, Niemöller responded in kind. "Why were there only 45 Protestant clergy in Dachau as compared with 450 Roman Catholic priests?" he asked. "No, the Church has not emerged from the war triumphant, [rather] she has failed and is still failing because she directs the blame all around her to the world but not to herself."[50]

At this point, the Nuremberg trials—held for the purpose of bringing twenty-two major Nazi war criminals to justice—were making daily headlines across the world. Images of Jewish corpses, piled in heaps, were omnipresent in the press. Amid the growing documentary evidence of the Holocaust, Niemöller turned more explicitly to the matter of the Jews. Whereas a year earlier in the Wiesbaden interrogation he had denied

German collective responsibility for the Holocaust, he now accepted it. In a May 1946 sermon in Herford near Münster, he declared:

> Six million Jews, an entire people was cold-bloodedly murdered in our midst and in our name. How shall we deal with this fact? If I should ask one of you here, he would say: "Ask the local party head about that. What could I have done?" And the local party head will refer me to the district party head, and so on and so forth until we get to the [Nuremberg] courtroom with the twenty-two defendants. And what about them? Well, we can hear that everyday—they blame it all on just three men. Three individuals who fortunately are no longer around: Hitler, Himmler and Goebbels. Yes, my dear friends, these three are dead. But the legacy of six million dead cannot be placed together with them in the grave. We have to accept the burden of that legacy; after all, we also accepted all those more favorable (or at least what seemed more favorable) legacies their actions bestowed on us over the course of the years.[51]

To demonstrate German collective guilt, Niemöller spoke of his own responsibility. He recounted what he saw on the day in November 1945 when he returned to Dachau with Else to show her the cell where he had been imprisoned. A plaque had been installed, commemorating the tens of thousands of inmates murdered there by the Nazis from 1933 to 1945. Else nearly collapsed as they stood reading the words, but what caused Niemöller to recoil was not the number of dead. What shook him were the dates, 1933 to 1945. His alibi, he had to acknowledge, accounted for the years 1937 to 1945. Now, he told his compatriots, he had to atone for the years 1933 to 1937.[52]

The vast majority of Germans did not want to hear about guilt because they did not think they were guilty. But there was also the political issue too. The Erlangen students booed Niemöller because they believed he was providing the occupying powers with an excuse to impose another Versailles-like treaty that would leave the country hobbled, as it had been after World War I. Niemöller understood this mentality. Following the

Erlangen protest, he admitted that he had responded in 1919 much the same as the students in 1946. "When a preacher told us that we Christians in Germany bore our own full measure of responsibility for the First World War and its outcome—and that at a time when the Versailles Treaty had just been signed—I could not help it, I had to leave." Now he saw things differently, for reasons both moral and pragmatic. Contrition was not only right and necessary, but also the key that would open the doors—and coffers—of the international Christian community.[53]

The gatekeepers of that community were present in February 1946 when Niemöller addressed members of the World Council of Churches in Geneva. He spoke in French, not wanting to offend the many church leaders whose countries were occupied and oppressed by German armies during the war. "We have discovered that the words sin and guilt are not empty and meaningless words which pastors brandish in their sermons," he told the assembled, "but that, on the contrary, they are clothed with a terrible truth and a terrible reality which leave man desolate and in despair and from which there is no escape." Foreign church leaders welcomed his person and message; Norwegian bishop Eivind Berggrav, who had suffered under Nazi occupation for his resistance, greeted Niemöller with an embrace and the words, "Dear Brother Niemöller, I have been looking forward to this moment for so many months."[54]

ALTHOUGH NIEMÖLLER EARNED in the early postwar years an international reputation for his stance on German responsibility for the war and Nazi atrocities, his interest in a thorough accounting of Nazism among the general populace was less than lukewarm. Indeed, Stewart Herman accurately predicted in July 1945 that Niemöller would fight the occupation authorities with the same tenacity and skill he had called on in his battles against the Nazis and German Christians. This was certainly the case when it came to the policy of denazification.[55]

Like many Germans, Niemöller opposed denazification from the moment the policy was unveiled in 1945 to its demise in 1948. The policy in the American zone required that every German adult fill out a multi-page questionnaire about his or her membership in Nazi organizations. Occupation authorities established five categories: major offenders, offenders, lesser offenders, followers, and exonerated persons. Sanctions, varying from travel restrictions and job loss to imprisonment and death, were imposed on those not exonerated. Although Niemöller, Wurm, Meiser, and others agreed that the Nazi leadership should be punished as war criminals, they also believed that nominal Nazi supporters had suffered enough and deserved no further penalty. "The German people have been punished already by God," Niemöller said. Punitive measures, he argued, would only turn people against the Allies and toward political radicalism.[56]

When asked in December 1945 what he thought was the most serious problem facing the German churches, Niemöller did not mention hunger, housing, or coming to terms with the Holocaust. Rather, his principal grievance was with what he perceived as overbearing denazification policies that had resulted, in the US zone alone, in the arrest and internment of some 117,000 Germans who had been members of a Nazi organization. Germans took to calling the American Counter Intelligence Corps—responsible for carrying out denazification—the "US Gestapo."[57]

Clerics complained that many card-carrying Nazis had never shared the party's ideology but instead took part in the Nazi Party out of necessity—for example, to hold on to a job. Now, ironically, many were being thrown out of their jobs. The arrest of low-level Nazis, Niemöller maintained, "was making the work of the church more difficult." How could the church encourage Germans to recognize their responsibility when occupation authorities were arresting anyone who acknowledged even the slightest affiliation with the Nazis? Germans learned quickly that they were better off lying about their past on the questionnaires than being truthful. In early 1946, Niemöller joined other church leaders in sending a declaration to the American Military Government criticizing the denazification procedures.[58]

The clergy's objections to denazification were rooted in part in self-preservation. Many, such as Martin's brother Wilhelm, had themselves been Nazis. Others, Martin Niemöller included, as well as Bishops Wurm and Meiser, had not joined the party but sympathized with the Nazi cause and so identified with the Germans who had joined Nazi organizations. Also, church leaders feared that the Allies would replace tainted individuals in the German bureaucracy and other professions with liberals and leftists, the enemies of the conservative churches. Time and again churchmen, including Niemöller, provided positive references—called *Persilscheine*, or "soap certificates"—for former Nazis to whitewash their past. This was most evident in the denazification of the churches themselves, which American officials permitted church leaders to carry out as they saw fit.[59]

Although Niemöller collaborated with his conservative colleagues in opposing denazification, they were opponents on almost every other issue. Indeed, even as his overall political worldview remained conservative, Niemöller was, as before, a reformer or even radical within the church. A June 22, 1946, letter to his colleagues on the EKD leadership council was full of wide-ranging and bitter complaints. Niemöller's impression was that, even as fellow churchmen cheered for him in the summer of 1945, his enemies in the church were really praying, "Lord God, protect us from the return of this lethal man." Niemöller felt that he was not consulted on many vital issues, that his colleagues on the council were undermining his outreach efforts to foreign churches and the ecumenical movement, and that a return to the old days of confessionalism, hierarchy, and bureaucratism was in the works. Most disturbing, he vented, was that no one seemed to be taking seriously the question of guilt or the message of repentance; he had spent a year preaching to a church that was not ready to listen.[60]

Leading clergy on the council, however, believed it was time to move on from the issue of German guilt. Hans Asmussen, now head of the church chancellery, urged Niemöller to tone down his public criticisms or risk being further ostracized.[61]

Karl Barth saw Niemöller's treatment by his colleagues as representative of the way the German church had always been and always would be. In a letter to Niemöller, Barth wrote that it was "quite clear" that his preaching about guilt, repentance, and the need for church reform "make them horribly uncomfortable."

> There is some corner in their souls in which they very well wish that in Dachau or somewhere else a beautiful little memorial chapel could be erected, to which they could go on an annual pilgrimage, and where they could . . . sing a mass in your honor. Instead of which, you are still driving around the country in your ramshackle car and saying tactless things, which they have to swallow.[62]

Needless to say, Niemöller did not heed Asmussen's advice to keep his criticisms private, but the Naples interview debacle had taught him to appreciate the importance of public relations. When he and Else arrived in the United States in December 1946 for a months-long speaking tour, his message to American Protestants was decidedly different from the harangue he had been feeding to German Protestants. Gone was the harsh rebuke of German Protestantism and German church leaders for not having done enough to resist the Nazi menace. Instead, he wooed the powerful and wealthy churches across the Atlantic with stories of persecution and resistance.

– EIGHT –

Barnstorming America
(1946–1947)

MARTIN AND ELSE SMILED GOOD-NATUREDLY AT THE EAGER REPORT-
ers on the tarmac. It was December 1946, and they were on American soil for the first time in their lives. Niemöller's natural inclination
was to bound down the plane's stairs, wade into the throng of reporters,
and expound on the plight of his countrymen. But the Americans who
had planned his five-month speaking tour were wary of his improving
English—and his impetuosity. No one wanted to repeat the disaster of
the Naples interview. "No answers to questions!" his hosts advised. "Save
your first comments for Seattle. And don't forget the famous Niemöller
smile."[1]

For Martin Niemöller and his US supporters, the stakes could not have
been higher. Germany's cities had been bombed into oblivion during the
last two years of the war. Winter was approaching, and shortages of food

Else and Martin Niemöller
arriving in New York at the
start of their five-month
US tour, December 1946.
(Associated Press)

and fuel meant that thousands would starve or succumb to the elements. Expelled from Poland, the Czech lands, and the rest of Eastern Europe, millions of Germans flooded into their occupied native land, exacerbating the crisis. As a leading national spokesman with international fame, Niemöller had the power to influence American public opinion of, and even policy toward, Germany—positively or negatively. Politicians and churchmen alike on both sides of the Atlantic would be scrutinizing his first address at the biennial meeting of the Federal Council of Churches in Seattle on December 4, 1946, to see what Niemöller had to say.

Officially, as vice president and head of foreign-church relations on the council of the Evangelical Church in Germany, Niemöller was in the United States to thank American churches for their support during and after Hitler's reign. Unofficially, there was a great deal more to the visit. Everything had to be choreographed to perfection, lest the harder and more important tasks come to nothing.

Niemöller hoped to convince Americans that he represented the "other Germany": the many Christians who had fought and prayed for an end to the Nazi menace and who were now eking out an existence in ruined cities and towns. It was essential that those Germans who had not been Nazis or silent bystanders become the face of the people, and that those who had been complicit were now seen to be repentant. American aid and occupation policies were matters of life and death, and Niemöller wanted Americans to understand that Germans deserved life. If he was to serve as an effective spokesman for the repentant German, he had to persuade his critics that, despite his longtime nationalist sentiments and early support for Nazism, he had become Hitler's most outspoken foe. Flashing the famous Niemöller smile and avoiding impromptu interviews was part of this larger strategy.

IT WAS NEVER certain that the Niemöllers would reach America. Of the obstacles they faced, the foremost was the US State Department. Dean Acheson, the undersecretary of state in charge of granting visas, was disappointed that the FCC had chosen Niemöller as their guest. Acheson had hoped that the first Germans selected to enter the United States "would be indisputably representative of democratic and peace-loving forces within Germany." This left FCC general secretary Sam Cavert with the unenviable job of convincing American officials that the pastor's views on German guilt had evolved since Naples. "As you probably know he is the leader in German Protestantism who is now taking the most clear-cut and outspoken stand for penitence on the part of the leaders of the church for their share in having let the evil spirit of Nazism loose in the world," Cavert wrote in April 1946 to the State Department.

> He has spoken so strongly along this line that he has come under very severe criticism from the more reactionary elements. As a result of seeing him daily for more than a week in Geneva, I am confident that the experience of meeting with representative church leaders from

America, England, France, Holland, Norway and other countries did a great deal to help him understand the spirit and outlook of our Western democracies and to strengthen him in his own efforts to bring the Church of Germany into line with our own point of view.[2]

But Acheson remained skeptical. Niemöller's nationalism, militarism, hostility to the Weimar Republic, and early support of Hitler left the undersecretary reluctant to grant the necessary visas. He applauded Niemöller's desire to "awaken the German conscience to a sense of individual guilt for the excesses of the Nazi regime," but did not believe that this meant Niemöller had repudiated his antidemocratic views. Acheson thought the intemperate words spoken in Italy proved that Niemöller's politics were "hostile to our occupation objectives."[3]

It was not just Americans who seemed bent on frustrating Niemöller's efforts. When he made plans to attend a World Council of Churches meeting in Cambridge, England, in August 1946, he had found himself unexpectedly denied entry to the United Kingdom. The British government instructed him to pick up his visa in Geneva; however, the British consulate there stymied him, allegedly because there was no room in his passport for the visa stamp. It was an absurd reason, and Niemöller knew it. Insulted, he petitioned the British authorities, who assured him that the visa denial was merely a bureaucratic hitch, not a deliberate rejection. Stewart Herman, the American Lutheran and evangelical traveling with Niemöller at the time, accused the British of anti-Niemöller and anti-German sentiments. Niemöller did not receive a visa in time to attend the WCC meeting, setting back his work as the EKD's ambassador to foreign churches and raising his anxiety about his planned trip to the United States.[4]

Finally, after nearly a year of persistent letter-writing and prodding by the likes of Bishop Henry Knox Sherrill of Boston, prominent Republican adviser and future secretary of state John Foster Dulles, and FCC president Bishop Garfield Bromley Oxnam, Acheson acquiesced. On November 14, 1946, the Niemöllers became the first German civilians granted US visas after the war. Cavert wasted no time reserving two seats on American Overseas Airline for December 1, departing from Frankfurt and arriving in New York the next day. Cavert cabled his contact in Frankfurt, "AMERICAN FRIENDS URGE HE MAKE NO STATEMENT TO PRESS ON ARRIVAL."[5]

American Jewish leaders were livid at the prospect of Niemöller's speaking tour. In late January 1946, John C. Bennett, a Congregationalist minister and professor of Christian theology and ethics, wrote Henry Smith Leiper at the FCC warning him that the evening before he had heard an address by Rabbi Stephen Wise, president of the American Jewish Congress, that was highly critical of Niemöller's stance on anti-Semitism. "It occurred to me that an ugly situation may arise if there is a Jewish demonstration against him when he comes." Wise's disapproval was published and read widely, drawing a rebuttal from Cavert. Referring to Niemöller's October 1945 talk in Stuttgart and his February 1946 address in Geneva, Cavert wrote Wise:

> I think you will regard them as indisputable evidence of Pastor Niemoeller's outspoken denunciation of the Nazi treatment of the Jews and other peoples. I find that some of my Jewish friends are surprised when they find that Pastor Niemoeller has been saying such things as these. I should greatly value your counsel as to whether there are steps which I should take to make the Jewish community more familiar with the facts about Pastor Niemoeller. I want to make certain that they do not, out of ignorance, attack one of the best friends the Jews have in Germany today.

When Wise replied that he found it hard to grasp how Niemöller could be considered such a fine friend of the Jews, Cavert responded,

> When I say that Pastor Niemoeller is "one of the best friends the Jews have in Germany today" I am convinced that this is the literal truth. . . . I cannot say too strongly that it is my firm belief that anyone who should speak against Pastor Niemoeller as he is today would be rendering a great disservice to the up-building of Germany on better moral foundations and also to the interests of the Jewish people.[6]

Cavert's tenacious defense of Niemöller is illuminating. It speaks both to how immensely important the FCC believed Niemöller's visit to be and to the willingness of American Protestant leaders to embellish his transformation from right-wing militarist and Nazi voter to Christian martyr and Jewish savior. In the United States, the tendency to launder Niemöller's prewar behavior continues even today. Wise might not have appreciated the degree to which Niemöller regretted his former enthusiasms, but the rabbi's cynicism regarding the portrayal of Niemöller as a saintly man of God who defied Hitler and befriended German Jews was understandable.

Public opinion in the United States was polarized. The FCC received hundreds of speaking requests for Niemöller from churches and seminaries. At the same time, the State Department received dozens of letters protesting the granting of Niemöller's visa. Whether they loved him or hated him, Americans knew about him and his ordeal in the concentration camps. Indeed, they were likely to know more about Martin Niemöller than any other living German at that time.

Although it is not surprising that the State Department and Jewish leaders had reservations about Niemöller's visit, few would have anticipated opposition from American Lutherans. Dr. Franklin Clark Fry, president of the United Lutheran Church in America, was reluctant to back Niemöller's proposed trip, but not because of the German pastor's political history. The problem was that Niemöller wasn't Lutheran enough. Whereas Niemöller supported a united Protestant Church, including Lutheran, United, and Reformed denominations, the most stalwart Lutheran leaders in Germany, Bishop Meiser of Bavaria chief among them, were eager to create a federation of exclusively Lutheran churches to forward Lutheran interests. The hope was that the denomination would gain a dominant voice. Niemöller was adamantly opposed to this plan because it would divide the Protestant Church, as the Nazis had done. American Lutherans worried that backing Niemöller would be a snub to Meiser and the Lutheran Council in Germany. In the end, they offered tepid support rather than opposition to the visit. Even the American Lutheran Stewart Herman, who fully supported

Niemöller's trip to America, hoped that the German pastor would be "properly chaperoned."[7]

That task fell to Pastor Ewart Turner, who saw his mission, in part, as an effort "to restore the stature" of Pastor Niemöller in American public opinion. The critics, he believed, could be silenced by the power of Niemöller's testimony of faith before the American people. Eleanor Roosevelt herself "may one day feel quietly ashamed that she judged such a man by his worst self," he wrote to Cavert. Turner also had high expectations for what Niemöller could accomplish. "If we do not make mistakes . . . this visit will have significance for American foreign policy," he said.[8]

As the tour got started in Seattle, Mrs. Roosevelt remained a serious public relations concern. The day after Niemöller's first address, Oxnam, the American Methodist bishop and FCC president, sent a telegram to her contesting her claim that Niemöller had not been a political opponent of the Nazis. "The record clearly shows," the telegram read, "that he repeatedly spoke against political aims of the Nazis as early as 1933. He was forbidden to preach as [a] result of his speaking against Hitler's racialistic [sic] program." The FCC went on to urge Roosevelt to revise the portrait of Niemöller she was promoting.[9]

But neither the telegram nor a subsequent letter from Bishop Oxnam swayed her. She responded that bringing Niemöller to the United States and allowing him to speak to large audiences would only create sympathy for Germany and mask the threat it posed to world peace. She concluded her letter to Oxnam by stating, "I want us to be vividly aware of the fact that the German people are to blame, that they committed horrible crimes. Therefore, I think you are doing something which is stupid beyond words in bringing this gentleman here and having him touring the country, no matter how much you like him." She even telephoned the foreign minister of Czechoslovakia, Jan Masaryk, whose country had suffered a brutal occupation by the Nazis, urging him to write an article countering Niemöller's "propaganda" on behalf of the "poor Germans." Masaryk was dismayed that a man who had offered to serve in the German navy in World War II was being greeted in the United States "as if he were Mahatma Gandhi."[10]

These criticisms stung the Niemöllers and their hosts, but their experience on the road was far different. In churches and auditoriums around the country, American Protestants greeted Niemöller like a celebrity. Tens of thousands of enraptured fans attended his addresses and listened to him on the radio. Turner advertised the experience of listening to Niemöller as "a spiritual atomic eruption" and advised local hosts, "Don't let this spirit of Pentecost take you by surprise. Prepare for it with all the traditional ingenuity and foresight of American church life at its best."[11]

Niemöller was as dynamic as promised, but the hectic schedule was taxing. Over the course of just fourteen days in December, he spoke in sixteen cities: Portland (Oregon), San Francisco, Oakland, Berkeley, San Jose, Los Angeles, Long Beach, Phoenix, Tucson, Fort Worth, Kansas City, St. Paul, Minneapolis, Cedar Rapids, and Davenport. Along the way, the fifty-four-year-old pastor experienced dizzy spells, chest pains, and pain in his right arm. The arm pain could be explained as neuralgia, which he developed in Sachsenhausen and Dachau as a result of malnutrition, but the chest pains and dizziness were new. He saw several doctors during the tour. To maintain his strength, a physician in Portland advised him to have a glass of equal parts milk and cream every hour and a half. Without the Niemöllers' knowledge, Turner requested that a doctor be present backstage at events whenever possible. He also admitted to Cavert that he was drawing attention to Niemöller's health problems in order to win favorable press coverage.[12]

Turner felt it was his responsibility to shield the Niemöllers from the endless numbers of people who wanted to greet them, be photographed with them, invite them to their homes, dine with them, drive them to and from their hotel and speaking venues, take them sightseeing, or simply wish them well. In addition to the anonymous crowds, there also seemed to be friends, relatives, and old schoolmates of Pastor and Mrs. Niemöller in every city they visited. These were Germans who had emigrated before the war. But the biggest obstacle, Turner found, was the Niemöllers' own unbridled enthusiasm and curiosity. Although they often complained about needing more rest, they were loath to decline any invitation or opportunity. "I have been resorting to every possible approach and technique to restrain the N's exuberance," a frustrated Turner said. He also realized that when Niemöller was overtired, his words got away from him, leading to misunderstandings. On one occasion, Turner invited reporters back to Niemöller's hotel room to clear up sensitive issues. "We discovered," he said, that "Pastor Niemöller cannot answer questions in a brief space."[13]

Traveling mostly by rail, the Niemöllers took advantage of the relative peace and quiet of train cars to sleep a few hours before a new set of city fathers, church dignitaries, and reporters met them at the next stop. The only significant break from the otherwise relentless schedule was the week around Christmas, which the Niemöllers spent near Chicago with Pastor Louis Goebel and his family.

The pastors and laity who organized local events were a constant source of surprise and color for the barnstorming German pastor. In New Haven, the dean of Yale Divinity School presented Niemöller with what was said to be the millionth copy of the Revised Standard Version of the New Testament. In San Jose, a leading layman, a mortician, drove the entourage in his palatial hearse. In Texas, the Niemöllers toured an "exotic" ranch. In Kansas City, they sat at a diner counter, where they enjoyed twirling around on the bar stools waiting for their orders.[14]

Los Angeles provided exciting diversions for the staid Germans. They ate dinner on the roof of the Biltmore Hotel while listening to jazz music, which they found rather jarring. They visited Telefilm Industries, where they made a twelve-minute newsreel intended for Americans who wouldn't get a chance to see them in person. Perhaps the highlight of the LA visit, however, was a stop at Paramount Studios, where the Niemöllers talked with the popular crooner and actor Bing Crosby, who professed himself a fan. Apparently, the feeling was mutual; the celebrated German pastor told the Academy Award winner that he had seen *Going My Way* three times in the past year in the American-occupied city of Büdingen. Crosby, quite pleased with this story, insisted on having his picture taken with the couple. At Paramount, Niemöller also met the director of the 1944 film *The Hitler Gang*, which featured a pastor in the resistance modeled on himself.[15]

Tucson left a lasting impression, not least for decidedly un-German winter temperatures in the high sixties and low seventies. The Niemöllers flew in from Phoenix in a chartered four-seater with the pilot pointing out the scenery en route. On arrival at their hotel, they were astonished that a local firm had loaned them a stenographer, an extra typewriter, and two radios. They had breakfast at the home of a teacher, Ada Peirce Mc-Cormick, who, nine years before, had created a small, room-size chapel near the University of Arizona in honor of Pastor Niemöller's 1937 arrest and imprisonment. She said that she had prayed daily with her students for his survival and liberation. So great was the local interest in attending the mass meeting in Tucson that over a thousand people were turned away. Else received enthusiastic applause when she told an audience that she wanted to retire in Arizona, while her husband described the whole experience as "out of this world."[16]

While the Niemöllers were enjoying bountiful meals and the excessive hospitality of their American hosts, members of their family and household back in Germany were doing their best to resume the routines of a normal life. Both daughter Hertha and son Hermann were students, she a philosophy student at the university in Frankfurt and he at medical school in Marburg. Hertha and Dora Schulz lived in the apartment in the Büdingen castle, which Hertha referred to as "the Schloss" when she wrote to Martha Turner, Ewart Turner's wife, thanking her for a much-needed care package.

Today tourists are charmed by Büdingen's half-timbered houses and the town's well-preserved, heavily fortified medieval wall, but life in the Schloss in the winter of 1946–1947 was anything but charming. The rooms were freezing, and Hertha's fingers were often so cold that she could barely write. Much of her time was spent fetching water, because the pipes were frozen, and trying to find wood for the stove. Yet Hertha soldiered on. As a means of escape, she listened to Bach on her father's radio and looked forward to weekend visits from Hermann, who was dating a friend of hers. Tini, who was temporarily living in Switzerland with Elsa and Adolf Freudenberg, also tried to help Dora and his older siblings by sending care packages. "We were moved by his care," Hertha told Mrs. Turner. While on winter break from the university, she worked in the mornings for the EKD's foreign bureau in her father's office, where the temperature was below freezing. She managed some fun—skiing for the first time in years and attending her first concert since the war's end, Handel's *Messiah*. But the day-to-day reality was grim. In the same letter to Martha Turner, she signed off by asking the Turners to rush a care package to an utterly destitute family she knew, refugees from the East who had lost everything.[17]

THE ULTIMATE PURPOSE of the Niemöllers' speaking tour was to alleviate German suffering at home. To do this Niemöller needed not only to convince American churchgoers to dig deep into their pockets but also to persuade political leaders of the need to change America's occupation policies. The latter aim depended on persuading as many Americans as possible that Germans were a peace-loving people with deep Christian roots—a people the American government should treat as friends rather than a defeated enemy.

Niemöller made sure to avoid the mistakes of Naples. Not only did he shun impromptu interviews, but initially he read his lectures and sermons nearly verbatim from a script. After a couple of weeks, however, he developed a repertoire of stories he was comfortable repeating without relying on his lecture notes. Although he returned again and again to themes that Americans were likely to find reassuring, he often managed to cause controversy.

From his first address in Seattle in early December to his last in Brooklyn in late April 1947, he began by thanking Americans for their prayers and support during his period of imprisonment and for the aid the United States was providing Germany. He thanked the Federal Council of Churches for inviting him abroad, extending a hand of friendship to the German churches. He emphasized that the world's prayers and his faith in God sustained him while he was in the Nazi concentration camps.[18]

He then told stories of Christian resistance. Church leaders, he explained, provoked Hitler's ire by proclaiming that "the Word of God is the supreme law of mankind." In particular, he drew attention to the 1934 Barmen Declaration of Faith, which asserted the absolute sovereignty of Christ as the backbone of the Confessing Church. Hitler thought that he could claim total authority over the churches, but that "was his fatal error." Instead, Hitler awakened a sense of faith and Christian brotherhood. "The empty churches of 1931 and 1932 became full churches, suddenly, in 1933 when the Church Struggle began."[19]

The impression Niemöller intended to give was that, all across Germany, persecuted Christians began gathering illegally in small groups to pray together and plot the end of Hitler's rule. He often implied that Christians, as a group, were Hitler's lone nemesis within Germany. When Niemöller did depict the opposition within the church as the minority it had been, he portrayed them as heroic and persecuted, the true followers of Christ. When Hitler arrested established church leaders, young pastors mounted the pulpit. When these younger men were forbidden to preach, lay elders rose to the task. When laymen were banned, the wives and children of the pastors took their place. "Nothing was left for Hitler than to rage in fury," he concluded triumphantly.[20]

Niemöller's self-proclaimed acts of defiance were central to his lectures. He regaled audiences with tales of preaching to fellow inmates in Sachsenhausen and Dachau. He narrated the 1934 meeting in which he confronted Hitler and said, he claimed, "Mr. Chancellor, God himself has entrusted us with the responsibility for our nation, and no power and no authority in the world is entitled to take it from us." Niemöller especially liked to tell the story of how, after being stripped of his possessions at Sachsenhausen, he demanded the return of one item: his Bible.[21]

Throughout the tour, Niemöller evoked Christians as gallant victims, martyrs to a spiritual cause whose destruction was a foremost Nazi goal. Hitler attempted to destroy the churches, he told listeners in Davenport, Iowa, but "the Word of God can't be bound and can't be murdered." He lauded Dietrich Bonhoeffer, Paul Schneider, Friedrich Weissler, and other heroes of the Confessing Church who were mur-

Poster advertising Niemöller address in Cincinnati in February 1947. (Ewart E. Turner Papers, Special Collections Research Center, Temple University Libraries, Philadelphia, PA)

dered by the Nazis "because they were Christians and because for them Christian faith was not only a private affair."[22]

When he sometimes briefly addressed Nazi racial persecution and the state-sponsored mass murder of Jews, he was particularly prone to elaborate on and embellish the actual role of the church. He usually presented the church—and sometimes the German people—as opposed to the Nazis' racial program. "The resistance of the church began with the Jewish question," he asserted. "When Hitler tried to extinguish the Jews, the Church had to pronounce and proclaim, 'Thou shalt not Kill.'" He pointed to the 1936 confidential memorandum to Hitler as proof that the Confessing Church condemned anti-Semitism as un-Christian and Hitler's regime as unlawful. He reassured American audiences that anti-Semitism was dead in Germany and would never live again.[23]

Although he devoted more time to Christian resistance than to Christian complicity or silence, he frequently and forthrightly acknowledged his own guilt and the guilt of his church and nation. The October 1945 Stuttgart Declaration of Guilt, he noted, was evidence of German Protestant Church leaders' recognition of and atonement for their inadequate response to Nazism. But he did not dwell on his or the church's complicity. As he saw it, the place for that type of breast-beating was in Germany, where his countrymen continued not only to refuse to acknowledge their responsibility for Nazism and the Holocaust but also to point to the guilt of others—Russians, Americans, the Brits—for Germany's desperate plight.

HISTORIANS HAVE LONG speculated that Niemöller first gave voice to his famous poetic confession "First they came for the Communists . . ." during his US tour. But this is not the case. Such speculation suggests a misunderstanding of the purpose of his visit. He did not come to the United States to highlight his and the Protestant Church's failure to resist the Nazis' attack on leftists, Jews, and others. That message was appropriate for German ears, not American ones, in the immediate postwar years.

The only speech where glimpses of the confession are seen is in a sermon Niemöller preached in German at Manhattan's Second Presbyterian Church on January 25. It was the only time during the tour that he addressed a mostly German audience and in his own tongue. The sermon reads very much like those he had been giving throughout Germany in 1946, in which he called on Germans to stop deflecting blame onto others. Our guilt, Niemöller told his compatriots in Manhattan, is that we did not follow God and love all people as brothers. The pastor admitted that he had personally failed in this respect. "I did not recognize the communists as brothers when they were locked up in concentration camps [and] I did not recognize the Jews as brothers when [the Nazis] smashed their windows and . . . a few months later hauled them off to concentration camps." To acknowledge that he did not recognize Jews as brothers was a heartfelt admission. But to admit this to English-speaking American audiences at that time would have greatly undermined the goal of his tour—to win over American support for Germany.[24]

Niemöller had different messages for different audiences. He says as much in a letter to a woman from Tucson, who informed Niemöller after his address there that a number of Jews had been in the audience and they had left disappointed that he did not mention their suffering in the Holocaust. Niemöller responded apologetically: "If I had known that beforehand, I should have liked to say a special word, just to them, as I often do. . . . But I was informed, that in Tucson the meeting was of a Christian interdenominational character, and therefore I made my address an example of Christian pronouncement." He asked the woman to convey to the Jewish group that "in Germany no single meeting goes by, without my mentioning the duty and obligation, which is laid upon our souls in helping those of our Jewish fellowmen, who have escaped the 'gates of hell' during the time of Hitler." He went on to tell her that his first arrest in 1933 was because he had dared to write a letter defending his Christian brethren of Jewish origin.[25]

In short, Niemöller's poetic confession confessed too much for American audiences in 1946 and 1947. The origins of the confession are no doubt in his 1946 addresses in Germany, where he admitted his own complacency in order to encourage Germans to do the same. The time and place of his first recitation of the rhythmic, poetic version of the confession that we know today, however, remains a mystery. Niemöller's responses to multiple queries by teachers, historians, librarians, and archivists about the original date and location were evasive because he was not sure himself when or where he said it. In response to a query from a New York librarian, he said, "I know this statement of mine; but I doubt that I ever gave this statement in writing or printing; it must be a quotation, probably from a discussion following one of my addresses." On another occasion, he responded to a persistent high school teacher from Philadelphia with a vague date and place—some years after 1948 in the United States. He did not have any documentation, he explained to the teacher, but

> if my memory serves me right I said something like this: At first, we Protestant Christians and the Protestant Church did not care about the atrocities of the Nazi regime. In 1933, the Communists and the So-cialists were imprisoned in concentration camps and we did not care about it, we kept silent. The trade unionists and others came next and we continued to remain silent, and we did not even open our mouths when the persecution of the Jews started and things got serious. Finally, we evangelical pastors came next and there was no one there who could and would have spoken.[26]

In this and other responses Niemöller does not take full ownership of the rhythmically repetitive version of the confession. He acknowledges that the sentiments are indeed his and that he said something like that in the postwar period, probably in America. It is quite possible that re-searchers will one day uncover evidence of Niemöller's original recita-tion of the poetic confession. However, it is also possible that Niemöller's admirers appropriated his frequent confessional statements and gave those confessions the poetic version that now graces the United States Holocaust Memorial Museum and other sites of Holocaust memory. But one thing is certain: there is no evidence in the archives that document his 1946–1947 speaking tour that he recited the oft-quoted confession during the US tour.

HE DID, HOWEVER, stress the need for brotherhood to his American audiences, an underlying theme of the famous quotation. He saw it as essential to present Germans as members of a world fraternity deserv-ing of forgiveness—and aid. "God's plan for Christian brotherhood doesn't stop short at the boundaries of nations nor at the borders of continents," Niemöller told the crowd in Seattle. He criticized denominational barriers and commended the nondenominational character of the Confessing Church.

But unity was more than a strong talking point. Indeed, Niemöller's embrace of ecumenism was genuine and had long inspired and sustained him during his incarceration. Speaking to audiences that might not always have been comfortable with denominational cooperation, he recalled sharing quarters in Dachau with three Catholic priests and praying together "according to the Roman customs every morning, every noontime, and every night." In the evenings the Catholics would listen to a Bible lesson by their Lutheran cellmate. "We became brethren in Christ not only by praying together but by common listening to the Word of God." And, without fail, he told the story of his international and multi-denominational congregation on Christmas Eve 1944 in Dachau.[27]

Another prominent message of his sermons was the need for the church to play a role in public affairs in Germany in particular, and in the world more generally. Niemöller lamented that, since the secularizing efforts of the French Revolution, religion had become a private affair in western and central Europe. Public matters were not guided by morality, and citizens did not feel a sense of moral responsibility. The absence of the Ten Commandments from public life, he suggested, led people to embrace demagogues who seemed to have all the answers. He made clear that the Confessing Church had learned its lesson. "When I came home, I found a different church than I had seen before my imprisonment," he told an audience in Schenectady, New York. "I found a church in which Jesus Christ had worked for eight years, and in which He had regained His place as Master and as Lord."[28]

Niemöller expressed concern that the average German had not yet embraced the lessons learned by the Confessing Church. This, he told his audiences, was no reason to condemn them. The German people were enduring terrible deprivations, and in their wretchedness they might fall prey to another charlatan or ideology offering simplistic and ultimately destructive solutions. Or, he worried, his countrymen would lose all hope and fall into despair. What they needed was food on their plates and coal to heat their apartments, yet the church alone could not fill their empty cupboards or warm their homes. Would the German church's message of wartime responsibility, repentance, and a new day in Christ fall on deaf ears? The first step in preventing unwanted outcomes was to alleviate physical suffering, and to that end, Niemöller was asking Americans for help in the form of monetary donations and relief packages. He also encouraged American pastors to travel to Germany to see the situation for themselves and to preach in German churches.[29]

In discussing the plight of the German people, Niemöller strayed into the territory that Dean Acheson and others skeptical about his past and his tour of America had hoped he would avoid. "The offices of our [American] military government are very nicely and cozily heated and our military government people live a good life as far as nourishment and everything else, even housing, is concerned," Niemöller said. "But they don't know how people really think and react who are hungry, who are on the way to starving." Germans, he claimed, were receiving no better than "the lowest ration ever heard of in a Nazi concentration camp." He said that this was what the occupation authorities should be focusing on, not denazification. He acknowledged that thousands of Germans would have starved to death if it hadn't been for the generosity of the British and Americans, but their generosity so far was not enough. Pressing his case, he told his listeners, who had made their own sacrifices during the war, that most Germans thought that the Allies were intentionally starving them to death. "That's the public opinion," he said. What Germany needed was parcels and pastors. Parcels to feed their stomachs and pastors to feed their souls. The alternative was starvation and the sort of nihilism that left people susceptible to extremist ideas.[30]

How should one assess Niemöller's message for America? There was much in it that embellished the truth. His claims about church and Christian resistance were exaggerated. Compared to left-wing opposition, Protestant Church resistance had been minuscule. More important, Protestant dissenters, Niemöller included, had not contested Hitler's domestic, foreign, or racial policies—only his church policy. To say, as Niemöller did, that church resistance began with the Jewish question was highly misleading because the Pastors' Emergency League did not challenge Hitler's treatment of Jews. The PEL's only true claim to anti-racist activism lay in its opposition to the German Christians' demand that pastors of Jewish heritage be excluded from the church—an effort on behalf of just twenty-nine pastors in the entire Protestant Church.[31]

Similarly, Niemöller implied that a Christian passion for resistance led parishioners back to once-empty churches, while conveniently skipping by the fact that many of the new churchgoers in 1933 wore SA uniforms and sang the Horst Wessel Song, the official anthem of the Nazi Party. The Confessing Church was never publicly aligned against Hitler. It spoke out against anti-Semitism only in its 1936 confidential memorandum to Hitler, which was not intended for the ears of parishioners. The Confessing Church did not share the German Christians' Nazi enthusiasms for an Aryan church, but it was silent about the Nuremberg Laws, *Kristallnacht*, the deportation of Jews, and daily acts of Jewish persecution and harassment.

While on tour, Niemöller never discussed the role of Christian anti-Semitism in desensitizing churchgoers to Jewish persecution. During his March 10 speech in Philadelphia, he asked, "Friends, how was it possible that in the midst of a continent with a Christian past for many, many centuries things could happen like that?" The "things" he spoke of were the murders of Christian churchmen. It was a valid question, but given how few Protestant martyrs there were, it would have been more pertinent to ask how was it possible for Christians in Germany and across Europe to actively participate in or passively acquiesce to the mass murder of six million Jews. At this stage in his postwar evolution, Niemöller was not prepared to answer that Protestant contempt for Jews was an essential factor.

NIEMÖLLER'S MIX OF fact, fiction, uplift, and penitence held American Protestants rapt. In Portland, five thousand people packed the civic auditorium, two thousand gathered in the overflow venue, and three thousand more were turned away. In Grand Rapids, Michigan, Niemöller addressed an audience of five thousand, and at the Brooklyn Academy of Music, he spoke before thirty-six hundred. And the money flowed in. Francis T. Cooke, executive secretary of the Portland Council of Churches, reported to Sam Cavert that audiences were "deeply moved and very enthusiastic." As Ewart Turner put it, "The cup runneth over." The donations from the entire tour amounted to more than $47,000 (approximately $528,000 in today's dollars). "It is really amazing to think that this large amount of money came in," Eleanor Kent Browne of the World Council of Churches wrote Niemöller. "We never anticipated any such total when you started out on the trip." The expenses for the trip were approximately $15,000, leaving approximately $32,000 for relief and reconstruction work in Germany. "You may remember that originally we had said it would be used in Europe," Browne wrote, "but we now feel that because the need in Germany is so great, we should send it there, and especially because it came in as a result of your visit here."[32]

Niemöller didn't just move Americans to reach for their wallets. There is also evidence that Niemöller's tour helped foster a sense of cross-border ecumenism. After Niemöller spoke at Davidson College, its president wrote Cavert to say that the visit went splendidly and that the German pastor made "a fine contribution to the ecumenical spirit of a community. He states clearly and persuasively that he is a Lutheran and expects to die a Lutheran, but that he must now also be a universal Christian." Willem Visser't Hooft, the general secretary of the WCC, believed that Niemöller was making a "deeply evangelistic impression on the American churches" and that there was "no other man in the world whose word and work is so clearly and visibly blessed." Cavert was pleased too, writing EKD president Bishop Wurm to express his appreciation. "I am confident that throughout the American churches there is a warmer feeling of fraternal fellowship with the Christian people of Germany as a consequence of the visit of Dr. and Mrs. Niemoeller."[33]

But Niemöller's critics remained steadfast. During the tour, several Federal Council of Churches donors, some of them Jews, withdrew their membership from the organization. Others wrote to express concern. One man wrote to the FCC, "I am sending you $5.00, but it has come to my attention from the reports I have received that you have given Nazi Neimueller [*sic*] a very grand reception. If I were not a Jew I probably would not give this another thought. It is only because it has affected me and my own that I am compelled to write." In a letter concerning the FCC's sponsorship of Niemöller's visit, a Maryland woman wrote, "I hope that the action you have taken may bring about the least possible harm." A veteran of the war, erroneously describing Niemöller as one of the first members of the Nazi Party, said in protest, "Now that Germany is down on her knees it exhibits the typical attitude of the majority of German intellectuals. With his eyes turned to heaven but with his mind pondering over revenge and a new war, he tries and apparently succeeds to stultify the American public. This Mephistopheles of German intellect is more dangerous than an outright Nazi. By using religion as his cloak he is going to make a fool of us unless he is stopped right now."[34]

Niemöller's speeches also did little to assuage the concerns of Eleanor Roosevelt or prominent American Jews. Rabbi Stephen Wise deplored the FCC's sponsorship of Niemöller and considered it a great disservice to the United States. "The record is that neither before nor during his incarceration in a concentration camp did Niemöller speak one word of protest against one of the foulest crimes in history," Wise said. He worried that Niemöller's visit would lead to further softening of America's occupation policy and that Germans would regard this as a sign of forgiveness—or even acceptance of antidemocratic and anti-Semitic views. In February 1947, Rabbi Abba Hillel Silver of The Temple in Cleveland, Ohio, called Niemöller unfit to lead postwar Germany because he opposed only the persecution of the church, not Nazism. A central figure in the mobilization of American support for the founding of the state of Israel, Silver agreed with Eleanor Roosevelt that Niemöller's speaking tour was being used "to allay the fears held by many American people that Germany will be rebuilt without a real moral regeneration of the German people. . . . I think it is bad for us to grow sympathetic to the Germans." And Henry Rubin of the Research Division of the Anti-Defamation League of B'nai B'rith objected to Niemöller's assurance that anti-Semitism was dead in Germany. He wrote the FCC asking for proof that Niemöller spoke against the mistreatment of Jews, as Cavert had claimed.[35]

There were critics within the Protestant Church too. William Spofford, managing editor of *The Witness: News-Magazine of the Episcopal Church*, opined that Niemöller might not have been a Nazi, but "has always stood for Pan-Germanism and does now." Spofford saw through Niemöller's professions of gratitude to the Allies, writing, "He is out to win a soft peace for his country." Exasperated by the criticisms from within, Cavert responded to another critic at the *Zion's Herald*: "I confess to much puzzlement as to why people who were praising Niemöller to the skies between 1937 and 1945 are now attacking him."[36]

FCC spokesmen such as Cavert, Leiper, Oxnam, and Reinhold Niebuhr did their best to convert critics into supporters. But when a critic like Rabbi Wise showed no signs of relenting, they took a different tack. In the pages of his *Christianity and Crisis*, Niebuhr told Wise to mind his own business. Christians "do not presume to pass judgments on the issues in the Jewish community [because] we do not know enough about the issues from the inside. [Wise] might accord us the same freedom from outside uninformed judgment." There was a regrettable tendency, Niebuhr admitted, for Christians to exaggerate church resistance. And it was true that Niemöller did not fully appreciate the Nazi peril in the beginning. But he did lead the fight of the Confessional Church against Nazism, and he was now revealing "a remarkable prophetic detachment from purely national considerations." For these reasons, "his record deserves a respect which ought always to be accorded genuine courage."[37]

In some rare instances, a conversion did take place. For instance, Estelle Sternberger, a well-known radio commentator in New York City and outspoken critic of Niemöller, changed her mind. Early in the tour, she told listeners, "Not even Pastor Martin Niemoeller, the former German U-boat commander, now a guest in this country, has, so far as I am aware, led a movement to have the German people put on sack cloths and ashes for these crimes of genocide." Cavert responded to her, explaining that Niemöller was doing more than anyone in Germany to talk about German guilt. The FCC inundated her with materials "proving" Niemöller's anti-Nazi credentials, and finally she conceded. Later, she even said on air "that the German pastor did do whatever he could to mobilize public opinion against the racial policies of the Nazis."[38]

On the whole, Niemöller's visit was unable to quell the dispute over his complicity and his resistance—and that of the German Protestant Church at large. Each side inflated and distorted the evidence. Niemöller's support for the Nazis in the 1924 and 1933 elections led to false accusations that he was a member of the Nazi Party and an unequivocal supporter of Hitler and his racial policies. At the same time, Niemöller's defiance of Hitler, opposition to the Aryan paragraph, and imprisonment in the camps led his defenders to make unsubstantiated claims that the pastor opposed Hitler's political and racial policies from the very start. These misrepresentations of Niemöller can be traced to the conflicted legacy of the Church Struggle—a legacy that includes, on the one hand, courageous opposition to the nazification of the churches, and, on the other, acceptance of most of the Nazi political and racial program.

In the end, even though he and Else enjoyed their time in America, and even though he raised more money than expected, Niemöller was disappointed in the tour's outcome. He was, he acknowledged, unable to win over his critics. Nor was his hope of moderating US occupation policies realized. The United States did significantly liberalize the occupation in 1947, but not because of Niemöller's public relations tour. Rather, the shift came in response to growing tensions with the Soviet Union, to which the United States responded by cultivating allies in Europe, including West Germany. Niemöller's tour did result in greater solidarity between German and American Christians, but this he would jeopardize in the coming years with frequent rants against the US foreign policy in the Cold War.[39]

NINE

Swords to Plowshares

(1947–1956)

W HEN THE NIEMÖLLERS RETURNED TO GERMANY IN MID-MAY 1947,
they were reunited with Hertha, then a nineteen-year-old philosophy student; oldest son Hermann, a twenty-three-year-old POW camp
escapee and medical student; and their youngest son Tini, all of eleven.
Along with housekeeper Dora Schulz and their little dachshund, they
settled into their apartment at Büdingen castle near Frankfurt. "We are
again something like a happy family," Martin Niemöller wrote Gladys
Boggess, his secretary and friend during the US tour. The use of "something like" indicated that not everyone was gathered around the hearth.
Brigitte, the firstborn, was living in Bavaria with her husband and three
daughters. Middle son Jan was still in a Russian POW camp. Martin's
brother Wilhelm had suffered a severe heart attack while Else and Martin
were in America and was recovering slowly.[1]

After six months in the land of plenty, war-ravaged Germany came as a shock. Niemöller spared no details in letters to Ewart Turner:

> The winter is over, but you feel it everywhere—in the cold which is still harboring in the rooms, especially in this old castle with its thick stone walls. The water pipes are broken. No running water in kitchen or toilet. Sitting at my desk I shiver from cold even now, and the only place where I feel some relief is once again in the bed. The food situation is more than difficult, and I scarcely dare to take a slice of bread, thinking that Hertha, Tini, and Hermann are far more in need of having it than I, and I can't help feeling guilty for being so well fed [in the United States]. The whole aspect of life is grim and dark; you see the traces of progressive starvation in every face you come to see.[2]

It wasn't only the material deprivations in Germany that troubled Niemöller. Even back home, he was dogged by controversy. "The attack of Mrs. Roosevelt," he wrote Boggess, "has pursued me . . . over here." American occupation officials, leftists, and Jews—"her friends," according to Niemöller—were investigating and highlighting his past, saying that he had been "an Antisemite, a Militarist and even a Nazi!" Exasperated and exhausted by the assaults on his honor, he yearned once again for the life of a simple pastor. But now he dreamed of a pastorate abroad. "Else and I are rather tired of the whole thing," he wrote, "and I am thinking earnestly of leaving Germany for good and of taking a small congregation in England or in your country. You see, there is not much left of the old 'fighting pastor,' at least of my old resistance."[3]

The physical and emotional toll of hunger, cold, and disillusionment, as well as the bureaucratic and logistical obstacles—all made life in the fatherland intolerable even to the tenacious pastor. "It was so much easier there than here," Else bemoaned when they got back from the United States. Her husband told Turner that if things didn't improve, "I should prefer to be back in my cell number 31 at Dachau." He blamed "the followers of the Morgenthau Plan," who, he said, had simply moved their "headquarters from Washington to the American Zone."[4]

Two incidents in July 1947 gave further impetus to those who believed that Niemöller was an anti-Semite. At a Berlin press conference on the first of the month, Niemöller claimed that a surfeit of Jews among the American occupation forces was causing the reemergence of anti-Semitism because Germans associated Jewish officials with what they felt were America's vengeful occupation policies. To stem the tide of "this basest form of hatred," as he called anti-Semitism, Niemöller suggested that the US military government reduce, in particular, the number of Jewish-German emigrants serving in Germany, many of whom operated "with an understandable spirit of hatred and revenge." These "astounding statements," in the words of a *Boston Globe* reporter, seemed to blame Jews themselves for the anti-Semitism they faced—a familiar anti-Semitic trope.[5]

Niemöller was one of the many Germans who sincerely believed that Jews in the occupation forces held some responsibility for their growing hunger. In another blunt letter to Turner in the fall of 1947, he described Germany's dire situation and implied Jewish responsibility for it:

> The [coming] winter will be a very severe test for all of us. The rations in fat and meat have been cut again to 25 grams of butter and 100 grams of meat a week! And no potatoes. The normal consumer probably will die this winter, and that Jew [in the occupation forces] will have been right who answered my question, what would become of the too many people in the Western Zones, by saying: "Don't worry, we shall look after that and the problem will be solved in quite a natural way!"

By "a natural way," Niemöller understood the Jewish occupation official to mean by starvation.[6]

The second incident occurred later that July, when evidence surfaced from Niemöller's 1938 trial. In his attempt to counter the Nazis' charge of treason, he had testified that he found Jews disagreeable and alien and that he had supported the Nazis in the 1920s and early '30s. When the postwar Association of Victims of Nazi Persecution—of which Niemöller was a member—learned of this testimony, they expelled him from the

Büdingen chapter and deprived him of the supplemental ration benefits that were his due as a former Nazi prisoner. He protested that his expulsion was part of a political vendetta, and he accused the head of the chapter of supporting only Jews. In a press conference held a few weeks later in Oslo, Niemöller defended himself. "I was never a friend of the Nazis and never the member of any political party," he declared, "but once between 1920 and 1930 I voted for the National Socialist party." (He neglected to mention his March 5, 1933, vote for the Nazis.) He complained that the German press ignored his record of resistance and failed to mention that the Nazis had wanted him dead. Although he was eventually reinstated in the victims' association, his reputation was tarnished.[7]

His friend and fellow pastor Adolf Freudenberg, who was forced to emigrate to England in 1939 because his wife Eva was a Christian of Jewish descent, thought it was ridiculous to allege that Niemöller was an anti-Semite on the basis of sentiments he had expressed ten or twenty years earlier. At the same time, Freudenberg thought Niemöller never should have approached the victims' group about supplemental rations, given all the wealthy and influential friends he might have relied on instead. Even if these friends could not help, it did not look good for a world-famous pastor, who shared a castle with the Büdingen prince, to demand special benefits. "It is my conviction," Freudenberg observed, "that Martin has been given more publicity than he can stand. . . . Martin and his friends would be well advised if they discontinued to focus too much sensational publicity on his person. As one of his critics rightly says: the Church cannot afford to have stars in her ranks." But a star was exactly what Niemöller had become.[8]

One person who rushed to Niemöller's defense was Senta-Maria Klatt, who a decade earlier had attended Niemöller's services in Dahlem and who wrote him praising his faith and resistance in 1936. In the fall of 1947, she wrote again on his behalf, this time to the Berlin newspaper *Kurier*, challenging his critics:

> As a "mixed breed," I acknowledge with great thankfulness that Pastor Niemöller always helped us non-Aryans whenever he could pos-

sibly do so. He was not at all ashamed of the fact that a large number of Jews attended his Church and his public evening meetings. . . . Moreover, Niemöller was the founder of the emergency committee of pastors whose first concern it was to banish from the Church the "Aryan Paragraph." As a pioneer in this struggle he risked his life. Do you call that anti-Semitism?

Of course, Klatt's defense of Niemöller addressed only his treatment of baptized Jews, while his detractors were mostly concerned with his lack of empathy toward Jews who never entered the church.

Critics also accused Niemöller of unfairly distributing some of the thousands of care packages from the United States. Upon their return to Germany, the Niemöllers had established themselves as key facilitators of aid arriving from America. Turner was the facilitator on the other end, notifying American pastors and parishioners who were organizing food drives when and where the need was greatest. But some critics alleged that, instead of sharing these treasured food parcels with the very needy, Martin and Else passed them on to friends, such as the prince's extended family. Although there is no proof of systematic abuse—the vast majority of food parcels were distributed to the destitute—there is evidence that the Niemöllers made some questionable decisions about who should receive the support from abroad. For instance, in December 1947, Niemöller asked Turner to send him parcels discreetly, for special cases. One was the widow of "the last Gestapo leader of Dachau, who was hanged according to a death-sentence from the Dachau Military Court." The woman and her children, Niemöller explained, "are dying from starvation and they have turned to us in their misery. I think it is our Christian duty to support them." Niemöller's leftist and Jewish critics would have certainly cried foul had they known about this.[9]

Although Freudenberg was not responding to a specific incident, his advice on how to handle the Niemöller phenomenon that fall was revealing for its restrained praise: "Let us love him as a man who, under the guidance of God, bears so wonderful witness for Jesus Christ, but let us not emphasize too much the personality with its charm and its defects." Niemöller's critics, however, were not concerned with mere personality defects. They saw an issue of character.[10]

One wonders if Freudenberg would have agreed with Niemöller's opponents had he known of Niemöller's reaction to his 1949 statement on anti-Semitism in Germany, "The Christian Attitude toward the Jews." Freudenberg's declaration was a response to reports of a dramatic increase in the desecration of Jewish graveyards in 1948 and 1949, especially in Bavaria in the American occupation zone. According to American military government surveys of Germans from that time, more than 50 percent—and in some areas as many as 65 percent—of Germans were racist or anti-Semitic. Freudenberg lamented the revival of public acts of anti-Semitism and strongly criticized the church's failure to condemn anti-Semitism unequivocally and embrace Christians of Jewish descent as equal members of the Christian community. "We are horrified that anti-Semitism still prevails in the ranks of the German people and is actually alive in some of our churches," Freudenberg exclaimed. When the FCC's Leiper asked Niemöller whether he agreed with Freudenberg's assessment, Niemöller replied by letter that he did not: "If anti-Semitism in Germany really is increasing, it is caused by increasing disapproval of the American occupation authorities. And as these authorities have many Jewish officials and employees—mostly German emigrants—, the Jews are made responsible for all the faults of the occupation forces." Nor did he agree with Freudenberg on Protestant disdain for baptized Jews. "Our Jewish fellow-Christians are in a way very pretentious which may be caused by what they have gone through. But (as I see things with my own eyes) the Jewish Christians are not treated like second-class Christians—and it has not been so in the past." In a further sign that Niemöller did not take anti-Semitism as seriously as he might have, after he was elected president of the Protestant Church in Hesse and Nassau (EKHN) in 1947, he used his position in 1950 to find a position for a former Nazi and German Christian, Wolf Meyer-Erlach.[11]

ALTHOUGH SOME OF his postwar statements and correspondence revealed Niemöller's nationalist and anti-Semitic predilections, he, at the same time, repeatedly and publicly condemned both nationalism and anti-Semitism. In fact, critics on the right attacked him for his supposed Communist sympathies. This accusation stemmed, at first, from a radical political statement he coauthored with colleagues in the Hessen city of Darmstadt in August 1947. The Darmstadt statement delineated where the Protestant Church had failed to reform itself politically and to embrace civil liberties, leading to the church's wholly inadequate response to Nazism. Influenced politically and theologically by Karl Barth, the authors broke decisively with the traditions of Christian politics in Germany, asserting that the four-hundred-year-old Lutheran propensity to back authoritarian regimes had contributed to the church's accommodating response to Hitler. "The alliance of the Church with the old and conventional conservative powers has taken heavy revenge upon us.... We rejected the right of revolution and tolerated and justified the evolution toward absolute dictatorship." Such a fundamental critique of German Lutheranism and defense of leftist revolution did not go unanswered by conservative Lutherans in the EKD. To the authors' surprise, however, the Darmstadt statement also evoked the fury of many beleaguered pastors and church leaders in the Soviet zone—some of them friendly with Niemöller—who read it as sympathetic to Communist rule.[12]

As critical as this statement was of the church's reactionary politics, it made no mention of the church's long history of anti-Semitism. This omission Niemöller and his colleagues tried to address—not entirely successfully—in the spring of 1948 and again in the summer of 1950. In "A Message Concerning the Jewish Question," published in 1948, they acknowledged that anti-Semitism flourished not only among the German people "but also among Christian leaders," and that this explained the church's virtual silence over Nazi crimes against the Jews. But while their statement condemned racial anti-Semitism, it showed little understanding of the role played by Christian anti-Semitism or theological anti-Judaism in the church's complicity in the Holocaust. The statement was replete with anti-Judaic rhetoric about the Jews' crucifixion of the Messiah, God's rejection of them as his chosen people, and God's choice of Christians as the new chosen people. The statement did not comment on the fact that Christian teaching about Jews had for centuries accused Jews of being Christ killers, laying the foundation for the more rabid anti-Semitism of the Nazis.[13]

In August 1950, Niemöller and church leaders gathered in the Weissensee suburb of Berlin to address the "Jewish question" again. This time they avoided much of the anti-Judaic rhetoric, calling on all Christians "to disassociate themselves from all anti-Semitism and earnestly to resist it." However, the authors maintained that the church's guilt for the Holocaust lay in its silence, not in its underlying contempt for Jews. And they ended with a prayer that Jews would one day be worshiping Christ alongside Christians.[14]

Although Niemöller was not the primary author of either of these statements, he was involved in their drafting and they represent well his understanding of the "Jewish question" after the Holocaust. It was not the place of a Christian to judge Jews as a race, he believed, but it was the duty of Christians to pray to God that as a religious people the Jews would one day see Jesus Christ as their savior. It was a major step, at the time, to reject racial objections to Jews. Niemöller was not a racial anti-Semite, who viewed Jews as inferior or inherently unscrupulous; his postwar anti-Semitism was predominantly the Christian variety that could be found in Christian churches throughout the world—in Britain, France, the United States, and elsewhere. Overcoming Christian anti-Semitism was a halting and incremental process for Niemöller and the Protestant Church in the postwar years. It would take a new generation of pastors born after the Second World War and the Holocaust to lead German Protestantism away from its anti-Judaic roots.

Although Niemöller had numerous adversaries in the late 1940s, he had many admirers too. Perhaps most important of all was his adopted regional church, the Church in Hesse and Nassau, which elected him to its highest office in September 1947. As president, Niemöller was finally able to move his family in early 1948 to a large house owned by the church on beautiful, tree-lined Brentanostrasse in the city of Wiesbaden, which was a short drive away from Frankfurt.

Located in a valley between the Rhine River and the Taunus Mountains, Wiesbaden—a celebrated spa city in Roman times—would be Niemöller's home for the rest of his life. As he wrote Gladys Boggess later that year, "We are happy enjoying our well heated new home and at the same time thinking much of our Berlin-friends sitting in cold and darkness"—no doubt a reference to the Soviet Union's eleven-month blockade of Berlin from June 1948 to May 1949, when American and British aircraft supplied West Berlin with over two million tons of food, fuel, and other necessities. In addition to celebrating their long-awaited move to a real home—the first for Niemöller since his 1937 arrest—the Niemöller family also rejoiced in the return of twenty-two-year-old Jan on April 20, 1948, after four years as a Russian POW, and the eightieth birthday of Martin's mother, Paula, on May 11.[15]

Niemöller used his position as president of the Church in Hesse and Nassau to carry on his fight against denazification. He outraged the US military government with a pastoral letter, read from every pulpit in Hesse and Nassau on February 1, 1948, calling on all Protestants to refuse to serve as prosecutors, assessors, or witnesses in denazification cases. He declared that clergy were "forbidden for the sake of their position and the welfare of the community to help justify this scandal any longer by doing any work in connection with denazification." General Lucius Clay, commander in chief of US Forces in Europe and military governor of the US zone in Germany, rebuked Niemöller, saying, "It is distressing to me that a minister of the religious faith advocates disrespect and violence to a law. Every citizen has the right to criticize and urge that a law be changed. It is not good citizenship to tell people to disobey the law." As it turned out, the Americans concluded on their own that the denazification program was an endless bureaucratic nightmare with few tangible benefits; they ended it not long after the pulpit declaration.[16]

But this hardly changed Niemöller's attitude toward the occupation. And even more troubling to Niemöller was the growing division between the Western occupation zones and the Soviet zone. The increasing divide, he told Turner, was poisonous for Germany's future. "We must find a new way." The "new way," Niemöller believed, would entail more than just an end to denazification. Searching for a path forward for Germany, Niemöller underwent his greatest transformation in a life full of them. He had already gone from U-boat to pulpit; from pulpit to leader of the Pastors' Emergency League; from PEL leader to camp inmate; from camp inmate to ecumenical activist. Throughout these changes, Niemöller held two things dear: his church and the German people. And to both he remained true as he, the former submarine commander, began to espouse pacifism.[17]

NIEMÖLLER LIKED TO explain his embrace of pacifism as the result of a 1954 conversation with Otto Hahn, the German "father of nuclear chemistry." The Nobelist told Niemöller that it had become possible to construct a thermonuclear hydrogen bomb that "would totally end life on this globe." A central aspect of the Cold War in the 1950s was the race between the United States and the Soviet Union to build more powerful bombs. In 1954, the United States tested a hydrogen bomb at Bikini Atoll, part of the Marshall Islands, which proved to be a thousand times more powerful than the atomic bombs dropped on Japan in 1945. According to Niemöller lore, Hahn's news so unnerved the pastor that he immediately read the entire New Testament for guidance. "What it said was quite clear to my eyes," he later claimed. "Jesus has NEVER allowed his disciples to act like this. His whole way of salvation was based on the other way around. War-acts and war-attitudes can only be done and held AGAINST Christ."[18]

Although Martin Niemöller would present his conversion to pacifism as the product of an epiphany at age sixty-two, his decision to reject all types of warfare came gradually. The record illustrates that 1954 was the culmination of a process that he began seriously in 1948. The evidence suggests that regular contact with pacifist clergymen in the ecumenical movement, such as A. J. Muste and John Nevin Sayre in the United States and Friedrich Siegmund-Schultze in Germany, played a critical role in swaying him.[19]

Although Niemöller's contact with pacifists in the ecumenical movement predates 1948, it was in that year, at the founding meeting of the World Council of Churches in Amsterdam, that he first discussed antiwar politics at length. Meeting with Sayre and the British pastor Lewis Maclachlan, two members of the pacifist Fellowship of Reconciliation (FOR), Niemöller told them,

> To follow the way of the Sermon on the Mount would indeed be to refuse to take part in war. I try to make decisions according to the rule of the Sermon on the Mount, but there are situations when I cannot make such decisions with good conscience. I have to decide between two wrongs and choose the less wrong. It is my duty to work against war as long as I can without laying a weight on my conscience that it cannot bear. . . . If there is war . . . then I must decide whether it is better to take part or not. If I participate in war I do so because I believe it to be a lesser evil. I cannot decide beforehand.

Sayre and Maclachlan might have been disappointed that Niemöller did not add his name to the FOR membership list at the time. But, while not yet a true pacifist, Niemöller had clearly come a long way from his earlier militarism. His position in 1948 could be summed up as antiwar—depending on the context. War was to be avoided, but not at all costs.[20]

Soon enough, Niemöller arrived at a less equivocal position. It was not the feared war in central Europe that drove him further toward doctrinaire pacifism, but one in the Far East.

Just weeks after North Korea invaded South Korea in June 1950, the WCC met in Toronto. Back on North American soil, Niemöller worked with American theologian Reinhold Niebuhr to draft a statement on the Korean situation. Although the troops sent to fight the North Koreans came from fifteen nations working under UN auspices, the bulk of the soldiers were from the United States, and the commander of the so-called UN police action was the American general Douglas MacArthur.

Niemöller, who had advocated neutrality in the Cold War in Europe, joined Niebuhr in defending the police action as a triumph of internationalism and defensive use of force. "An act of aggression has been committed," their statement began.

> The United Nations Commission in Korea, the most objective witness available, asserts that "all evidence points to a calculated, coordinated attack prepared and launched with secrecy" by the North Korean troops. Armed attack as an instrument of national policy is wrong. We therefore commend the United Nations, an instrument of world order, for its prompt decision to meet this aggression and for authorizing a police measure which every member nation should support.[21]

"We in Germany do not think of what is happening in Korea as war," said Niemöller, "but police action against armed violence in defiance of authority." Niebuhr was exuberant: "This is the first time in the modern world that a police action has been taken by the community of nations. We support it in this statement, as we should." The WCC adopted the statement by a vote of 45 to 2. The FCC came out in support of the action, as did the liberal Protestant weekly *The Christian Century.*[22]

Reverend Edwin T. Dahlberg, an American Baptist and a founder of the American FOR, and Dr. Algie I. Newlin, a Quaker, were the two members to oppose the statement, both for reasons of conscience. (Dahlberg was one of two recipients in 1960 of the Gandhi Peace Prize; the other was Eleanor Roosevelt.) The American branch of FOR condemned the statement, favoring "mediation and persuasion" over military action. Intervention, FOR asserted, "deprives the UN of the moral force" it might have used to persuade both sides to come to a ceasefire and negotiate.[23]

The FOR position seems to have moved Niemöller in a way he did not anticipate. Some weeks after drafting the Toronto statement, he began to have misgivings. He soon went to New York to meet A. J. Muste, another FOR leader who opposed the Toronto statement and had written an open letter accusing Niebuhr of holding political views identical to those of John Foster Dulles, one of the chief architects of US foreign policy in the Cold War. Muste and other leading US Christian pacifists had produced a petition, the "Affirmation and Appeal," calling on all Christians to reject war and "support the use of the methods of reconciliation and nonviolent action, such as Gandhi has demonstrated in our time."[24]

The meeting in New York came at Muste's request. The Dutch-born American clergyman, seven years Niemöller's senior, wanted to speak with the author of the July 1950 article "Does the Church Want Peace?," which expressed sentiments and philosophies similar to those of the petition rejecting war. In the article, Niemöller delineated his position on war in light of the increasingly hot Cold War. He argued that peace could not be achieved if, at the same time, the East and West continued to prepare for war: "He who prepares for war also inevitably creates the spirit of war." In the past, Niemöller admitted, churches had too easily been convinced of war's necessity, of conflict as a lesser evil than inaction—a position Niemöller had held for most of his life. But now he declared, "People must not be left in doubt that we Christians, and therefore the church, can no longer be rallied to violent solutions."[25]

Muste pointed out to Niemöller the contradiction between the article and his work with Niebuhr. Niemöller conceded that the Toronto statement increasingly troubled him. He told Muste that he intended to get in touch with the moderator of the central committee of the WCC, his friend George Bell, to express his misgivings. Bell, he hoped, might support a new statement clarifying that the WCC did not back war in Korea and "would refuse to line up in the Russian-US war."[26]

At this point, Niemöller remained adamant that his rejection of war did not make him a pacifist. "I whole heartedly agree with your tendency," Niemöller wrote Muste, but "I should like to make clear that I am not a pacifist by principle but that in the present days' situation I think that any solution of the problems in a warlike way is a crime against humanity." In other words, the context of each case still mattered.[27]

As the war in Korea intensified, Niemöller saw implications for the debate in Germany over the question of rearmament. On one side, Chancellor Konrad Adenauer and his supporters redoubled their efforts to rearm West Germany so that it could participate in its own defense should the Soviets and their East German allies invade, just as the Communist North Koreans had invaded South Korea. On the other side were the likes of Niemöller and his closest allies, Karl Barth and Gustav Heinemann, who was both president of the EKD synod and minister of the interior in Adenauer's cabinet. They argued that the ferocity of the Korean War was evidence that Germany should be united, unarmed, and neutral. Niemöller believed that a divided and rearmed Germany would jeopardize peace and, in effect, "amount to suicide."[28]

Niemöller also objected to rearmament for social reasons. Rearmament, he believed, would divert resources from more urgent problems, primarily the provision of homes and jobs for refugees from the East. And he had religious misgivings about Germany's division because it meant abandoning Germans, most of them Protestants, behind the Iron Curtain. With Germany's forty million Protestants spread almost equally between East and West, Niemöller saw the division of the nation as a catastrophe for Protestantism.[29]

His concern stemmed in part from his fear that Catholics would control the fate of Protestants in West Germany. Each faith numbered around twenty million in West Germany, but Catholics enjoyed more influence in the government. Whereas Protestants were geographically, institutionally, and politically divided, Catholics were "one political body with one political program." German Catholics also benefited from close relations with the US occupation authorities. Niemöller complained to the FCC's Henry Smith Leiper that, with the appointment of US Catholics to leading positions in the US High Commission in Germany, "America is propagating a counter Reformation." As he put it, West Germany was "a child conceived in the Vatican and born in Washington" and German Protestantism had "lost a battle" in the process. Niemöller held out hope that the Protestant Church could play a significant role in achieving German unity if it refused to take sides in the Cold War, but it would need help.

"Is there any possibility for the American Protestant churches to free us from becoming overruled by Roman Catholics in the name of the USA?" he implored.[30]

By October 1950, the aggressiveness that had won Niemöller so many admirers and enemies alike over the decades was again in evidence. Early that month he wrote to Adenauer alleging that the chancellor was subverting the democratic process by ordering rearmament against the will of the majority. Niemöller demanded that elections be held so that the people could decide whether to rearm. He said that the EKD was unified in its opposition, "unable to pronounce in favor of remilitarization." Yet at that very moment, amid rising Communist antagonism in Asia and Eastern Europe, EKD unity on disarmament was in fact disintegrating.[31]

Niemöller's attempted intervention in national politics was not popular with many of his German church colleagues. Hanns Lilje, the bishop of Hanover and a leading Lutheran on the EKD council, called on an American official to express his "great anger" about Niemöller's insolence toward Adenauer and his claim to speak for the EKD. Lilje and others on the council hoped to publicly announce their disagreement with Niemöller, or at least to admonish him in private.[32]

In November 1950, German church leaders convened a special meeting in Berlin-Spandau at which Niemöller's opponents on the EKD council were expected to censure him. But the pastor, newly aflame with pacifist sentiment, got the better of them. As an eyewitness described the encounter, "Niemoeller went into the meeting, took the offensive immediately, and launched into a vigorous and courageous attack on the conservative wing of the EKD (represented by Bishop Meiser of Bavaria and others) and for three hours held forth on their miserable record of opposition to the Nazis, their refusal to deal courageously with the social and political issues of today, and when he finished literally no one was willing to take him on." At the end of the twelve-hour meeting, Bishop Dibelius papered over the discord by drafting a declaration that concluded, "Rearmament should be treated with great circumspection."[33]

Niemöller found himself in the minority within the church, again. Most of the members of the EKD leadership council took a hawkish stance toward the Soviet Union, as did theologians and activists in the American Federal Council of Churches. Communist rhetoric that religion was the opium of the people, as Marx had said, and that as pillars of conservative authoritarianism the churches must be destroyed sowed fear among the clergy. This was no time to be embracing pacifism, they insisted. Many of Niemöller's longtime allies from the Church Struggle, such as Pastor Hans Asmussen and Bishops Otto Dibelius and Hanns Lilje, believed that Western Christendom should side unabashedly with the United States and its allies in the struggle against the godless Communists.

Observing Niemöller's isolation at the Spandau meeting and his pariah status in Washington and in the West German capital of Bonn, the German peace activist and FOR supporter Friedrich Siegmund-Schultze saw an opportunity to recruit a powerful ally. He believed that as remilitarization gained approval in the United States and in West German churches, Niemöller would realize that his true allies were to be found in the Fellowship of Reconciliation. "I am sure that Niemöller will need more organizational help in the future," Siegmund-Schultze wrote Muste. "I should give him the advice in his own interest to co-operate a little more with the Fellowship." Not that Siegmund-Schultze was under any illusions regarding Niemöller's ambiguous antiwar position. In another letter to Muste, he summarized his observations:

> On the one hand [Niemöller] naturally feels that he needs allies; on the other hand he would not like to join allies who follow certain principles regarding war. He repeats again and again . . . that he does not oppose war as such and that after some years he will support the remilitarization of Germany, but that he is now against it because it would mean a civil war between East and West Germany and because it is inopportune for other reasons. Besides that he is . . . very individualistic in all his ways, also within the church, so in spite of our willingness, real co-operation will not succeed. But we are very glad that Niemöller is so bravely pushing things forward.[34]

The more Niemöller pushed things forward, the more he was viewed as a traitor to the West and a patsy for the Soviets. Already in June 1950, when he gave an anti-rearmament speech in Mannheim, he had come to the attention of the US Army's Counterintelligence Corps. Agents noted that the German Communist Party helped to publicize the speech and distributed leaflets to the audience. In October, agents alerted their superiors to another set of Communist leaflets enthusiastically quoting Niemöller's harsh letter to Adenauer. One agent concluded that the Communists wanted the masses to know that Niemöller's aims were the same as their own. Another agent attending a sermon in Korbach near Kassel in December 1950 concluded:

> Niemoeller is, by his speeches, exerting a very dangerous influence upon the people in Western Germany. His fight against remilitarization coincides with the Communist propaganda campaign. It is not believed that Niemoeller is a Communist but the fact remains that he is directly aiding the attempts of the Communists to undermine the morale of Western Germany. He commands great authority and influence over the better classes of the population, the religious people who put their implicit trust in Ministers and Presidents of the Church.[35]

It was in this atmosphere of heightened anti-Communism that Niemöller went to Moscow for a week in December 1951, at the invitation of Patriarch of Moscow Alexy I. Niemöller's daughter Hertha, who had studied Russian at the University of Frankfurt, accompanied him as an interpreter. Niemöller was adamant about the trip's apolitical, spiritual, and peace-loving motivations. He maintained that he only wanted to assess the strength and independence of the Russian Orthodox Church under Communist rule and to develop an ecumenical relationship between churches in the East and the West. Two months later, on a lecture tour in the United States, he tried to explain that he went to Russia because he felt that it was his Christian duty to tell the Russians that Western Europeans and Americans did not want a third world war. He was in America to say that the Russians did not want one either. Niemöller reported on the vibrancy of the churches in Moscow, which "are not only filled on high holy days but are visited constantly during the week." Although most Russians saw the West as the aggressor in the Cold War, Niemöller said that he "was received and treated in a manner that convinced me that Russian Christianity harbors a real and conscious sense of ecumenicity." He had also sought to convince Russian church leaders that the World Council of Churches was not a tool of the West.[36]

Many responses to Niemöller's Moscow trip were sharply critical. The *Stuttgarter Zeitung* carried a cartoon depicting a grinning Stalin with Niemöller in the shape of a parrot perched on his forearm. As though the image was not sufficiently clear, the caption added, "Niemöller in Moscow. Polly wanna cracker." Bishop Dibelius, a strident cold warrior, veiled his disagreement in a truism: "All operations of Dr. Niemöller have an astonishing power of division. Whatever he does, one group will agree passionately and the other will reject passionately as well." Niemöller's neighbors on Brentanostrasse in Wiesbaden hung a huge sign across the street reading, BACK TO MOSCOW COMRADE NIEMÖLLER. Asmussen warned against the "mortal danger of the churches adjusting themselves to communism under the influence of Pastor Martin Niemöller's ecumenical work." He went on, "The danger of the ecumenical movement engaging in politics has never been so great as it is at present with Pastor Niemöller in charge of the Church's foreign relations."[37]

Reaction was similarly severe on the other side of the Atlantic. *Christian Century* declared, "Martin Niemöller seems always to live at the center of a storm. That is because he says and does what his conscience approves without bothering too long about consequences." Myron Taylor, a former US envoy to the Vatican and religious adviser to President Truman, kept the president informed about Niemöller's activities, especially the Moscow trip and the US speaking tour that followed two months later. To better understand Niemöller's intentions, Taylor sought the opinion of Bishop Dibelius. The bishop was a careful informant, noting that "we all must keep in mind the sincerity of conscience of Niemöller and his suffering under the Nazi regime." But Dibelius also made clear that Niemöller's enthusiastic description of church life in Russia raised concerns in Germany. "He does not take seriously enough the dark sides of the communistic regime. . . . Most of the members [of the EKD council] clearly and decidedly are against" Niemöller's positions, he added, explaining that the council intended to bring the quarrel into the public eye. Taylor, in turn, warned President Truman:

> Niemoeller has embarked for the United States, apparently to present to the American people a point of view contrary to our thought or plan of re-arming Germany—which would put him in a class of propaganda contrary to American interests and leads me to question whether an avowed propagandist friendly to the Soviets should be allowed to lecture in this country.

Two days later Truman responded, "I don't know what his objective is but I think your caution, that he ought to be watched, is a good one."[38]

It is not clear exactly what actions the US government took, if any, regarding Niemöller's visit in 1952, but Taylor wrote Truman in April stating that Niemöller's efforts to spread propaganda were "thwarted." Niemöller had of course come to the United States and spoken to American Christians, without any apparent interference from American authorities. Taylor might have been referring to the negative press coverage Niemöller received. Eugene Tillinger, who had written several highly critical articles on the alleged Communist sympathies of the renowned and prolific German writer Thomas Mann, also wrote a harsh assessment of Niemöller for the liberal anti-Communist magazine *The New Leader*. His article "Niemöller: Germany's 'Red Dean'" carried the subtitle "A Fellow-Travelling Churchman Promotes Moscow's Campaign to Undermine the West" and described Niemöller as "a man whom many consider one of the most dangerous pro-Soviet figures in Western Germany." The phrase "Red Dean" was a reference to the Stalinist dean of Canterbury, Hewlett Johnson, whom the State Department had banned from speaking in the United States because of his political views. Government officials believed that refusing Niemöller a visa would only lead to protests by American Protestants.[39]

The comparison was certainly unfair—Niemöller was no Stalinist. Indeed, Niemöller had returned from Russia not only lauding the efforts of Russian Christians but warning of communism's evils in a manner that would have impressed the House Un-American Activities Committee. "The threat of Bolshevism is a hundred times more dangerous than that of Nazism," he told a Wiesbaden audience in 1952. "I would a thousand times rather live on this side of the Iron Curtain than the other. There, people are being stripped piece by piece of all that makes human living worth while."[40]

As was so often the case with Niemöller, his views were subtler than their expression sometimes suggested. The nuances were intolerable to hard-liners who saw every political problem in black and white. Thus did Niemöller and Niebuhr, the latter a staunch anti-Communist, increasingly find themselves at odds over the Cold War. Niebuhr was openly critical of Eastern Bloc Christians' failure to defy Communist tyrants in the way Christians supposedly had defied Hitler. The two men clashed over how to treat churches that conformed to Communist rule, such as those Niemöller had visited in Russia and praised. Although he did not mention Niemöller by name, Niebuhr made clear that he considered him an appeaser. After citing Niemöller's noble line of defiance, "We must obey God rather than men," Niebuhr inserted the knife. "It is now apparent that we will not have the same inspiring record of heroic resistance by the churches to the second wave of tyranny, the Communist one," he said.[41]

Cold warriors refused to take seriously Niemöller's contention that Orthodox Christianity in Russia was, while not entirely free, tolerated and flourishing. Where Niemöller saw an opening for engagement between Eastern and Western churches, Niebuhr insisted that Christians not allow themselves to "be hoodwinked when communism ceases to annihilate Christianity, but tries merely to corrupt it." He asserted that "the price for the state support of a church in a Communist nation is the corruption of the church." Where Niemöller asked, "What can the Church do for peace?" Niebuhr asked, "What can the Church contribute to the health and the power of survival of a free society?"[42]

Niemöller followed his conscience even to the highly suspect World Peace Council, a Soviet-backed propaganda organization. In 1953, he traveled to Budapest to participate in one of its congresses in the hope of engaging colleagues in the East. Asked whether his presence at the conference lent Soviet propaganda the appearance of sincerity, Niemöller responded that the Soviets' true motives did not matter. As long as the Russians allowed such meetings to go on, he was prepared to encourage them.[43]

His evident commitment to a peaceful resolution to the Cold War was leading Niemöller away from the likes of Niebuhr and closer to his pacifist friends on both sides of the Atlantic. A 1953 interview with the American ecumenicist and Quaker Douglas Steere is revealing. When Steere asked about his position on war in principle, Niemöller was ready to make a firmer commitment: "In our time, the Christian must witness to peace and against the sin of war. . . . Unless the Christian world gets rid of war there is no way of our passing on to other races the Christian heritage in the years to come," he told him.[44]

By 1954, Niemöller's journey to pacifism was complete. Where once he preached in favor of German neutrality in the Cold War, at the Second Assembly of the World Council of Churches held in August in Evanston, Illinois, he lectured on "The Way of Peace." "When Jesus said, 'Blessed are the peacemakers,' I have come to see, he really meant it. It is not just a pious and nice sounding phrase. . . . I do not see in the New Testament any encouragement for the use of force." In another address, "How I Became a Pacifist," he said that had he died in 1953, his obituary would have read, "Although an opponent of Nazism because it claimed to supersede and be superior to the requirements and judgments of God, Niemöller remained always of the military caste of mind that his national heritage and early profession had created." But in 1954, following his conversation with the nuclear chemist Hahn, he realized that it was not a question of whether war was good or bad, just or unjust. He decided that war was simply madness. After concluding that war was anti-Christian, Niemöller declared, "I wrote to my friend, Professor Friedrich Siegmund-Schultze of Dortmund, that I was now joining the Fellowship of Reconciliation." Soon after, he became the president of the German Peace Society, Germany's oldest pacifist organization, founded in 1892.[45]

Leaving militarism behind represented a genuine rupture in Niemöller's thought, career, and life. A further rupture came with the recognition that, for models of Christian pacifism, he would have to look far beyond the German Lutheran Church. He turned to the teachings of a non-Christian who had lived on another continent: Mahatma Gandhi. In December 1952, he and Else had flown to India and participated the following month in an international seminar on the "Contribution of Gandhian Outlook and Techniques to the Solution of Tensions between and within Nations," which had a major impact on his thinking. Niemöller said at the conference that "World War II had taught Germany that violence and war was now outmoded and that war could no longer be an effective instrument of policy." He explained to the audience in Evanston, Illinois, in 1954 that "Gandhi became a blessing for his nation and I believe God means that he should become a blessing for the Christian world by causing us to examine ourselves. He has demonstrated that in a 'hopeless' situation other means than violence can be devised to achieve something for the bettering of this world of ours." Gandhi's way of nonviolence, Niemöller insisted, was the way of Christ. "I wish that Christians would not be the last group of men and women in the world to learn this lesson that God is teaching us through this prophet."[46]

In fact, Niemöller was disturbed by the possibility that Christians would be the last such group. Among Christians in Germany, he pointed out, there was a long history of considering pacifism anti-Christian. Outside the tiny circles of Christian pacifists in FOR and similar groups, most of the Christian world evidently had failed to grasp the message of Christ. "God calls us to ask ourselves today whether we really are Christians or whether we are using the words of Jesus Christ written on a banner to lead the Christian army in exactly the opposite direction from the one He pointed out," Niemöller lamented. Pacifists, he said, were often thought of as bad Christians, especially in Germany, where to be a church member had meant unhesitating obedience to the state.[47]

The earlier reservations of Fellowship of Reconciliation members disappeared after Niemöller's Evanston address. Sayre, from the American branch of FOR, wrote Siegmund-Schultze to praise Niemöller's appearance at the conference and described a recent sermon by Niemöller as "excellent . . . on the basic Christian commandments of non-violence and love to our enemies."[48]

From 1954 on, Niemöller made it his primary goal to expand the circle of pacifists, person by person, through example and education. By way of example, he not only became president of the German Peace Society but also joined the German branch of FOR and marched in pacifist demonstrations. As for education, he adopted the methods of the pacifist colleagues who had convinced him—if not converted him—through dialogue and debate. He traveled the globe, frequently visiting Communist nations, preaching nonviolence, extolling Gandhi, and telling anyone who would listen that we live in either a united world or a world with no future.

– TEN –

Ambassador of God
(1956–1984)

NUMBER 3 BRENTANOSTRASSE IN WIESBADEN REMAINED NIEMÖLLER'S home from 1948 to the end of his life. But as with most of Niemöller's homes, whether in Münster, Dahlem, Büdingen, or Wiesbaden, he spent at least as much time on the road as he did there. Just as he had taken his father's advice, "Make home visits, my boy," when he accepted his first parish in Dahlem, now as the president of a regional church he made his first task that of visiting the congregations within the regional Church in Hesse and Nassau (EKHN), of which there were approximately eight hundred parishes. "I enjoy this sort of work," he told Ewart Turner, "for the pastors are very thankful to be visited after a long period of having been neglected by their church authorities." Niemöller believed that the revival of the church should begin at the parish level, and he began his tenure by preaching in a different parish every week. To make clear his preference for a more democratic church, he refused to adopt the title of bishop, which many of his fellow church leaders had taken, because he associated it with a top-down hierarchy.[1]

In addition to his new position in the Church in Hesse and Nassau, Niemöller continued as chairman of the Protestant Church's foreign office, which required not only fostering ecumenical relations but tending to the care of German Protestant churches abroad in Europe, America, Africa, Asia, and Australia. He also sat on the twelve-man executive council of the World Council of Churches and held positions in other ecumenical and peace organizations. All of which required Niemöller to travel all over the world.

Some of his colleagues in the Hessen Church thought their church president should spend more of his time in his Wiesbaden office and less time gallivanting around the globe. More than anything, his absence from Wiesbaden was due to his status as a highly sought after speaker who received invitations to lecture and preach on every continent. And Niemöller liked to travel, not least because he could temporarily escape the feuding within the leadership council of the Protestant Church in Germany (EKD). Abroad he was the famous pastor who had defied Hitler and a leading light in ecumenical Christianity; at home his colleagues on the council considered him an annoyance, while the postwar West German government continued to view him as a rabble-rouser.[2]

In several European nations, including Sweden, Norway, Denmark, the Netherlands, and the United Kingdom, Niemöller was the first German to be honored with an invitation to address the public. He visited the British Isles and the United States more frequently than any other nations except Switzerland—even making it to the US Territory of Hawaii, where he was photographed grinning in a Hawaiian shirt and lei with his arm around Else. At the same time, he kept up his visits to the Communist side of the Iron Curtain, making multiple stops in Russia, Czechoslovakia, Hungary, Yugoslavia, and East Germany, where the authorities were always ready to literally roll out the red carpet for the famous critic of Western imperialism. Niemöller also went farther afield, to Africa, Asia, the Middle East, Latin America, and Oceania, where his reception was that of a celebrity.[3]

"An ambassador of God" was the label Henry Smith Leiper of the Federal Council of Churches used for Niemöller following one of his many trips to the United States in November 1956. "It seems to me beyond question true," Leiper said, "that your contact with the churches in many lands where you have gone as an ambassador of God has done much to strengthen the convictions of Christians in our time concerning the primacy of Christ's claims upon the hearts and minds of men." Else accompanied him on many of these trips and often gave addresses herself in English. Niemöller's message on these trips was frequently threefold: he emphasized the futility of war, the importance of church engagement in public affairs, and the need to build a worldwide Christian brotherhood.[4]

"The danger of the church in the present situation," Niemöller told theology students in Marsh Chapel at Boston University in 1955, "lies in the fact, that she may fall back on the line of least resistance and that she may retire into her 'purely religious' mission." By giving a free hand to the secular authority in political matters, he argued, the church left people without Christian counsel or guidance in these matters. "The church has to become the conscience of the political powers, reminding politicians of the limitations of their authority." This wasn't just the task of the organized church but also of everyday Christians in their roles "as judges, politicians, industrialists, workers, and businessmen"—and, he might have added, "pastors." As he saw it, all Christians had to demonstrate Christian responsibility in their public life and demand it of their leaders.[5]

Niemöller's pacifism was now at the foundation of his political beliefs and his public persona. In speeches, he rejected remilitarization, attacked Chancellor Adenauer, criticized chaplains in the military, voiced opposition to conscription, and advocated dialogue with the Communist world. He always provided a religious explanation for his arguments—often pointing to the Sermon on the Mount or another example in the life and teachings of Jesus Christ. Niemöller's political pronouncements, no matter that he grounded them in faith, elicited rebuke after rebuke from fellow churchmen, especially the conservative Lutheran faction in the EKD, who believed that the job of a church leader was to preach the Gospel and administer church affairs—not offer advice to the West German chancellor. The Lutherans, Niemöller didn't hesitate to point out, were as politically engaged as he was, the only difference being they supported the West German government.

The irreconcilable differences between Niemöller and the Lutheran members of the EKD leadership council led his opponents on the council to finally oust him from the church's foreign office in 1956. Niemöller accused them of militant confessionalism and wrote a detailed rebuttal of the charges made against him. "Persecution by the Church," as he put it to a friend, "following [the Nazi] persecution of the Church." But in truth, he no longer needed or wanted to be EKD ambassador to the churches abroad. He now had a global pulpit from which he could promote ecumenism and reconciliation between nations. Thus, losing his place on the EKD council freed him from the constraints the council had imposed and allowed him to preach his message of East-West unity without the council's criticisms. And anyway, back in his home Church in Hesse and Nassau, he still had enough of a following to be reelected to another term as church president in 1958.[6]

FROM THE MID-1950S to the late 1970s, Niemöller was a sought-after speaker at peace demonstrations, disarmament marches, and antinuclear protests. He was president of the German Peace Society, sat on the council of the World Peace Committee, represented Germany in the Campaign against Atomic Death, and walked in the "Easter Marches" against atomic weapons. In these roles, he necessarily came into conflict with the West German government, especially during Konrad Adenauer's long reign as chancellor from 1949 to 1963. Niemöller's conviction that Western militarism was by far a greater threat to peace than the Soviet Union did not sit well with a government obsessed with defending its border with Communist East Germany.[7]

Niemöller's international appeal continued to expand as he traveled to the four corners of the globe. The Indian literary critic Amiya Chakravarty wrote Niemöller in 1955: "We revere you in India because of the deep accord that binds India's spiritual pacifism as expressed by Mahatma Gandhi and [Rabindranath] Tagore with your own spirituality centered pacifism."[8]

More and more in the 1950s and '60s, he began to draw connections between pacifism, anticolonialism, and racial justice, joining on several occasions with Martin Luther King Jr. and his former nemesis Eleanor Roosevelt in signing and sponsoring petitions against racism and imperialism. A pacifist policy that focused solely on the abolition of war and the elimination of armaments, he came to believe, was not enough. Beginning with his trip to India in the winter of 1952–1953, six years after that country won independence from Great Britain, his focus gradually broadened to include the struggle for human rights and social justice in the non-Western world. In 1957, Niemöller was one of many world Christian leaders who signed the "Declaration of Conscience" written by the American Committee on Africa (ACOA), which supported African struggles against colonialism and apartheid. "We support the overwhelming majority of South African people, non-white and white," the declaration read, "in their determination to achieve the basic human rights that are the rightful heritage of all men."[9]

Signing a petition is not hard, but Niemöller did not readily attach his name to every piece of paper put in front of him. He believed that, whenever possible, he should visit a region to gather facts before making a pronouncement one way or another. He wrote to the ACOA, for example, explaining that the declaration "expresses fully my own conviction." In this case, he added, he "would have preferred to go to South Africa personally and tell the responsible people of that country what the world and especially the Christian church is thinking of their attitude and behavior." (In 1966, Niemöller did go to South Africa for four weeks and told newsmen there that Christian morality was sixty years behind the times in South Africa and that it reminded him of the narrow-minded Germany of his youth.)[10]

Niemöller's condemnations of racism at times focused on specific events. When he learned in 1959 of the arrest of Asbury Howard, a black labor leader and voting rights activist in Alabama, and of his savage beating by a white mob in front of the police, he wrote Nevin Sayre of the US Fellowship of Reconciliation to express his outrage. "Now, I am not a citizen of your country," he began, "but as a member of the human family I cannot but protest on the ground of unalienable human rights against the inhuman treatment of people (whoever they are) under the eyes of legal authorities (wherever this happens). If this would pass by without being condemned, the end of human civilization, culture and history would inevitably be at hand; God Forbid!"[11]

In 1959, Martin Luther King Jr. responded enthusiastically to a friend's suggestion that he meet Niemöller, writing in a letter that the German pastor "is certainly one of the outstanding figures of the world. I have always longed to meet him. It will be a real pleasure if he finds the time to come to Alabama on his next visit to the United States. I will be more than happy to entertain him." Although this particular meeting did not take place, Niemöller was as much an admirer of King as King was of him. He wrote the civil rights leader in 1962, thanking him for his work on the ACOA and asking for copies of the "Appeal for Action against Apartheid" so that he could share it with churches in Germany.[12]

In 1964, Niemöller publicly lent his voice to the campaign to award King the Nobel Peace Prize. After King received the prize later that year, Niemöller received hate mail from a man in Atlanta who deemed MLK a troublemaker, his followers rapists, and Niemöller a dupe for nominating a black man. Most people would not have dignified the racist letter writer with a response, but Niemöller could not let it rest. He told the man that he was entitled to his own opinion, but that his conviction "that Negros are human beings of minor value and lesser importance than you are, I do not participate in. I pray that those of your type will dwindle away and disappear soon because if they will prevail the end of humanity will be at hand." Here was a sign of another shift in his thinking. In the 1960s, he had come to see racism as threatening the continued existence of human civilization, and this fear superseded his worries about nuclear war.[13]

Still, Niemöller's pronouncements on race were not always so unambiguous and progressive. He never fully escaped his upbringing and continued to conceive of humanity as divided into racial groups often at odds with each other. Unlike racists in the American South, Niemöller laid the blame for racial conflict on white bigotry. How he articulated this view, however, at times led to misunderstandings.

In speeches and sermons in predominantly white nations, he divided humanity into white and dark races. In Claremont, California, in August 1957, he declared that the most important concern at present was not Cold War tensions but the future existence of the white race. "You know the dark races constitute five-sevenths of the people on this earth and there is a great movement among them." He feared that the colored races would unite and overtake the white Christian world. "The dominance of the world," he wrote in 1957 to a woman in Los Angeles, "will change over to what we call the 'colored races' and our main question is whether this transition from the white to a colored dominance of the world will happen in peace or in a spirit of retaliation."[14]

California attorney Samuel C. McMorris took exception to Niemöller's claim that the "darker races" sought retaliation against whites. "Contrary to Pastor Niemoeller's fears, the darker races do not seek revenge upon or domination of their former persecutors. They seek to live simply as equal members individually and collectively in the family of men and nations." Niemöller's articulation of the racial divide might have been unsophisticated and awkwardly expressed—but he fundamentally agreed with McMorris.[15]

The populations of Africa and Asia and their descendants in Europe and the United States had legitimate reasons for feeling vengeful, Niemöller thought. White control of the world for the past five hundred years, as he put it, "was an exploitive stewardship." The struggle between the races was at heart a struggle between the haves and the have-nots. With the majority of the world's population starving, it was just a matter of time before an "explosion point" was reached, he wrote for the Confessing Church's news magazine. If racist attitudes toward the people of Africa and Asia were not reformed, whites would face obliteration by the colored races. Here Niemöller drew an interesting and, in some respects, distinctive connection between racism and the Cold War of his era. He argued that the legacy of white racism required that whites in the present day, whether living in the Communist East or the capitalist West, cooperate with each other—not merely for the sake of peace, but to save themselves from the vengeance of the peoples they had oppressed.[16]

Niemöller also urged whites to "replace hatred with love," though, again, his view mixed moral urgency with pragmatism. He believed that whites should "be as friendly as we can to non-whites while we still have a chance." He urged an audience in Raleigh, North Carolina, in 1966 to "fight against every type of race-discrimination. Man needs it and God wills it!" Only by demonstrating a spirit of brotherhood and sharing food and other material resources could whites hope for peaceful racial coexistence. Niemöller feared that men like the racist from Atlanta who criticized his support of King and the white mob that beat Asbury Howard in Alabama were dooming humanity to a race war with their prejudice.[17]

While in New Orleans in 1964 for a week of preaching, Niemöller was interviewed in Kolb's German restaurant—after finishing a plate of oysters—by three southern churchmen. They were interested in his views on Christian responsibility as it related to race relations. Christians, he maintained, had a responsibility "to demand for any member of a different race the same basic rights as he himself enjoys. We must demonstrate that the love of God is not for a special race because all human beings are of one flesh in Christ. We must demonstrate at the table of the Lord we belong together." When asked how he would respond to the question, "Would you let your daughter marry a Negro?" Niemöller responded immediately, "Of course, it is up to my daughter, not to me." In his opinion, intermarriage between blacks and whites, while not common, usually "turns out well." His concluding advice to white Christians was straightforward: "Do not treat the Negro as a second class human being and do open the door for the Negro woman."[18]

Niemöller's relatively enlightened views on race seem to have developed from two influences particular to his post–World War II life. The first was the realization that the Gospel, the good news of Christ's love and mercy, was for all of humankind and not just Germans. Germany's total defeat in the war and the revelations of the Holocaust had shattered Niemöller's commitment to national Protestantism. Ostracized and isolated in the immediate postwar years, Germans now had the responsibility to try to convince the peoples of the world that they too deserved the Gospel. Christ's message, Niemöller came to appreciate, was not defined or restricted by national borders. It was one of the lessons he took from Dachau and his experiences with ecumenism after the war. He now applied this revelation to all races.

The second influence on Niemöller's views on race stemmed from and complemented the first—international travel. From the Gandhi seminar he attended in New Delhi in 1953 with civil rights activist and Nobel Peace Prize recipient Ralph Bunch to the numerous World Council of Churches meetings across the globe, Niemöller learned firsthand the absurdity of racial theories that placed one race ahead of another. Through personal contact with men and women of different races, he overcame his earlier prejudices.

NIEMÖLLER LOVED TO have Else by his side on his travels, and she enjoyed the time she spent with him abroad and the chance to work toward the same ends he sought. But Else's travels were curtailed when she was diagnosed with Parkinson's disease in the late 1950s. She became more dependent than ever on Dora, especially when Martin was on the road. As the disease progressed, he tried not to stray too far. During the first half of 1961, Niemöller confined himself to short European trips: to Basel, Geneva, Berlin, Moscow, Belfast, Prague, back to Switzerland,

and finally to East Germany in July to protest the EKD's pro-Western orientation.

His multiple trips to the other side of the Iron Curtain ignited another controversy that made his summer of '61 vacation with Else in Denmark all the more appealing. To make this particular vacation even more special, their eight-year-old grandson Martin von Klewitz (Hertha's oldest child) was to accompany them, along with Dora.[19]

Tragically, neither Else nor Dora would return home alive from Denmark.

With Martin driving, the four left Wiesbaden on August 6 and headed north, spending the night in Nordheim before continuing on to Denmark the following day. In the early afternoon, a terrible accident occurred. In stormy weather, Niemöller lost control of their Volkswagen Beetle on a hillside curve just north of the German-Danish border, near the seaside town of Aabenraa. There were no seat belts in cars at the time; the small VW struck a tree, and Niemöller was knocked unconscious when his head hit the windshield, while Else and Dora were thrown from the car. When Martin regained consciousness in the hospital, he learned that his wife of forty-two years, who had been by his side through the most difficult of times, had died instantly. Dora, who was like a younger sister to Martin and Else and a second mother to many of the Niemöller children, died en route to the hospital. Their grandson escaped major injury with only a broken arm.[20]

Martin suffered no life-threatening injuries, but he had a serious concussion and body and facial lacerations, and he had lost a lot of blood. On August 14, 1961, one day after the East Germans erected the Berlin Wall to seal off West Berlin, the funeral for Else and Dora took place in Luther Church in Wiesbaden. Else and Dora were laid to rest side by side in the Wiesbaden cemetery. Niemöller, still lying in a hospital bed in Denmark, could not attend. A week later, he was driven by ambulance 120 miles to the Hamburg airport and flown to Frankfurt, where he was taken to St. Mark's Hospital to recuperate near friends and family. "I killed them. I killed them both," he kept repeating. Burdened by guilt and despair, he wondered whether life without Else would be worth living.[21]

Six copresidents of the World Council of Churches at a meeting in New Delhi, 1961 (Niemöller second from left). (World Council of Churches Archives Geneva, ref. code ND51-08)

In October, he wrote a friend, "I am now over the shock, and have resigned myself inwardly to taking up again this life and its tasks. That it must go on without my wife and Dora . . . remains daily very difficult." With Else's death, he lost his most loyal companion. "I do not know what would have become of me," he confided to an American friend, "if I had not been supported by her courage, energy and strength of conviction and faith. Many people have been a blessing for me in my lifetime, but none of them is to be compared with the blessing God gave me in her." He took some solace knowing that Else would not have to suffer the debilitating effects of Parkinson's disease and that she was now in heaven.[22]

He told his friend Ewart Turner, who visited him in the Frankfurt hospital, that he intended to participate in the World Council of Churches assembly in November in New Delhi, India. At that meeting, his ecumenical colleagues not only consoled him but also elected him one of the six WCC presidents. The WCC assembly in New Delhi was significant for Niemöller for at least two additional reasons. It was the first assembly held outside of Europe, indicating the WCC's desire to reach nonwhite Christians; and the Russian Orthodox Church joined the WCC in New Delhi, a move that Niemöller had lobbied for persistently after his first visits to Russia in the early 1950s. The last time Niemöller had been to India was with Else in the winter of 1952–1953, and they both had had many fond memories of that trip. But in 1961 Niemöller traveled alone.

JUST AS NIEMÖLLER'S views on race had evolved by the 1950s and '60s, there are some indications that his attitude on Jews did as well. In connection with the publication and staging in 1963 of German playwright Rolf Hochhuth's highly critical play centered on Pope Pius XII, *The Deputy*, Niemöller spoke frequently on the topic "Germany, the Jews, and the Christian Church" in the spring of 1964. Hochhuth's play had ignited a controversy, as it suggested that Pope Pius XII knew about the Nazi extermination of Jews in the early 1940s but refused to condemn it publicly. The reasons for Pius's silence, Hochhuth believed, were anti-Semitism and fear of the consequences for German Catholics and the institution of the Catholic Church in Germany. Niemöller used the controversy as an opportunity to publicly consider the behavior of the German Protestant Church during the Nazi period.

The Pastors' Emergency League, and later the Confessing Church, Niemöller recalled, had boldly claimed the right in 1933 to continue proselytizing Jews, baptizing them, and accepting them as full members of the Protestant Church. In this respect, the PEL differed from the Nazis and German Christians, who believed that Jews, regardless of their religion, were racially unredeemable. By the 1960s, however, Niemöller had come to see the PEL's response to Nazi anti-Semitism as inadequate, because it expressed nothing more than "the church's own interest and [demonstrated] no regard for the human beings outside the church who happened to be Jews."[23]

Niemöller emphatically denounced the anti-Semitism behind the Confessing Church's silence and inaction. In a televised broadcast in the United States on NBC, Niemöller told viewers that the problem of anti-Semitism in the Protestant Church could be traced as far back as Martin Luther and his 1543 anti-Semitic screed, *The Jews and Their Lies*, in which Luther encouraged violence against Jews. "Anti-Semitism inside the Protestant churches in Germany and its population," Niemöller remarked, "certainly is as old as Protestantism in Germany." But he did not believe that the church was guilty of *fostering* anti-Semitism, only that it reflected broader social currents and failed to stand up for what was right. "[The churches] did not oppose it," Niemöller admitted. "And that's a real sin of the churches as far as I'm concerned. As a Christian I know that the dangers of the sins of omission are much more dangerous than the dangers of committed sins." He applauded Hochhuth's play for challenging both Catholics and Protestants to examine their sins of omission, specifically the Christian failure to come to the aid of the very people "for whom their Lord and Savior died"—that is, Jews. By addressing Protestant complacency during the Nazi era, especially in the context of Hochhuth's indictment of Pope Pius XII and the Catholic Church, Niemöller offered his most direct challenge to the myth of Protestant resistance.[24]

Correcting this falsehood distinguished Niemöller from the many German Protestants who sought to favorably contrast the so-called Protestant resistance with the failures of Pius XII. Still, Niemöller did not engage in a forthright discussion of the church's sins of commission. Protestant anti-Semitism did not manifest itself simply as a failure to speak out against the persecution of Jews. The problem ran much deeper, as his reference to Luther's rabid anti-Semitism implied. That Christian anti-Semitism paved the way for Nazi anti-Semitism was something only a minority of Christians were ready to acknowledge in the 1950s and 1960s. Coming to terms with Christian complacency toward anti-Semitism required agreeing to speak out against Jewish persecution in the future and condemning it in the past. Coming to terms with Christian complicity in the rise and perpetuation of anti-Semitism required a fundamental rethinking of centuries of Christian doctrine on Jews. Niemöller was prepared to do the former, but was still wrestling with the logic behind the latter.

The staging of Hochhuth's play coincided with the first tentative steps by Catholics and Protestants to address the two-thousand-year-old practice of Christian anti-Semitism. By this point, many of the church leaders from the Nazi period had retired or died, including Pope Pius XII, and new leaders had emerged who were more willing to rethink their faith's traditional attitude toward Jews. Beginning in 1961, the Protestant Church's biennial congresses not only included the topic of "Judaism and the Church" on the agenda but also invited Jewish scholars and theologians to participate. This marked the beginning of the post-Holocaust Jewish-Christian dialogue in the Protestant Church, a dialogue between Jewish scholars and religious leaders, including Rabbi Robert Rafael Geis, and a group of forward-thinking pastors from the Rhineland. That there were Jews willing to act as teachers and dialogue partners with postwar Christians was essential to the halting and painful process of addressing the church's long history of Christian anti-Semitism. The process culminated with the 1980 publication of a remarkable statement by the Rhineland pastors, "Towards the Renewal of the Relationship of Christians and Jews." The statement recognized Christian co-responsibility and guilt for the Holocaust; rejected the Church's mission to convert Jews (*Judenmission*); and affirmed the permanent election of the Jewish people as the people of God. Although Niemöller was not particularly active in this process of self-criticism, reflection, and reappraisal, he was supportive.[25]

IN DECEMBER 1964, forty years after his ordination in Münster, Niemöller retired as head of the Church in Hesse and Nassau, where he had overseen hundreds of congregations for sixteen years. In retirement, he still struggled to respond to the piles of correspondence he received every week. "In my study I am surrounded—now for more than six months—by a mountain of unanswered correspondence," he grumbled to a friend. As church president, he had three, and in special cases four, secretaries working for him. But after retiring, he had only one, his foster daughter Ingrid. "No wonder, that we both sometimes feel discouraged—we never see any real progress in getting rid of the mountain."[26]

As Niemöller's family kept growing through his children's marriages and their offspring, he relished his time with them and proudly noted their successes to his acquaintances. In October 1964, he became a great-grandfather when Brigitte's oldest daughter, Jutta—named after the sister she had lost in 1944 to diphtheria—had a son. Divorced from her attorney-inventor husband Benno Johannesson, Brigitte and her children had lived in Georgetown, Connecticut, for many years. That same year Martin and Else's youngest child, "little Tini," now thirty and a judge near Wiesbaden, married. Niemöller's two oldest boys, Hermann and Jan, were also married with children and living in Germany; Hermann had recently returned from several years of employment at Yale University's medical school. Hertha lived with her husband, Wilhelm von Klewitz, and five children in Yugoslavia, where Wilhelm was a German consul in Zagreb.[27]

But Niemöller was not one to spend his retirement bouncing grandchildren on his knee. As his itinerary for the first six months of his retirement indicates, he planned to devote his time almost entirely to travel connected with his ecumenical and peace work. In January 1965, he went to French Equatorial Africa (now Gabon) on Africa's west coast to visit his friend Albert Schweitzer at his famous missionary hospital in Lambaréné. Schweitzer, the Nobel Peace Prize recipient in 1952, was active in the anti–atomic weapons movement. After his visit with Schweitzer, Niemöller attended the WCC central committee meeting in Enugu, Nigeria, and later traveled to Ghana. After a brief stop in Wiesbaden to replenish his energy, he was off to the United States for the entirety of Lent and the two weeks after Easter. Another quick respite in Wiesbaden was followed by a trip to southwest England (Somerset, Devonshire, and Cornwall). He was in Bangkok and Vietnam in July

1965 and soon enough went back to Geneva for another WCC meeting. Later that same summer, he went to Puerto Rico for the World Convention of Churches of Christ, where he shared the stage with Martin Luther King Jr. From there he flew to Southern Rhodesia before going back to the United States to take a two-week summer vacation with Brigitte in Connecticut. The fall brought more of the same. He spent more than two hundred days abroad in 1965.[28]

Niemöller's trip to South Vietnam in July 1965 was in response to President Lyndon Johnson's announcement of Operation Rolling Thunder, the sustained aerial bombardment of Communist North Vietnam that had begun in March. The American Fellowship of Recognition called for an immediate cessation to the bombing in a full-page ad in the April 4 edition of the *New York Times*: "Mr. President, In the Name of God, Stop It!" Twenty-five hundred American clergymen signed the letter. The bombing campaign and the almost simultaneous arrival of American ground troops in South Vietnam motivated Niemöller to take action.

Niemöller joined Alfred Hassler, the FOR executive secretary, and a dozen American pacifists and clergy on a fact-finding mission to South Vietnam in the summer of 1965. While in Saigon, the delegation received a cablegram from Martin Luther King Jr., commending them on their "all-important mission to Vietnam." Niemöller was one of two European members of FOR on the trip; the other was the Frenchman André Trocmé, who had served as a pastor in the French town of Le Chambon-sur-Lignon in south-central France during the Nazi occupation. Pastor Trocmé and his wife Magda urged their congregation of Protestant Huguenots to shelter Jews in the hilly region of Le Chambon during the roundups and deportations in 1942. Their efforts and those of surrounding parishes saved as many as five thousand lives.[29]

The twelve Americans and two Europeans spent five days in Vietnam meeting with journalists, government and military officials, students, trade unionists, and prominent Vietnamese Buddhists and Catholics. Niemöller and the delegates were most impressed with the active role of the Buddhist monks in the political struggle against US intervention.

FOR delegates published a report following their trip calling on the United Nations to convene a peace conference. The report concluded with a paragraph that could have come from one of Niemöller's sermons following his embrace of pacifism and racial harmony.

> We have lived too long within the traditional concepts of nation against nation, ideology against ideology, race against race. Today we see the true enemies of man to be what they have always been: injustice, poverty, disease, national pride, the abuse of power, and the hatred and war that are their creatures and creators. To be complacent about these is to deny humanity itself. To focus our attack on these evils rather than to fight within the family of man is to stand with the God of History.[30]

In January 1967, when he was seventy-four years old, Niemöller traveled to Vietnam again, but this time he went to Hanoi, the capital of North Vietnam. The purpose was to find out for himself what the Communists stood for and how he and other pacifists could help end the war and aid its victims. A. J. Muste, the eighty-two-year-old American pastor and political activist, led the four-man delegation, having received an invitation from North Vietnamese president Ho Chi Minh. Along with Muste and Niemöller were two younger men—both sixty-seven years old—Rabbi Abraham Feinberg of Toronto and Ambrose Reeves, an assistant bishop of the diocese of Chichester, England.[31]

Their two-week stay in North Vietnam was both illuminating and depressing. They visited the Hanoi suburb of Nhat Tan, which American pilots had bombed several months earlier, and were horrified by the destruction. They met two girls in the local hospital who had been paralyzed by shrapnel; their little sister had been killed along with twenty-three other villagers. "It was more than a person could bear," Muste said. "I just couldn't take it." But the mostly Catholic inhabitants impressed the visitors with their fortitude; they had already rebuilt their church and kindergarten. The pastors also met with two American pilots being held prisoner, who praised the treatment by their captors. Were they brainwashed or tortured, the visitors wondered? Apparently neither, they

Martin Niemöller during a controversial visit with Ho Chi Minh in Hanoi, North Vietnam, 1967. (Associated Press)

concluded. On two occasions, Niemöller and the others had to take cover in concrete bunkers as bombers flew over the area, though no bombs were dropped.[32]

Before leaving Hanoi, the four men met with Ho Chi Minh and Premier Pham Van Dong. They conversed in English, which Ho said he had learned as a cook in Soho and Harlem as a young man in New York. At seventy-seven, the president seemed pleased to be meeting with other men of advanced age. After some casual back-and-forth, Ho turned serious. He had a message for the Americans in the group to take back home. If the United States stopped the bombing, he would be glad to invite President Lyndon Johnson for tea, he told them.

> Mr. Johnson has said that he would meet anyone, anywhere, anytime to talk about peace. I invite him to come here as our guest, sitting where you are. Let Mr. Johnson come with his wife and daughter, his secre-

tary, his doctor and his cook. Let him not come with a gun on his hip or with generals and admirals. As an old revolutionary, I pledge my honor that Mr. Johnson will have complete security.

JUST TWO WEEKS after returning from Hanoi, Niemöller's American comrade, A. J. Muste, died of a heart attack. Muste, along with others in the international pacifist movement, had been instrumental in the German pastor's conversion to the antiwar movement. The visit to Hanoi and the death of Muste further galvanized Niemöller to work to stop the war.[33]

Back in Germany, Niemöller told the popular news weekly *Der Spiegel* that Ho Chi Minh was neither a fanatic nor a pawn of Communist China, but a proud and humane man who would continue to fight until the Americans left Vietnam. When the Americans stop the bombing, Niemöller said, they can expect Ho to extend an invitation to tea. He left no doubt about his opinion of the war. "What the US is doing today in Vietnam is not just a crime in the sense of its irresponsible inhumanity, it is a supreme stupidity because it will sow hatred and enmity" toward Americans for years to come. He went even further during a commemoration speech at Dachau, describing the US war in Vietnam as comparable "in every aspect" with what took place in the concentration camp. His harsh criticism of the US presence in Vietnam and his praise for Ho Chi Minh did not go over well with many Americans.[34]

In a speech to the West German Women's Peace Movement on October 29, 1967, in Cologne, Niemöller said that US soldiers being held prisoner in North Vietnam were not POWs but—legally speaking—criminals, because the United States had not officially declared war; he added that the North Vietnamese were treating the American prisoners well. The *Philadelphia Daily News* covered Niemöller's address the next day. An agitated *Daily News* reader challenged Niemöller. She wrote him wanting to know why Germans were so concerned with the US presence in Vietnam. Niemöller responded, "Surely the fate of 32 million human beings in Vietnam are our concern just as well and even more urgent than yours." Next to the Statue of Liberty in New York, he would say later, "should stand the Statue of Responsibility!"[35]

Later that year, the Soviet Union awarded Niemöller the Lenin Prize, the Communist counterpart to the Nobel Peace Prize, which included a cash award of 25,000 rubles, or $28,000. A government-appointed panel chose half a dozen Lenin Prize awardees each year, typically bestowing the honor on foreign Communists, such as Fidel Castro in 1961, or individuals friendly to the Communist cause. After participating in the WCC central committee meeting on the island of Crete in August 1967, Niemöller made his seventh trip to the Soviet Union to formally accept the award and meet with Russian church leaders. He announced from Moscow that he would donate nearly half of the prize money to the North Vietnamese Red Cross. The Soviet Union's Tass news agency quoted Niemöller saying, "With this money the Democratic Republic of Vietnam [North Vietnam] Red Cross will be able to purchase medicines and medical instruments and the money will thus bring much more use than if I had kept it." Afterwards he went on holiday eighty miles north of Moscow in Zavidovo, known during the Soviet era as the "politburo hunting preserve" and the "Soviet equivalent of Camp David." "I'm spending most of my beautiful holiday in the Russian woods," he told Henry Smith Leiper in a letter, "walking every day 15 to 20 miles, which surely is the most profitable way to get rid of the world and its troubles: no mail, no newspapers, no radio, no television, but only sunshine and rain, woods and water, days and nights—the ideal Indian summer!"[36]

It is truly remarkable that the same Martin Niemöller who had led a battalion of right-wing extremists in 1920 against German Communist workers during the Ruhr uprising was by the late 1960s praising the likes of Ho Chi Minh and vacationing in Zavidovo as a recipient of the Lenin Prize. Appearances aside, Niemöller had not become a Communist, but his hatred for the ideology had subsided. He now saw communism as both an appealing ideology for poor people and poor nations and an alternative to the consumerist and capitalist tendencies of the United

States and much of the Western world. Nevertheless, his desire to bridge East and West, North and South, through dialogue and mutual trust seems to have blinded him to the harsh realities and criminal nature of communism—the material deprivations, the lack of freedom and due process, and the mass incarcerations and executions. His willingness to work with Communist regimes rather than fight them was a product of the convergence of several factors: naïveté, an overestimation of the effectiveness of dialogue, and an aversion to Western imperialism and self-importance.[37]

ALTHOUGH HE HAD many friends and a large family, Niemöller told his friend Ewart Turner on several occasions that, since Else's death, "I am the loneliest man in the world." The sudden death in 1968 of Gladys Boggess, a close American friend from his first US visit, further depleted the ranks of his personal friends and of "those who kept a loving memory of Mutti." His "family" at 3 Brentanostrasse in Wiesbaden now consisted of Grete Lemke, the Niemöllers' former cook from Dahlem, who had taken Dora Schulz's place as his housekeeper. Grete had left the Dahlem parsonage in 1939 when she married, but she lost her husband in the fighting in 1941. After the war, Niemöller adopted her daughter, Ingrid. Niemöller, Grete, and Ingrid acted as parents of the youngest resident of the house, Hertha's son Martin. The boy, who had been in the tragic car accident, was now fourteen and attending high school in Wiesbaden because there was no German school in Zagreb, where his parents lived. Rounding out the household were two small Dachshunds, Racker and Rascal, who, Niemöller explained, "regarded themselves as full members of the family—and they are!" Slowing down in his later years, Niemöller was no longer insistent on fixing the world himself. "I have to acknowledge that I have become old after all," he confided to a friend, "and I feel not even sorry for that, since there is a younger generation demanding its own, and they must have it and live it as we did. But I do hope that they will do it in a better and more Christian way than we did!"[38]

Despite Niemöller's record of dramatic life changes, no one, least of all himself, could have guessed what was to come next. In the spring of 1968, though he was dealing with heart troubles, he traveled to the East Coast of the United States for various speaking engagements. There was no shortage of old friends, colleagues, and well-wishers who wanted to meet with the famed pastor for a meal, a glass of wine, or a photo opportunity. One invitation, however, caught his attention, coming as it did from a former Dahlem parishioner he had confirmed as a young girl, Sibylle von Sell.

Niemöller had first met Sibylle and her family forty years earlier, in June 1931, on the day that the retiring Dahlem pastor introduced the young Martin Niemöller as his replacement to St. Anne's parishioners. Among the churchgoers was a reluctant eight-year-old girl, the daughter of Prussian nobles, Baroness Augusta von Sell and Baron Ulrich von Sell. Her father, a decorated army officer, was a close confidant of the exiled kaiser, Wilhelm II, and manager of his estate. During the Nazi regime, Baron von Sell's contacts with the resistance among the officer corps led to his arrest after the failed July 20, 1944, plot to assassinate Hitler. He was spared the fate of Claus von Stauffenberg and the other conspirators but died from exposure and starvation in November 1945 in a Soviet POW camp near Berlin.[39]

Sibylle later wrote that her first encounter with Pastor Niemöller in 1931 had two significant consequences. First, her parents developed a close relationship with the pastor and his wife Else. And second, she formed friendships with the six Niemöller children (Brigette, Jochen, Hermann, Jan, Hertha, and Jutta), then ages four to twelve. She loved the antics and high spirits at the rectory, so different from the subdued atmosphere in her own home. Even then Dora was a member of the household—and apparently the only one able to control the pandemonium.

After the war, appalled by the failure of so many of her Protestant countrymen to take responsibility for the Holocaust, Sibylle left the Lutheran Church, emigrated to the United States, and became an American citizen. When Sibylle and Martin reconnected in 1968, she was living in a brownstone in Brooklyn Heights with her teenage son, having been recently abandoned by her second husband. She read in a newspaper about Niemöller's scheduled appearance at a Brooklyn church, wondering, as she later recounted, "Should I dare to contact him? Would the man who had risen to world fame remember the freckled child who had once roamed the rectory in Dahlem with his own children over thirty years ago?" She braved a call to his hotel. Not only did he remember her, but he invited her to lunch at the Gramercy Park Hotel. Soon she was visiting him in Wiesbaden. They fell in love, and Martin proposed.

Ten years a widower in August 1971, seventy-nine-year-old Martin Niemöller married forty-eight-year-old Sibylle von Sell in a simple ceremony in the old Wiesbaden City Hall. The marriage of the retired pastor to his former confirmation student thirty years his junior became a topic of conversation that summer in Germany. "It's typical of his independence," one of his colleagues from the church resistance offered. That a religious ceremony did not follow the civil one led to some tongue-wagging. "The scandalous fact that I was not a member of the church," Sibylle explained in her autobiography, "remained a deep, dark secret between my husband and myself." Since Niemöller, a grandfather and great-grandfather, had previously announced his intention to move to a senior citizens' residence in Darmstadt, the marriage was at first met with surprise and some resistance by his children. Sibylle's son, stung by his first stepfather's desertion, was wary of yet another stepfather, but the new man in his mother's life turned out to be so welcoming and loving that the boy took his last name, becoming U. Marcus Niemoeller. Marcus moved into the Wiesbaden villa with his mother and attended the American military high school in Wiesbaden. Later, like his stepbrother Hermann, he became a medical doctor.[40]

After the marriage, Sibylle went right to work cleaning house at 3 Brentanostrasse. First to go was Niemöller's old housekeeper Grete. His wardrobe and furniture followed soon after. She replaced Grete with a "competent new housekeeper," his clothes with tasteful tweeds, and the furniture with von Sell family heirlooms. Martin remained in charge of purchasing his treasured cigars, and his study remained his personal fiefdom. He still pulled out his old typewriter from his Dahlem days to write lectures and listened to recordings of American musicals on his old phonograph.

"My home has returned to normalcy again," Niemöller wrote Turner. Sibylle did not marry to wait on her new husband hand and foot—she spent long hours as a volunteer at the American Red Cross at the Wiesbaden US Air Force Hospital a block from their home—but she did provide him with the love and attention he desired. And he liked that his wife was not a stereotypical pastor's wife. She wore makeup, nail polish, and fashionable clothes and chauffeured him around in her American car with its New York license plates. From the backseat, he entertained his stylish chauffeur with songs from his favorite American musicals and stories about his meetings with everyone from Hitler and Ho Chi Minh to Bing Crosby and Billy Graham.[41]

ADVANCED YEARS MIGHT have slowed Martin Niemöller down, but he still kept a busy schedule, attending WCC meetings, guest preaching, officiating at baptisms, weddings, and funerals, and, of course, keeping up with his correspondence. Into his eighties, he managed to put in long days, broken up by welcome naps. He was too busy to write the autobiography that his friend Turner was always prodding him to do. It was not only that such a project would have been time-consuming. It was that Niemöller believed few memoirists were capable of escaping the temptation of self-justification. "I don't like to influence criticism of history in any way by my own 'judgment,'" he told the disappointed Turner. "The tomorrow still keeps so many tasks waiting, which is quite sufficient for my thinking and working."[42]

Niemöller was pleased that a younger generation in Germany, born after 1945 and coming of age in the late 1960s and '70s, eagerly wanted to take West Germany in a liberalizing direction. The 68ers, as they were called, demanded a thorough reckoning with the Nazi past, a genuine commitment to democratic institutions, and an end to Western imperialism. Similar to youth in other Western nations, they railed against the materialism and conservatism of the middle class. The German 68ers did have distinguishing features, of course. They took particular issue with the fact that many former Nazis and Nazi sympathizers had escaped punishment and were ensconced in the government, armed forces, economic institutions, and universities. Although the political and social commitments of the 68ers overlapped with Niemöller's desire to see a complete reorientation of German society, the younger generation was not motivated, for the most part, by Christianity. Some factions on the student left were atheistic, including the militant wing of the protest movement, the Red Army Faction (RAF), also known as the Baader-Meinhof Gang, which sought the violent overthrow of the "fascist" and "imperialist" West German government.

Even as an octogenarian, Niemöller participated in peaceful demonstrations organized by 68ers. He was appalled, however, by the militancy of the Baader-Meinhof Gang, as well as the West German government's inordinately violent response to it. The RAF was an urban guerrilla group that, in the name of the exploited Third World, engaged in bombings, assassinations, kidnappings, bank robberies, and shoot-outs with police. By the fall of 1977, many of the RAF's original leaders had been arrested and were held in a new "super-max" prison designed to make their lives unbearable. Hoping to win their comrades' freedom, on July 30, 1977, three RAF militants attempted to kidnap the president of Dresdner Bank at his home in Frankfurt; they planned to use him as a bargaining chip for their colleagues' release. But when he resisted, they killed him. And so the RAF struck again: on September 5, they abducted Hanns Martin Schleyer, president of two powerful business organizations. Ambushing his motorcade, the kidnappers took Schleyer alive but murdered his chauffeur and three police escorts.

Niemöller became entangled in this bloody affair when the kidnappers demanded an airplane to take them where they wanted, that imprisoned RAF members be released, and that two hostages accompany them to their destination—in order to ensure that the government did not try to stop them. One of the proposed hostages was the eighty-five-year-old Martin Niemöller. Although Niemöller was prepared to play his assigned role to save Schleyer's life, the Bonn government refused the RAF's demands. When on October 18 the kidnappers learned that their three imprisoned leaders, including Andreas Baader, had been found dead in their cells, two with gunshot wounds to the head, they executed Schleyer. The authorities maintained that the deaths of the RAF prisoners were suicides, but the militants insisted that they were murdered by the "neofascist" West German authorities.

Ardent pacifist that he had become, Niemöller was sickened by the leftist violence. But he was also deeply concerned, as many on the left were, by the extreme antiterrorist measures passed by the West German government in the 1970s that limited the freedoms of speech and association and subjected imprisoned terrorists to long periods of solitary confinement. He feared that the government's attack on the far left signaled a resurgence of right-wing nationalist tendencies on the part of the West German state.[43]

The last few years of Niemöller's life were quiet by comparison. His newfound contentment and happiness with Sibylle were tempered in 1976 when a terrible sadness enveloped the family. Hertha's eldest son Martin—the boy who had survived the car crash that killed his grandmother—committed suicide in Copenhagen when he learned that the girl he deeply loved had left him. He was not quite twenty-three.[44]

Martin and Sibylle made their last overseas trip together in 1979 to attend Marcus's graduation from Greensboro College in North Carolina. Beginning in the summer of 1981 and for the two years that followed, the greatest commotion Niemöller had to endure was the filming in his home of a feature-length documentary about his life, entitled *What Would Jesus Say?* His health deteriorated to such a degree that he could only do interviews twice a week for a few hours at a time. Just as the crew was wrapping up the film in 1983, Niemöller was diagnosed with cancer and told he had only months to live.

One of his last visitors in the summer of 1983 was his friend Linus Pauling, the winner of two Nobel Prizes, the Nobel Prize in Chemistry in 1954 and the Nobel Peace Prize in 1962. Pauling and Niemöller had become acquainted in the late 1950s as a result of their mutual efforts in the peace movement. In 1960, Niemöller was invited to a "garden party" in California to honor the work of Pauling and his wife. The invitation asked if he would be an "Honorary Sponsor" of the garden party. "I am not very well informed with the social habits in these kind of affairs as they are common and natural in California," Niemöller responded, "but in any case I should be only too glad for your kind invitation to join with you in paying tribute to the Paulings and to become an Honorary Sponsor of the planned garden party." When the two met twenty-three years later in the Niemöllers' Wiesbaden garden, Pauling was there to pay tribute to Niemöller. "On an enchanted Indian summer afternoon," Sibylle recalled, "Marcus carried his father, now light as a feather, into the garden, and we were touched to see the two seasoned old peace veterans holding hands, laughing, and crying with joy over their unexpected reunion."[45]

On January 14, 1984, on Niemöller's ninety-second birthday, Sibylle and Marcus invited the entire family and many of his friends to celebrate his extraordinary life and to say their good-byes. A trombone trio played all of Martin's favorites. Even in his debilitated state, propped up in bed by pillows, he managed a smile and responded gratefully to his visitors.

On March 6, 1984, Martin Niemöller died peacefully in his own bed surrounded by family. He was laid to rest in the cemetery in the small Westphalian village of Wersen, his family's ancestral home. The gravesite bears a cross of black granite with the words, LORD, WHAT WILLST THOU HAVE ME DO? and a granite plate inscribed with the following words:

D. Martin Niemöller
Pastor in Berlin-Dahlem 1931–1945
Hitler's prisoner 1937–1945
President of the Church in
Hessen and Nassau 1947–1964
President of the World Council
of Churches 1961–1968
Confessor of Faith
Defender of Peace

Conclusion

MARTIN NIEMÖLLER IS REMEMBERED TODAY AS THE PRINCIPLED PAStor who defied the Nazis and wrote the famous postwar confession, "First they came for the Communists. . . ." His name is linked with anti-Nazi resistance and the moral imperative to come to the defense of persecuted minorities. His standing in popular culture is not without merit. He did defy Hitler's attempts to Nazify the Protestant Church, and he was arrested and imprisoned on Hitler's personal orders. Later, he encouraged people to speak out when other human beings were being attacked, whatever their race, religion, or political beliefs.

But he was also an influential pastor who voted for the Nazis, welcomed Hitler's rise, and showed contempt for groups he deemed anti-Christian and anti-German. His dissent during the Nazi era was a defense of the German Protestant Church. In this respect, it is just as legitimate to group him with—as his critics do—Hitler's early enablers.

It is tempting for admirers to rationalize Niemöller's earlier years by speaking in terms of a clean break between a young, imprudent Niemöller, on the one hand, and a mature, wiser Niemöller, on the other. But Martin Niemöller was a forty-one-year-old father of six, with two decades of professional experience, when he applauded Hitler's ascension to power. He was a middle-aged man who had read *Mein Kampf* and knew very well what Hitler stood for. And even after he watched Hitler abolish the national parliament, ban political parties and trade unions, and persecute his opponents, Niemöller refused to distance himself from radical nationalism and anti-Semitism—even on occasion after 1945.

Once the legend is stripped away, Niemöller necessarily disappoints us. In contrast to other great foes of tyranny, including Mahatma Gandhi and Aleksandr Solzhenitsyn, or even his younger German colleague Dietrich Bonhoeffer, Niemöller was on the wrong side of history for much of his life. He was a fantastically capable administrator, an effective orator, and a tireless devotee of whatever cause he was supporting at a given time. Yet in some ways he was an ordinary, and ordinarily flawed, human being.

But it is the imperfection of Niemöller's moral compass that makes him all the more relevant today. This middle-class, conservative Protestant, who harbored ingrained prejudices against those not like him, did something excruciatingly difficult for someone of his background: he changed his mind. Hitler's persecution of the churches and Niemöller's arrest and imprisonment initiated a process of rethinking his biased and narrow-minded convictions. Niemöller did not emerge from Dachau a completely changed man. His evolution was gradual, halting, and in many respects incomplete. But change he did. And in his fifties, sixties, and seventies, he labored relentlessly to make a better, more equal, and more peaceful world. His impact was most evident in the way he inspired those who came out to see and hear him speak, whether in a church in Arizona, at an antinuclear rally in England, or at a World Council of Churches meeting in Nigeria. And of course, his most inspirational words—even if they were not as central to his life as we would like to believe—survive him.

Niemöller reminds us of the difficulty of recognizing our faults and renouncing our most cherished convictions. He often posed the question, "Lord, what will you have me do?" when he was troubled. But in the final count, he relied on his own judgment. When the facts indicated that he had taken the wrong path, the former U-boat pilot changed course, albeit grudgingly and often very slowly. Niemöller was neither chameleon nor opportunist; at his core was a resolute certainty that his conscience, dictated by love of God and homeland, would lead him down the right path.

Many of his German contemporaries—people born at the end of the nineteenth century and living into the post-1945 period—were unwilling to criticize their own actions during the Third Reich. Nor were they willing to adapt to the world that emerged from the war. In this sense, Niemöller is something of an exception, and an admirable one. But while his willingness to change is laudable, Niemöller is far too complex a character for hero worship.

Niemöller's legacy to the twenty-first century is mixed. On the one hand, the bigotry and radical nationalism that characterized the first half of his life are repellent in an increasingly global and diverse world. On the other hand, he also provides an example of how we can all change—an imperfect example to be sure, but a useful one nevertheless. By coming to terms with his past and dedicating his later life to the service of justice, peace, and love for one's neighbor, he inspires us to look at our own prejudices and to try to do better.

Acknowledgments

I N THE PROCESS OF WRITING *THEN THEY CAME FOR ME*, I HAVE benefited from the support and encouragement of many people and institutions.

Most of all I would like to thank John Conway, whose death in 2017 was a major loss to the field of German church history. From his office at the University of British Columbia, John did more than anyone to foster a sense of community among German church historians in North America. His personal attention to my scholarship and generosity with his time since the mid-1990s was unparalleled. I would also like to thank Victoria Barnett, director of the United States Holocaust Memorial Museum's Programs on Ethics, Religion, and the Holocaust, for her unflagging support for this project. Her balanced and insightful scholarship on Dietrich Bonhoeffer and the German Church Struggle is a model I have striven to emulate. I also owe a debt of gratitude to Doris Bergen at the University of Toronto and Mark Ruff at Saint Louis University for their encouragement and willingness to act as referees for several grants I applied for. And finally, I would like to thank Benjamin Ziemman at the University of Sheffield and Harold Marcuse at the University of California–Santa Barbara, for their collegiality and assistance. The opinions and theses in this book are entirely my own, and I do not assume that any of the colleagues I've thanked will share all or any of them with me.

More generally, I owe a considerable debt to the growing corpus of scholarship on German church history, which I have drawn on to contextualize Martin Niemöller's life. Colleagues who sit with me on the editorial board of the *Contemporary Church History Quarterly*—a periodical founded by John Conway—are responsible for a good deal of this scholarship. German scholars, however, many of whom I have not met personally, have produced the bulk of this scholarship, and it is to them that I also wish to extend my gratitude.

But what really brought Niemöller to life for me was reading his correspondence with family, friends, and colleagues—and not a few adversaries—held in archives in Europe and the United States. For the opportunity to view this material, it gives me great pleasure to thank the archivists and their associates for assisting with my research. The primary source of archival material was the Zentralarchiv der Evangelischen Kirche in Hessen und Nassau in Darmstadt, Germany, which holds the papers and correspondence of Martin Niemöller. I also consulted the archives affiliated with the World Council of Churches in Geneva, Switzerland, the Presbyterian Historical Society and the Swarthmore College Peace Collection in Philadelphia, and the US National Archives and Records Administration in College Park, Maryland, among others. Crucial to carrying out my research was funding I received from the German Academic Exchange Service (DAAD), the American Philosophical Society, and Skidmore College.

For their editorial advice and assistance, I would like to thank Anne Hockenos, Paul Hockenos, Simon Waxman, and my editor at Basic Books, Dan Gerstle. My literary agent, Rob McQuilkin of Massie & McQuilkin, has been a constant source of encouragement and useful advice. I would also like to thank my research assistants at Skidmore College for taking time from their busy academic schedules to assist me.

Notes

INTRODUCTION

1. In fact, the death toll on the plaque was wrong. Although the actual figure is closer to 42,000, according to Dachau scholars, it is no less distressing. The number of people cremated was likely 15,000 to 20,000, according to Harold Marcuse. See Barbara Distel, "Dachau Main Camp," trans. Stephen Pallavicini, in *The United States Holocaust Memorial Museum Encyclopedia of Camps and Ghettos, 1933–1945*, ed. Geoffrey P. Megargee (Bloomington: Indiana University Press, 2009), 442–446; Harold Marcuse, "Dachau," in *Europe since 1914: Encyclopedia of the Age of War and Reconstruction*, vol. 2, ed. John Merriman and J. M. Winter (Detroit: Charles Scribner's Sons, 2006), 764; Harold Marcuse, "The Origin and Reception of Martin Niemöller's Quotation 'First They Came for the Communists . . . ,'" in *Remembering for the Future: Armenia, Auschwitz, and Beyond*, ed. Michael Berenbaum et al. (St. Paul, MN: Paragon, 2016), 173–199.

2. Niemöller tells the Dachau story in his 1946 address and essay "Der Weg ins Freie" ("The Path to Freedom"). The essay appears in several collections of essays by Niemöller, including Martin Niemöller, *Gewissen vor Staatsräson: Ausgewählte Schriften*, ed. Joachim Perels (Göttingen: Wallstein, 2016), 47–72, 56–58.

3. Quoted in Eberhard Busch, *Karl Barth: His Life from Letters and Autobiographical Texts*, trans. John Bowden (Philadelphia: Fortress Press, 1976), 233.

CHAPTER 1: WITH GOD FOR KING AND FATHERLAND (1892–1914)

1. Martin Niemöller, *From U-Boat to Pulpit* (Chicago: Willett, Clark & Co., 1937), 182; Heinrich Niemöller, *Aus 56 Amtsjahren* (Bielefeld: Ludwig Bechauf Verlag, 1948), 5; Wilhelm Niemöller to "Meine lieben Kinder," August 26, 1940, Zentralarchiv der Evangelischen Kirche in Hessen und Nassau (ZA EKHN), Bestand 62 (record group 62), Aktenzeichen 1295 (file number 1295) (hereafter, for example, ZA EKHN, B. 62/1295); interview with Günter Gaus in Martin Niemöller, *Was würde Jesus dazu sagen? Reden, Predigten, Aufsätze 1937–1980* (Berlin: Union, 1980), 173–190. Wilhelm Niemöller's letter to his children is a thirty-five-page, single-spaced document about his family.

2. Wilhelm Niemöller to "Meine lieben Kinder," August 26, 1940, ZA EKHN, B. 62/1295.

3. Franz Hildebrandt, *Pastor Niemöller and His Creed* (London: Hodder & Stoughton, 1939), 31; interview with Günter Gaus in Niemöller, *Was würde Jesus dazu sagen?*, 174; Martin Niemöller, speech, Boston University, December 2, 1955, ZA EKHN, B. 62/500.

4. Hannes Karnick and Wolfgang Richter, *Niemöller: Was Würde Jesus dazu Sagen?* (Frankfurt: Röderberg, 1986), 16.

5. Magdalene Niemöller, "Mein Bruder Martin," Ewart E. Turner Papers, SCRC 81, Special Collections Research Center, Temple University Libraries, Philadelphia, PA (hereafter Turner Papers, Temple University).

6. Karnick and Richter, *Niemöller: Was Würde Jesus dazu Sagen?*, 15.

7. Magdalene Niemöller, "Mein Bruder Martin," Turner Papers, Temple University.

8. Hannes Karnick and Wolfgang Richter, eds., *Protestant: Das Jahrhundert des Pastors Martin Niemöller* (Frankfurt: Evangelischer Presseverband in Hessen und Nassau, 1992), 18–21.

9. Magdalene Niemöller, "Mein Bruder Martin," Turner Papers, Temple University.

10. Jonathan Sperber, "The Transformation of Catholic Associations in the Northern Rhineland and Westphalia, 1830–1870," *Journal of Social History* 15, no. 2 (Winter 1981): 253–263; Jonathan Sperber, "Roman Catholic Religious Identity in Rhineland-Westphalia, 1800–70: Quantitative Examples and Some Political Implications," *Social History* 7, no. 3 (October 1982): 305–318; Helmut Walser Smith, *German Nationalism and Religious Conflict: Culture, Ideology, Politics, 1870–1914* (Princeton, NJ: Princeton University Press, 1995), 95; Wolfgang Altgeld, "German Catholics," in *The Emancipation of Catholics, Jews, and Protestants: Minorities and the Nation State in Nineteenth-Century Europe*, ed. Rainer Liedtke and Stephan Wendehorst (Manchester, UK: Manchester University Press, 1999), 100–121, 121.

11. *German-Jewish History in Modern Times*, vol. 3, *Integration in Dispute, 1871–1918*, ed. Michael Meyer (New York: Columbia University Press, 1997), 27; Martin Niemöller, notes on stationery from the Biltmore Hotel, Los Angeles, 1947, Turner Papers, Temple University; interview with Günter Gaus in Niemöller, *Was würde Jesus dazu sagen?*, 189; Wolfgang Gerlach, *And the Witnesses Were Silent: The Confessing Church and the Persecution of the Jews*, trans. Victoria Barnett (Lincoln: University of Nebraska Press, 2000), 47.

12. Holger H. Herwig, *Hammer or Anvil? Modern Germany 1648–Present* (Lexington, MA: D. C. Heath and Co., 1994), 174.

13. John C. G. Röhl, *Kaiser Wilhelm II, 1859–1941: A Concise Life* (Cambridge: Cambridge University Press, 2014), 25, 28; John C. G. Röhl, *Young Wilhelm: The Kaiser's Early Life, 1859–1888* (Cambridge: Cambridge University Press, 1998), 825.

14. Isabel Hull, "Prussian Dynastic Ritual and the End of the Monarchy," in *German Nationalism and the European Response 1890–1945*, ed. Isabel Hull et al. (Norman: University of Oklahoma Press, 1985), 13; Holger Herwig, *Luxury Fleet: The Imperial German Navy 1888–1918* (London: George Allen & Unwin, 1980), 23; Bernd Sösemann, "Hollow-Sounding Jubilees: Forms and Effects of Public Display in Wilhelmine Germany," in *The Kaiser: New Research on Wilhelm II's Role in Imperial Germany*, ed. Annika Mombauer and Wilhelm Deist (Cambridge: Cambridge University Press, 2003), 39–40.

15. Barry Stephenson, *Performing the Reformation: Public Ritual in the City of Luther* (Oxford: Oxford University Press, 2010), 91–93.

16. Niemöller, *Aus 56 Amtsjahren*, 15; Dietmar Schmidt, *Pastor Niemöller* (Garden City, NY: Doubleday, 1959), 18.

17. Frank Nägler, "Operational and Strategic Plans in the Kaiser's Navy prior to World War I," in *Jutland: World War I's Greatest Naval Battle*, ed. Michael Epkenhans, Jörg Hillmann, and Frank Nägler (Lexington: University Press of Kentucky, 2015), 25–62, 25; Michael Epkenhans, "The Imperial Navy, 1914–1915," in Epkenhans et al., *Jutland: World War I's Greatest Naval Battle*, 118.

18. Herwig, *Luxury Fleet*, 52.

19. See Jan Rüger, *The Great Naval Game: Britain and Germany in the Age of Empire* (Cambridge: Cambridge University Press, 2007); Geoff Eley, *Reshaping the German Right: Radical Nationalism and Political Change after Bismarck* (New Haven, CT: Yale University Press, 1980), 218–226.

20. Eley, *Reshaping the German Right*, 218–221; Holger H. Herwig, *The German Naval Officer Corps: A Social and Political History, 1890–1918* (Oxford: Oxford University Press, 1973), 8.

21. Michael Epkenhans, "Wilhelm II and 'His' Navy, 1888–1918," in Mombauer and Deist, *The Kaiser*, 12–36, 17.

22. Thorsten Neubert-Preine, "The Founding of German Protestant Institutions in Jerusalem during the Reign of Kaiser Wilhelm II," in *Germany and the Middle East: Past, Present, and Future*, ed. Haim Goren (Jerusalem: Hebrew University Magnes Press, 2003), 31.

23. Niemöller, *Aus 56 Amtsjahren*, 24; Heinrich Niemöller, *Hinauf gen Jerusalem: Gedenkbuch der offiziellen Festfahrt zur Einweihung der Erlöserkirche in Jerusalem* (Berlin: Mittler, 1899), 1–2, 151–157.

24. John C. G. Röhl, *Wilhelm II: The Kaiser's Personal Monarchy, 1888–1900* (Cambridge: Cambridge University Press, 2004), 952; *The Kaiser's Speeches: Forming a Character Portrait of Emperor William II*, trans. Wolf von Schierbrand (New York: Harper & Brothers, 1903), 318.

25. Niemöller, *Hinauf gen Jerusalem*, 23, 72.

26. Magdalene Niemöller, "Mein Bruder Martin," Turner Papers, Temple University; Wilhelm Niemöller to "Meine lieben Kinder," August 26, 1940, ZA EKHN, B. 62/1295; Martin Niemöller, *Briefe aus der Gefangenschaft, Konzentrationslager Sachsenhausen (Oranienburg)*, ed. Wilhelm Niemöller (Frankfurt: Otto Lembeck, 1975), 135.

27. Wilhelm Niemöller to "Meine lieben Kinder," August 26, 1940, ZA EKHN, B. 62/1295.

28. Niemöller, *From U-Boat to Pulpit*, 183.

29. Wilhelm Niemöller to "Meine lieben Kinder," August 26, 1940, ZA EKHN, B. 62/1295; Karnick and Richter, *Protestant*, 20–21; Karnick and Richter, *Niemöller: Was Würde Jesus dazu Sagen?*, 14.

30. Harry Liebersohn, "Religion and Industrial Society: The Protestant Social Congress in Wilhelmine Germany," *Transactions of the American Philosophical Society*, New Series, 76, no. 6 (1986), 1–63, 18; Daniel R. Borg, *The Old-Prussian Church and the Weimar Republic: A Study in Political Adjustment, 1917–1927* (Hanover, NH: University Press of New England, 1984), 23.

31. Niemöller, *From U-Boat to Pulpit*, 183; Herwig, *The German Naval Officer Corps*, 33–34.

32. Holger H. Herwig, "Admirals versus Generals: The War Aims of the Imperial German Navy, 1914–1918," *Central European History* 5, no. 3 (September 1972): 208–233, 208–209.

33. Herwig, *Luxury Fleet*, 117–119; Herwig, *The German Naval Officer Corps*, 41–43, 45, 69.

34. Schmidt, *Pastor Niemöller*, 30–31; interview with Heinrich Werner of *Neuen Stimme* in Niemöller, *Was würde Jesus dazu sagen?*, 272–285, 282; Karnick and Richter, *Niemöller: Was Würde Jesus dazu Sagen?*, 16.

35. Herwig, *Luxury Fleet*, 119–120.

36. Jeffrey R. Smith, "The Monarchy versus the Nation: The 'Festive Year' 1913 in Wilhelmine Germany," *German Studies Review* 23, no. 2 (May 2000): 257–274, 257.

37. Smith, "The Monarchy versus the Nation," 262, 264.

38. See David Blackbourn, "The Politics of Demagogy in Imperial Germany," *Past and Present* 113 (November 1986): 152–184; Röhl, *Kaiser Wilhelm II, 1859–1941*, 57; Eley, *Reshaping the German Right*, 201.

39. See Martin Kitchen, *The German Officer Corps, 1800–1914* (Oxford: Oxford University Press, 1968), 187–221.

40. V. R. Berghahn, *Germany and the Approach of War in 1914* (New York: St. Martin's Press, 1973), 174; David Schoenbaum, *Zabern 1913: Consensus Politics in Imperial Germany* (London: George Allen & Unwin, 1982), 181; John C. G. Röhl, *Wilhelm II: Into the Abyss of War and Exile, 1900–1941* (Cambridge: Cambridge University Press, 2014), 972–979.

41. W. O. Henderson, *The Rise of German Industrial Power, 1834–1914* (Berkeley: University of California Press, 1975), 239–240.

CHAPTER 2: SERVING THE KAISER ON THE HIGH SEAS (1914–1918)

1. Niemöller, *From U-Boat to Pulpit*, 1–2.

2. Röhl, *Wilhelm II: Into the Abyss*, 1089; Hermann Franke, *Kriegspredigten 1914: gehalten in der Peter-Paul-Kirche zu Liegnitz* (Liegnitz: Seyffarth, 1914), 11, 30.

3. Jeffrey Verhey, *The Spirit of 1914: Militarism, Myth, and Mobilization in Germany* (New York: Cambridge University Press, 2000); Bernd Ulrich and Benjamin Ziemann, eds., *German Soldiers in the Great War: Letters and Eyewitness Accounts* (Barnsley, UK: Pen & Sword Military, 2010), 22; Volker Ullrich, *Kriegsalltag: Hamburg in Ersten Weltkrieg* (Cologne: Prometh, 1982); Benjamin Ziemann, *War Experiences in Rural Germany, 1914–1923* (Oxford: Bloomsbury Academic, 2007); Christian Geinitz, *Kriegsfurcht und Kampfbereitschaft: Das Augusterlebnis in Freiburg: Eine Studie zum Kriegsbeginn* (Essen: Klartext, 1998); Verhey, *The Spirit of 1914*, 159.

4. Wilhelm Niemöller to "Meine lieben Kinder," August 26, 1940, ZA EKHN, B. 62/1295; Jacob Peter Bang, *Hurrah and Hallelujah: The Spirit of New-Germanism: A Documentation* (London: Hodder and Stoughton, 1917), 75.

5. Ulrich and Ziemann, *German Soldiers in the Great War*, 94–95.

6. Quoted in "For What I Am," *Time*, June 18, 1945.

7. Paul G. Halpern, *A Naval History of World War I* (Annapolis, MD: Naval Institute Press, 1994), 287; Robert Weldon Whalen, *Bitter Wounds: German Victims of the Great War, 1914–1939* (Ithaca, NY: Cornell University Press,

1984), 71; C. Paul Vincent, *The Politics of Hunger: The Allied Blockade of Germany, 1915–1919* (Athens, OH: Ohio University Press, 1985), 20.

8. A. J. Hoover, *God, Germany, and Great Britain in the Great War: A Study in Clerical Nationalism* (New York: Praeger, 1989), 12–13.

9. Paul Halpern, "'Handelskrieg mit U-Booten': The German Submarine Offensive in World War I," in *Commerce Raiding: Historical Case Studies, 1755–2009*, ed. Bruce A. Elleman and S. C. M. Pain (Newport, RI: Naval War College Press, 2013), 135–150, 139; Epkenhans, "The Imperial Navy, 1914–1915," 124.

10. Lawrence Sondhaus, *The Great War at Sea: A Naval History of the First World War* (Cambridge: Cambridge University Press, 2014), 151.

11. Niemöller, *From U-Boat to Pulpit*, 2, 6.

12. *United States Naval Institute Proceedings* 42 (1916): 1044; Niemöller, *From U-Boat to Pulpit*, 18.

13. Halpern, *A Naval History of World War I*, 310–334.

14. Halpern, *A Naval History of World War I*, 329.

15. John Brooks, *Battle of Jutland* (Cambridge: Cambridge University Press, 2016), 515; Whalen, *Bitter Wounds*, 39–42; Richard Bessel, *Germany after the First World War* (Oxford: Clarendon Press, 1993), 6; Matthias Schreiber, *Martin Niemöller* (Hamburg: Rowohlt, 1997), 14.

16. Niemöller, *From U-Boat to Pulpit*, 27, 32.

17. "World War I U-boats: U 39," uboat.net, https://uboat.net/wwi/boats /?boat=39 (accessed December 28, 2017).

18. Walter Forstmann, *U39 auf Jag im Mittelmeer* (Berlin: Ullstein, 1918), 100–106, 105–106; Niemöller, *From U-Boat to Pulpit*, 45–46, 47.

19. See Hoover, "The Just War," chap. 7 in *God, Germany, and Great Britain in the Great War*, 103–118; Bang, *Hurrah and Hallelujah*, 75.

20. Bang, *Hurrah and Hallelujah*, 75, 112–113, 117.

21. Niemöller, *From U-Boat to Pulpit*, 184.

22. Lawrence Sondhaus, *German Submarine Warfare in World War I: The Onset of Total War at Sea* (Lanham, MD: Rowman & Littlefield, 2017), 28.

23. Dirk Bönker, "A German Way of War? Narratives of German Militarism and Maritime Warfare in World War I," in *Imperial Germany Revisited: Continuing Debates and New Perspectives*, ed. Cornelius Torp and Sven Oliver Müller (New York: Berghahn Books, 2011), 227–237, 229; Herwig, *Luxury Fleet*, 196–197; Halpern, *A Naval History of World War I*, 337–338, 341.

24. Halpern, *A Naval History of World War I*, 341.

25. Niemöller, *From U-Boat to Pulpit*, 49.

26. Niemöller, *From U-Boat to Pulpit*, 49–50; Edita Sterik, ed., *Else Niemöller, Die Frau eines bedeutenden Mannes: Ausstellung des Zentralarchivs der Evangelischen Kirche in Hessen und Nassau, 20 Juli 1990* (Hemsbach: Druckhaus Beltz, 1990), 12, 114.

27. Herwig, *Luxury Fleet*, 226.

28. Niemöller, *From U-Boat to Pulpit*, 42; Sondhaus, *The Great War at Sea*, 261; Herwig, *Luxury Fleet*, 243.

29. Niemöller, *From U-Boat to Pulpit*, 61.

30. Belinda Davis, *Home Fires Burning: Food, Politics, and Everyday Life in World War I Berlin* (Chapel Hill: University of North Carolina Press, 2000), 28–29, 83, 105, 140, 194; C. Paul Vincent, *The Politics of Hunger: The Allied Blockade of Germany, 1915–1919* (Athens: Ohio University Press, 1985), 137.

31. Niemöller, *From U-Boat to Pulpit*, 83; Ute Daniel, *The War from Within: German Working-Class Women in the First World War* (Oxford: Berg, 1997), 196.

32. Herwig, *Hammer or Anvil?*, 208.

33. Carl Schorske, *German Social Democracy, 1905–1917: The Development of the Great Schism* (Cambridge, MA: Harvard University Press, 1983), 312–321; F. L. Carsten, *War against War: British and German Radical Movements in the First World War* (Berkeley: University of California Press, 1982), 92–95; Ulrich and Ziemann, *German Soldiers in the Great War*, 171.

34. Herwig, *Hammer or Anvil?*, 209; Ulrich and Ziemann, *German Soldiers in the Great War*, 178.

35. Carsten, *War against War*, 184; Ulrich and Ziemann, *German Soldiers in the Great War*, 155.

36. Daniel Horn, *The German Naval Mutinies of World War I* (New Brunswick, NJ: Rutgers University Press, 1969), 57.

37. Carsten, *War against War*, 113; Herwig, *Luxury Fleet*, 250.

38. Horn, *The German Naval Mutinies of World War I*, 71.

39. Horn, *The German Naval Mutinies of World War I*, 94–95; Herwig, *Luxury Fleet*, 233; Michael Epkenhans, "'Red Sailors' and the Demise of the German Empire, 1918," in *Naval Mutinies of the Twentieth Century: An International Perspective*, ed. Christopher M. Bell and Bruce A. Elleman (Abingdon-on-Thames, UK: Taylor & Francis, 2004), 91.

40. Niemöller, *From U-Boat to Pulpit*, 97; Sterik, *Else Niemöller, Die Frau eines bedeutenden Mannes*, 114.

41. Isabel V. Hull, *Absolute Destruction: Military Culture and the Practices of War in Imperial Germany* (Ithaca, NY: Cornell University Press, 2004), 309; Röhl, *Wilhelm II: Into the Abyss*, 1149.

42. Niemöller, *From U-Boat to Pulpit*, 98, 112.

43. Epkenhans, "'Red Sailors' and the Demise of the German Empire," 98; Horn, *The German Naval Mutinies of World War I*, 205.

44. Niemöller, *From U-Boat to Pulpit*, 112.

45. Niemöller, *From U-Boat to Pulpit*, 112.

46. Nicolas Wolz, *From Imperial Splendour to Internment: The German Navy in the First World War* (Barnsley, UK: Seaforth, 2015), 179; Epkenhans, "'Red Sailors' and the Demise of the German Empire," 99.

47. Niemöller, *From U-Boat to Pulpit*, 116.

48. Niemöller, *From U-Boat to Pulpit*, 118.

CHAPTER 3: FROM U-BOAT TO PULPIT (1918–1933)

1. Sterik, *Else Niemöller, Die Frau eines bedeutenden Mannes*, 114.

2. Eric Weitz, *Weimar Germany: Promise and Tragedy* (Princeton, NJ: Princeton University Press, 2007), 32.

3. Karl-Wilhelm Dahm, "German Protestantism and Politics, 1918–39," *Journal of Contemporary History* 3, no. 1 (January 1968): 29–49; Karnick and Richter, *Niemöller: Was Würde Jesus dazu Sagen?*, 16–17.

4. Niemöller, *From U-Boat to Pulpit*, 124–125.

5. Niemöller, *From U-Boat to Pulpit*, 128.

6. Karnick and Richter, *Niemöller: Was Würde Jesus dazu Sagen?*, 23; Ernst von Salomon, *The Outlaws* (*Die Geächteten*), trans. Ian Morrow (London: J. Cape, 1931), 57.

7. Bernhard Sauer, *Schwarze Reichswehr und Fememorde: Eine Milieustudie zum Rechtsradikalismus in der Weimarer Republik* (Berlin: Metropol, 2004), 23; Karnick and Richter, *Niemöller: Was Würde Jesus dazu Sagen?*, 23, 41.

8. Niemöller, *From U-Boat to Pulpit*, 121.

9. Niemöller, *From U-Boat to Pulpit*, 128.

10. Karnick and Richter, *Niemöller: Was Würde Jesus dazu Sagen?*, 125; Bentley, *Martin Niemöller*, 21.

11. Ben Fowkes, *The German Left and the Weimar Republic: Selection of Documents* (Leiden and Boston: Brill, 2014), 204; Borg, *The Old-Prussian Church*, 218.

12. "Martin Niemöller Talking," interview with Paul Oestreicher, *The Listener*, February 27, 1964; Bentley, *Martin Niemöller*, 22.

13. Niemöller, *From U-Boat to Pulpit*, 139, 180–181.

14. Eberhard Kolb, *The Weimar Republic* (London: Unwin Hyman, 1988), 36; Robert G. Waite, *Vanguard of Nazism: The Free Corps Movement in Postwar Germany, 1918–1923* (Cambridge, MA: Harvard University Press, 1952), 150.

15. Waite, *Vanguard of Nazism*, 170.

16. Niemöller, *From U-Boat to Pulpit*, 148; Martin Niemöller to Harold J. Gordon, February 28, 1953, ZA EKHN, B. 62/510.

17. Niemöller, *From U-Boat to Pulpit*, 152.

18. Nigel Jones, *A Brief History of the Birth of the Nazis* (New York: Carroll & Graf, 2004), 199; Heinrich August Winkler, *Germany: The Long Road*

West, 1789–1933 (Oxford: Oxford University Press, 2006), 371; Niemöller, *From U-Boat to Pulpit*, 153.

19. Niemöller, *From U-Boat to Pulpit*, 155.

20. Borg, *The Old-Prussian Church and the Weimar Republic*, 1–8; Otto Dibelius, *Das Jahrhundert der Kirche* (Berlin: Furche-Verlag, 1928), 75; Klaus Scholder, *Die Kirchen zwischen Republik und Gewaltherrschaft* (Berlin: Siedler, 1988), 133.

21. Martin Kitchen, *A History of Modern Germany, 1800–2000* (Malden, MA: Blackwell, 2006), 233.

22. Niemöller, *From U-Boat to Pulpit*, 160.

23. Niemöller, *From U-Boat to Pulpit*, 165.

24. Niemöller, *From U-Boat to Pulpit*, 167.

25. Niemöller, *From U-Boat to Pulpit*, 172; Bentley, *Martin Niemöller*, 39.

26. Conan Fischer, *A Vision of Europe: Franco-German Relations during the Great Depression, 1929–1932* (Oxford: Oxford University Press, 2017), 17; Peter Collar, *The Propaganda War in the Rhineland: Weimar Germany, Race, and Occupation after World War I* (London: I. B. Tauris, 2013), 76–93; Niemöller, *From U-Boat to Pulpit*, 171.

27. Niemöller, *From U-Boat to Pulpit*, 173.

28. Niemöller, *From U-Boat to Pulpit*, 171.

29. Niemöller, *From U-Boat to Pulpit*, 175.

30. Niemöller, *From U-Boat to Pulpit*, 177.

31. Volker Ullrich, *Hitler: Ascent 1889–1939* (New York: Alfred A. Knopf, 2016), 133, 147, 155.

32. Winkler, *Germany: The Long Road West*, 401; Jurgen Schmidt, *Martin Niemoller im Kirchenkampf* (Hamburg: Leibniz-Verlag, 1971), 41.

33. Niemöller, *From U-Boat to Pulpit*, 178.

34. Klaus Scholder, *The Churches and the Third Reich*, vol. 1 (Philadelphia: Fortress Press, 1988), 325.

35. Bernd Widdig, *Culture and Inflation in Weimar Germany* (Berkeley: University of California Press, 2001), 48; Kolb, *The Weimar Republic*, 87.

36. Niemöller, *From U-Boat to Pulpit*, 180–181.

37. Matthias Schreiber, *Martin Niemöller* (Reinbek: Rowohlt, 1997), 43; Karnick and Richter, *Protestant*, 57.

38. Bentley, *Martin Niemöller*, 35; Michael Heymel, *Martin Niemöller: Vom Marineoffizier zum Friedenskämpfer* (Darmstadt: Lambert Schneider, 2017), 39; Benjamin Ziemann, "Schiffe versenken: Martin Niemöllers Bericht über die deutsche U-Bootflotte im Ersten Weltkrieg," *Krieg und Literatur* 23 (2017): 21–46, 26.

39. Busch, *Karl Barth*, 233.

40. Thomas Childers, *The Nazi Voter: The Social Foundations of Fascism in Germany, 1919–1933* (Chapel Hill: University of North Carolina Press, 1983); Thomas Friedrich, *Hitler's Berlin: Abused City* (New Haven, CT: Yale University

Press, 2012), 204; Clarissa Start Davidson, *God's Man: The Story of Pastor Niemoeller* (New York: Ives Washburn, 1959), 34.

41. Schmidt, *Martin Niemöller im Kirchenkampf*, 36–43.

42. Ferdinand Schlingensiepen, *Dietrich Bonhoeffer, 1906–1945: Martyr, Thinker, Man of Resistance* (London: T&T Clark, 2010), 82; Victoria Barnett, "Dietrich Bonhoeffer's Ecumenical Vision," *Christian Century*, April 26, 1995, 454–457.

43. Wilhelm Niemöller to "Meine lieben Kinder," ZA EKHN, B. 62/1295; Niemöller, *Was würde Jesus dazu sagen?*, 282.

CHAPTER 4: TRUSTING GOD AND HITLER (1933)

1. Martin Niemöller, *Here Stand I!*, trans. Jane Lymburn (Chicago: Eillett, Clark & Co., 1937), 1–9.

2. Ian Kershaw, *Hitler 1889–1936: Hubris* (New York: W. W. Norton & Co., 1999), 404; Hermann Beck, "Anti-Semitic Violence 'from Below': Attacks and Protestant Church Responses in Germany in 1933," *Politics, Religion, and Ideology* 14, no. 3 (2013): 395–411, 397, n. 6.

3. Jürgen W. Falter, *Hitlers Wähler* (Munich: C. H. Beck, 1991), 177; Kolb, *The Weimar Republic*, 120.

4. H. A. Turner, *Thirty Days to Power: January 1933* (Reading, MA: Addison-Wesley, 1996), 17, 194, 117.

5. Larry Eugene Jones, "Franz von Papen, Catholic Conservatives, and the Establishment of the Third Reich," *Journal of Modern History* 83 (June 2011): 272–318, 272–274.

6. Jones, "Franz von Papen," 279.

7. Niemöller, *Here Stand I!*, 3, 8.

8. Turner, *Hitler's Thirty Days to Power*, 36–37; *Völkischer Beobachter* 348 (December 13, 1932), in Detlef Mühlberger, *Hitler's Voice: The Völkischer Beobachter 1920–1933*, vol. 1, *Organization and Development of the Nazi Party* (Bern: Peter Lang, 2004), 608–610.

9. Schmidt, *Martin Niemöller im Kirchenkampf*, 41–43; Scholder, *Die Kirchen zwischen Republik und Gewaltherrschaft*, 133.

10. Richard J. Evans, *The Coming of the Third Reich* (New York: Penguin Press, 2004), 303; Jones, "Franz von Papen," 280.

11. Evans, *The Coming of the Third Reich*, 308; Hermann Beck, *The Fateful Alliance: German Conservatives and Nazis in 1933: The Machtergreifung in a New Light* (New York: Berghahn, 2008), 228–233.

12. *Dokumente zur Kirchenpolitik des Dritten Reiches*, ed. Georg Kretschmar (Munich: Kaiser, 1971), 1; Ernst Christian Helmreich, *The German Churches under Hitler: Background, Struggle, and Epilogue* (Detroit: Wayne State University Press, 1979), 129.

13. Manfred Gailus, "Overwhelmed by Their Own Fascination with the 'Ideas of 1933': Berlin's Protestant Social Milieu in the Third Reich," *German History* 20, no. 4 (October 2002): 462–493, 483; Hildebrandt, *Pastor Niemöller and His Creed*, 32.

14. Anson Rabinbach, "Staging Antifascism: The Brown Book of the Reichstag Fire and Hitler Terror," *New German Critique* (Winter 2008): 97–126; Wolfgang Benz, *A Concise History of the Third Reich*, trans. Thomas Dunlap (Berkeley: University of California Press, 2006), 26; Otto Dibelius, *In the Service of the Lord: The Autobiography of Bishop Otto Dibelius*, trans. Mary Ilford (New York: Holt, Rinehart and Winston, 1964), 135.

15. Niemöller, *Here Stand I!*, 10–12; Schmidt, *Martin Niemöller im Kirchenkampf*, 48.

16. Niemöller, *Here Stand I!*, 12–13.

17. Eugene W. Miller, "The Reich Interior Ministry and the Evangelical Kirchenkampf, 1933," *Journal of Church and State* 21, no. 3 (Autumn 1979): 507–523; Samuel Koehne, "Were the National Socialists a Völkisch Party? Paganism, Christianity, and the Nazi Christmas," *Central European History* 47 (2014): 760–790.

18. Niemöller, *Here Stand I!*, 13–14.

19. On the planning of the event, see Matthias Grünzig, *Für Deutschtum und Vaterland: Die Potsdamer Garnisonskirche im 20. Jahrhundert* (Berlin: Metropol-Verlag, 2017), 144–161; Ullrich, *Hitler: Ascent*, 433.

20. Grünzig, *Für Deutschtum*, 164–173; "State Opening of the Reichstag," *Manchester Guardian*, March 22, 1933, 11.

21. Ullrich, *Hitler: Ascent*, 227; Dibelius, *In the Service of the Lord*, 138.

22. Grünzig, *Für Deutschtum*, 171–173; Peter Longerich, *Goebbels: A Biography*, trans. Alan Bance, Jeremy Noakes, and Lesley Sharpe (New York: Random House, 2015), 214; Kershaw, *Hitler: 1889–1936*, 465.

23. Kretschmar, *Dokumente zur Kirchenpolitik des Dritten Reiches*, 24.

24. Doris Bergen, "Storm Troopers of Christ: The German Christian Movement and the Ecclesiastical Final Solution," in *Betrayal: German Churches and the Holocaust*, ed. Robert P. Ericksen and Susannah Heschel (Minneapolis: Fortress Press, 1999), 40–67, 40; Shelley Baranowski, "The 1933 German Protestant Church Elections: Machtpolitik or Accommodation?" *Church History* 49 (1980): 298–315, 306; see also Robert Ericksen, *Theologians under Hitler: Gerhard Kittel, Paul Althaus, and Emanuel Hirsch* (New Haven, CT: Yale University Press, 1985), and Robert Ericksen, "Assessing the Heritage: German Protestant Theologians, Nazis, and the 'Jewish Question,'" in Ericksen and Heschel, *Betrayal*, 22–39.

25. Gailus, "Overwhelmed by Their Own Fascination with the 'Ideas of 1933,'" 475–476; Manfred Gailus, *Protestantismus und Nationalsozialismus: Studien zur nationalsozialistischen Durchdringung des protestantischen Sozialmilieus*

in Berlin (Cologne: Böhlau, 2001), 139–196; Doris Bergen, "Christianity and Germanness: Mutually Reinforcing, Reciprocally Undermining?" in *Religion und Nation, Nation und Religion: Beiträge zu einer unbewältigten Geschichte*, ed. Michael Geyer and Hartmut Lehmann (Göttingen: Wallstein, 2004), 76–98; Scholder, *The Churches and the Third Reich*, vol. 1, 521.

26. Gailus, *Protestantismus und Nationalsozialismus*, 97; Bergen, "Storm Troopers of Christ," 43; Gailus, "Overwhelmed by Their Own Fascination with the 'Ideas of 1933,'" 483–485; Olaf Kühl-Freudenstein, "Berlin-Dahlem," in *Kirchenkampf in Berlin 1932–1945*, ed. Olaf Kühl-Freudenstein, Peter Noss, and Claus P. Wagener (Berlin: Institut Kirche und Judentum, 1999), 396–411, 397.

27. Niemöller, *Here Stand I!*, 17, 27–28.

28. Richard Bessel, *Nazism and War* (New York: Modern Library, 2004), 43; Victor Klemperer, *I Will Bear Witness: A Diary of the Nazi Years* (New York: Random House, 1998), 9.

29. "Rabbis Fear Hitler as Enemy of Jews," *New York Times*, February 6, 1933, 13.

30. Gerlach, *And the Witnesses Were Silent*, 35.

31. Richard Gutteridge, *The German Evangelical Church and the Jews, 1879–1950* (Oxford: Basil Blackwell, 1976), 94; Baranowski, "The 1933 German Protestant Church Elections," 302.

32. Karl Barth, *Theological Existence Today (A Plea for Theological Freedom)* (London: Hodder and Stoughton, 1933), 62–85.

33. Carsten Nicolaisen, Ernst-Albert Scharffenorth, and Larry L. Rasmussen, eds., *Dietrich Bonhoeffer Works*, vol. 12, *Berlin, 1932–1933* (Minneapolis: Fortress Press, 2009), 361–370.

34. Samuel McCrea Cavert, "Hitler and the German Churches" *Christian Century*, May 24, 1933, 683–685; Reinhold Niebuhr, "Religion and the New Germany," *Christian Century*, June 28, 1933, 843–845.

35. Keith Clements, ed., *Dietrich Bonhoeffer Works*, vol. 13, *London, 1933–1935* (Minneapolis: Fortress Press, 2007), 135.

36. Niemöller, *Here Stand I!*, 39–43.

37. Kurt Meier, *Kreuz und Hakenkreuz: Die evangelische Kirche im Dritten Reich* (Munich: Deutscher Taschenbuch Verlag, 1992), 42; Eberhard Bethge, *Dietrich Bonhoeffer: A Biography* (Minneapolis: Fortress Press, 2000), 284.

38. Dibelius, *In the Service of the Lord*, 144–145; Gailus, *Protestantismus und Nationalsozialismus*, 114.

39. Scholder, *The Churches and the Third Reich*, vol. 1, 359–360; Gerti Graff, Hertha von Klewitz, Hille Richers, and Gerhard Schräberle, eds., *Unterwegs zur mündigen Gemeinde: d. evang. Kirche im Nationalsozialismus am Beispiel der Gemeinde Dahlem; Bilder u. Texte e. Ausstellung im Friedenszentrum Martin-Niemöller-Haus, Berlin-Dahlem* (Stuttgart: Alektor-Verlag, 1982), 13.

40. Graff et al., *Unterwegs zur mündigen Gemeinde*, 11.

41. Baranowski, "The 1933 German Protestant Church Elections," 313; Doris L. Bergen, *Twisted Cross: The German Christian Movement in the Third Reich* (Chapel Hill: University of North Carolina Press, 1996), 6; Schmidt, *Pastor Niemöller*, 88; Helmreich, *The German Churches under Hitler*, 142.

42. Schlingensiepen, *Dietrich Bonhoeffer, 1906–1945*, 133; Heymel, *Martin Niemöller*, 62; Dibelius, *In the Service of the Lord*, 145; Karnick and Richter, *Niemöller: Was Würde Jesus dazu Sagen?*, 44; Helmreich, *The German Churches under Hitler*, 143.

43. Schmidt, *Martin Niemöller im Kirchenkampf*, 107; Scholder, *The Churches and the Third Reich*, vol. 1, 468–469.

44. M. Niemöller, "Die Jungereformatorische Bewegung und die Kirchenpolitik: 16 Thesen," *Junge Kirche* 9 (August 24, 1933): 99–101, 99–100.

45. Graff et al., *Unterwegs zur mündigen Gemeinde*, 17; Schmidt, *Martin Niemöller im Kirchenkampf*, 107, 466, n. 180; Gailus, *Protestantismus und Nationalsozialismus*, 128, 138.

46. This anecdote comes from Manfred Gailus's excellent history of Berlin parishes in the Nazi era, *Protestantismus und Nationalsozialismus*, 228–232 and Gailus, "Overwhelmed by Their Own Fascination with the 'Ideas of 1933,'" 478–479.

47. Bethge, *Dietrich Bonhoeffer*, 301.

48. Nicolaisen et al., *Dietrich Bonhoeffer Works*, vol. 12, 375.

49. Schmidt, *Martin Niemöller im Kirchenkampf*, 118; Clements, *Dietrich Bonhoeffer Works*, vol. 13, 45; Scholder, *The Churches and the Third Reich*, vol. 1, 472.

50. Siegfried Hermle, "Die Bischöfe und die Schicksale 'nichtarischer' Christen," in *Nationalprotestantische Mentalitäten*, ed. Manfred Gailus and Hartmut Lehmann (Göttingen: Vandenhoeck & Ruprecht, 2005), 263–306, 274.

51. Bethge, *Dietrich Bonhoeffer*, 306.

52. "Circular Letter by Niemöller, 21 September 1933," in *The Third Reich and the Christian Churches: A Documentary Account of Christian Resistance and Complicity during the Nazi Era*, ed. Peter Matheson (Edinburgh: T&T Clark, 1981), 36–37.

CHAPTER 5: FIGHTING PASTOR (1934–1937)

1. Davidson, *God's Man*, 71; Memorandum by Bishop Bell, February 1937, in *Brethren in Adversity: Bishop George Bell, the Church of England, and the Crisis of German Protestantism 1933–1939*, ed. Andrew Chandler (Woodbridge, UK: Boydel & Brewer, 1997), 121–133, 123.

2. Nicolaisen et al., *Dietrich Bonhoeffer Works*, vol. 12, 181–183, 183; "An die Nationalsynode der Deutschen Evangelischen Kirche zu Wittenberg," September 27, 1933, ZA EKHN, B. 62/6040.

3. Victoria Barnett, *For the Soul of the People: Protestant Protest against Hitler* (New York: Oxford University Press, 1992), 28–29, 146–151.

4. Scholder, *The Churches and the Third Reich*, vol. 1, 491–492; Bethge, *Dietrich Bonhoeffer*, 318–320.

5. Barnett, *For the Soul of the People*, 4; Scholder, *The Churches and the Third Reich*, vol. 1, 492; "Hitler Wins Church Control; 2,000 Clergymen Protest," *Chicago Daily Tribune*, September 28, 1933, 9.

6. Clements, *Dietrich Bonhoeffer Works*, vol. 13, 21–24, 39–41.

7. Niemöller to Reichskanzler, October 15, 1933, ZA EKHN, B. 62/6040; *Junge Kirche*, 1, no. 16, October 19, 1933, 252; Schmidt, *Martin Niemöller im Kirchenkampf*, 142.

8. Bethge, *Dietrich Bonhoeffer*, 323.

9. Martin Niemöller, "Sätze zur Arierfrage in der Kirche," *Junge Kirche*, November 2, 1933, 269–271; Amon Cresswell and Maxwell Tow, *Dr. Franz Hildebrandt: Mr. Valiant-for-Truth* (Macon, GA: Smyth & Helwys, 2000), 63–65.

10. Mary Solberg, *A Church Undone: Documents from the German Christian Faith Movement, 1932–1940* (Minneapolis: Fortress Press, 2015), 169; Niemöller, *Here I Stand!*, 60–62.

11. Schmidt, *Martin Niemöller im Kirchenkampf*, 145–146.

12. Graff et al., *Unterwegs zur mündigen Gemeinde*, 48; Sibylle Sarah Niemoeller, *Crowns, Crosses, and Stars: My Youth in Prussia, Surviving Hitler, and a Life Beyond* (West Lafayette, IN: Purdue University Press, 2012), 52.

13. Solberg, *A Church Undone*, 249–262.

14. Scholder, *The Churches and the Third Reich*, vol. 1, 554.

15. Schmidt, *Martin Niemöller in Kirchenkampf*, 169; Scholder, *The Churches and the Third Reich*, vol. 1, 555–556.

16. Clements, *Dietrich Bonhoeffer Works*, vol. 13, 52–53, 56.

17. Niemöller to Hildebrandt, December 27, 1933, in Clements, *Dietrich Bonhoeffer Works*, vol. 13, 64–65.

18. Hildebrandt, *Pastor Niemöller and His Creed*, 39; Chandler, *Brethren in Adversity*, 78.

19. Schmidt, *Martin Niemöller im Kirchenkampf*, 164; Klaus Scholder, *The Churches and the Third Reich*, vol. 2, *The Year of Disillusionment: 1934* (London: SCM Press, 2012), 23–24.

20. J. S. Conway, *The Nazi Persecution of the Churches, 1933–1945* (Vancouver, BC: Regent College Publishing, 1997), 76–77.

21. Scholder, *The Churches and the Third Reich*, vol. 2, 38.

22. Carsten Nicolaisen, *Dokumente zur Kirchenpolitik des Dritten Reiches*, vol. 2 (Munich: Kaiser, 1975), 17–19.

23. Bentley, *Martin Niemöller*, 85; Scholder, *The Churches and the Third Reich*, vol. 2, 41–42.

24. Nicolaisen, *Dokumente zur Kirchenpolitik des Dritten Reiches*, vol. 2, 23–25.

25. Schmidt, *Martin Niemöller im Kirchenkampf*, 172.

26. Schmidt, *Martin Niemöller im Kirchenkampf*, 173.

27. See Davidson, *God's Man*, 56–59; Schmidt, *Martin Niemöller im Kirchenkampf*, 173; Martin Niemöller, radio address, KVI Seattle, December 5, 1946, World Council of Churches Archive, "Germany Wartime, Martin Niemöller's Visit to the USA 1946–1947," Yale Divinity School, series 4, microfische 247 (hereafter, for example, WCC, "Niemöller Visit," YDS 4, mf. 247).

28. The most accurate account, in my opinion, is from Scholder, *The Churches and the Third Reich*, vol. 2, 40–42. Scholder does not mention that Niemöller spoke to Hitler when they shook hands. The relevant documents are found in Nicolaisen, *Dokumente zur Kirchenpolitik des Dritten Reiches*, vol. 2; and Wilhelm Niemöller, *Hitler und die Evangelischen Kirchenführer* (Bielefeld: Ludwig Bechauf, 1959).

29. Cresswell and Tow, *Dr. Franz Hildebrandt*, 63; Paula Bonhoeffer to Dietrich Bonhoeffer, February 5, 1934, in Clements, *Dietrich Bonhoeffer Works*, vol. 13, 99–101, 101.

30. Louis P. Lochner, *What About Germany?* (New York: Dodd, Mead & Co., 1942), 254–255; Sigrid Schultz, "Fighting Pastor Defies Hitler's Church Dictator," *Chicago Daily Tribune*, March 5, 1934, 7.

31. Heinrich Hermelink, *Kirche im Kampf: Dokumente des Widerstands und des Aufbaus in der Evangelischen Kirche Deutschlands von 1933 bis 1945* (Stuttgart: Rainer Wunderlich Verlag, 1950), 87.

32. Eberhard Busch, *The Barmen Theses Then and Now* (Grand Rapids, MI: Eerdmans, 2010), 19.

33. Busch, *The Barmen Theses Then and Now*, 5; Eberhard Bethge, "Barmen und die Juden—eine nicht geschreibene These?," in *Das eine Wort für alle: Barmen 1934–1984*, ed. Hans-Ulrich Stephan (Neukirchen-Vluyn: Neukirchener Verlag, 1986), 114–133; Eberhard Bethge, *Erstes Gebot und Zeitgeschichte: Aufsätze und Reden, 1980–1990* (Munich: Chr. Kaiser, 1991), 173.

34. Bentley, *Martin Niemöller*, 3–4; Busch, *Karl Barth*, 382.

35. Ziemann, "Schiffe versenken," 36; Martin Niemöller to Goebbels, November 22, 1934, ZA EKHN, B. 62/6040.

36. Scholder, *The Churches and the Third Reich*, vol. 2, 273; Niemöller to H. Teute, August 6, 1935, ZA EKHN, B. 62/6040.

37. Scholder, *The Churches and the Third Reich*, vol. 2, 269.

38. Scholder, *The Churches and the Third Reich*, vol. 2, 267–269; Wilhelm Niesel, *Kirche unter dem Wort: Der Kampf der Bekennenden Kirche der altpreussischen Union 1933–1945* (Göttingen: Vandenhoeck & Ruprecht, 1978), 38.

39. Schmidt, *Martin Niemöller im Kirchenkampf*, 181–182; Niemöller, *Here Stand I!*, 117–123.

40. Schmidt, *Martin Niemöller im Kirchenkampf*, 271; Gerhard Besier, *Die Kirchen und das Dritte Reich: Band 3: Spaltungen und Abwehrkämpfe 1934 bis 1937* (Berlin: Propyläen Verlag, 2001), 62; Gerlach, *And the Witnesses Were Silent*, 80; Niemöller, Amtskalender, March 17, 1935, ZA EKHN, B. 62/6096.

41. Niemöller, *Here Stand I!*, 187; Martin Niemöller, *God Is My Führer* (New York: Philosophical Library, 1941), 37; Niemöller to Pastor Amelung (Plauen), January 28, 1936, ZA EKHN, B. 62/6001.

42. Niemöller, *Here Stand I!*, 139.

43. On Niemöller, the Confessing Church, and anti-Semitism, see Leonore Siegele-Wenschkewitz, "Die Judenfrage ist eine Arierfrage," in Karnick and Richter, *Protestant*, 109–136; Martin Stöhr, ". . . habe ich geschwiegen: Zur Frage eines Antisemitismus bei Martin Niemöller," Martin Niemöller Stiftung, 2006, www.martin-niemoeller-stiftung.de; Robert Michael, "Theological Myth, German Antisemitism, and the Holocaust: The Case of Martin Niemöller," *Holocaust and Genocide Studies* 2, no. 1 (January 1987): 105-122; Richard Gutteridge, *Open Thy Mouth for the Dumb: The German Evangelical Church and the Jews, 1879–1950* (Oxford: Blackwell, 1976); Otto Kulka, "Popular Christian Attitudes in the Third Reich to National-Socialist Policies toward Jews," in *Judaism and Christianity under the Impact of National Socialism, 1919–1945*, ed. Otto Dov Kulka and Paul R. Mendes-Flohr (Jerusalem: Historical Society of Israel and Zalman Shazar Center for Jewish History, 1982).

44. Gerlach, *And the Witnesses Were Silent*, 46.

45. Niemöller, *Here Stand I!*, 195, 192–198.

46. Senta-Maria Klatt to Niemöller, March 10, 1936, ZA EKHN, B. 62/6009; on Senta-Maria Klatt, see "Senta-Maria Klatt," Gedenkstätte Deutscher Widerstand, www.gdw-berlin.de/en/recess/biographies/index_of_persons/biographie/view-bio/senta-maria-klatt/?no_cache=1 (accessed January 6, 2018); "Testifies Niemoeller Not an Anti-Semite," *Christian Century*, December 3, 1947, 1477.

47. Bethge, *Dietrich Bonhoeffer*, 488–489; Gerlach, *And the Witnesses Were Silent*, 95–100.

48. Niemöller, *God Is My Führer*, 50.

49. Peter Hoffmann, ed., *Behind Valkyrie: German Resistance to Hitler: Documents* (Montreal: McGill-Queen's University Press, 2011), 101–116, 111; Martin Greschat, ed., *Zwischen Widerspruch und Widerstand: Texte zur Denkschrift der Bekennenden Kirche an Hitler (1936)* (Munich: C. Kaiser, 1987), 83, 97, 101.

50. Hoffmann, *Behind Valkyrie*, 108.

51. Manfred Gailus, *Friedrich Weissler: Ein Jurist und bekennender Christ im Widerstand gegen Hitler* (Göttingen: Vandenhoeck & Ruprecht, 2017), 160.

52. Niemöller, *God Is My Führer*, 271–273.

53. Gerald D. Feldman, *Allianz and the German Insurance Business, 1933–1945* (Cambridge: Cambridge University Press, 2001), 309.

54. Niemöller, *God Is My Führer*, 276–277, 279; Schmidt, *Martin Niemöller im Kirchenkampf*, 431.

CHAPTER 6: HITLER'S PERSONAL PRISONER (1937–1945)

1. Bentley, *Martin Niemöller*, 130.

2. Wilhelm Niemöller, *Macht geht vor Recht: Der Prozess Martin Niemöllers* (Munich: Chr. Kaiser, 1952), 30.

3. Karnick and Richter, *Protestant*, 99; Bethge, *Dietrich Bonhoeffer*, 579.

4. Martin Niemöller, *Briefe aus der Gefangenschaft Moabit*, ed. Wilhelm Niemöller (Frankfurt: Otto Lembeck, 1975), 31; Schmidt, *Pastor Niemöller*, 102.

5. Gerhard Schäberle-Koenigs, *Und sie waren täglich einmütig beieinander: Der Weg der Bekennenden Gemeinde Berlin/Dahlem 1937–1943 mit Helmut Gollwitzer* (Gütersloh: Kaiser, 1998), 36.

6. Martin Niemöller, *Exile in the Fatherland: Letters from Moabit Prison*, ed. Hubert G. Locke, trans. Ernst Kaemle, Kathy Elias, and Jacklyn Wilferd (Grand Rapids, MI: Eerdmans, 1986), 25.

7. Ullrich, *Hitler: Ascent*, 655, 924, n. 105; Goebbels, December 22, 1937, in *Die Tagebücher von Joseph Goebbels*, part 1, vol. 5, *Dezember 1937–Juli 1938*, ed. Elke Fröhlich (Munich: K. G. Saur, 2000), 65; Niemöller, *Macht geht vor Recht*, 31–32.

8. Holger Roggelin, *Franz Hildebrandt: Ein lutherischer Dissenter im Kirchenkampf und Exil* (Göttingen: Vandenhoeck & Ruprecht, 1999), 122; Bethge, *Dietrich Bonhoeffer*, 580.

9. Niemöller, *Briefe aus der Gefangenschaft Moabit*, 16.

10. Dibelius, *In the Service of the Lord*, 155; Niemöller, *Briefe aus der Gefangenschaft Moabit*, 23.

11. Graff et al., *Unterwegs zur mündigen Gemeinde*, 74–75; Lothar Gruchmann, *Justiz im Dritten Reich 1933–1940: Anpassung und Unterwerfung in der Ära Gürtner* (Munich: Oldenbourg, 1988), 73–74.

12. Schäberle-Koenigs, *Und sie waren täglich einmütig beieinander*, 39–40; Graff et al., *Unterwegs zur mündigen Gemeinde*, 84; Barnett, *For the Soul of the People*, 166–168.

13. Roggelin, *Franz Hildebrandt*, 122–127.

14. Graff et al., *Unterwegs zur mündigen Gemeinde*, 75–76.

15. Bishop George Bell, *The (London) Times*, July 3, 1938.

16. Niemöller, *Briefe aus der Gefangenschaft Moabit*, 9; Niemöller, *Exile in the Fatherland*, 37.

17. Niemöller, *Exile in the Fatherland*, 133.

18. Niemöller, *Exile in the Fatherland*, 132, 125.

19. Niemöller, *Macht geht vor Recht*, 30; Niemöller, *Exile in the Fatherland*, 55.

20. Niemöller, *Exile in the Fatherland*, 30.

21. Niemöller, *Exile in the Fatherland*, 49.

22. Niemöller, *Exile in the Fatherland*, 110, 122, 81, 136.

23. *Dietrich Bonhoeffer Works*, vol. 15, *Theological Education Underground, 1937–1940*, trans. Victoria J. Barnett, Claudia D. Bergmann, Peter Frick, and Scott A. Moore (Minneapolis: Fortress Books, 2011), 27; Niemöller, *Exile in the Fatherland*, 55; Niemöller, *Macht geht vor Recht*, 30–31.

24. Niemöller, *Exile in the Fatherland*, 135.

25. Graff et al., *Unterwegs zur mündigen Gemeinde*, 73; Helmreich, *The German Churches under Hitler*, 210–211, 214, and 510, n. 18; Hans Buchheim, ed., "Ein NS-Funkionär zum Niemöller-Prozess," *Vierteljahrshefte für Zeitgeschichte* 4, no. 3 (July 1956): 307–315, 310.

26. Goebbels, January 21, 1938, in Fröhlich, *Die Tagebücher*, 108–109.

27. Niemöller, *Exile in the Fatherland*, 157.

28. Buchheim, "Ein NS-Funkionär zum Niemöller-Prozess," 313; Niemöller, *Exile in the Fatherland*, 157; Goebbels, February 8, 1938, in Fröhlich, *Die Tagebücher*, 143.

29. Niemöller, *Macht geht vor Recht*, 64, 58; Niemöller, *Exile in the Fatherland*, 159.

30. Schmidt, *Martin Niemöller im Kirchenkampf*, 441; Goebbels, February 27, 1938, in Fröhlich, *Die Tagebücher*, 179.

31. Niemöller, *Exile in the Fatherland*, 167.

32. Schreiber, *Martin Niemöller*, 83.

33. Schreiber, *Martin Niemöller*, 83–84; Toby Thacker, *Joseph Goebbels: Life and Death* (Basingstoke: Palgrave Macmillan, 2009), 193; Goebbels, March 2, 1938, in Fröhlich, *Die Tagebücher*, 185.

34. Goebbels, March 4, 1938, in Fröhlich, *Die Tagebücher*, 187.

35. "Sachsenhausen Main Camp," in Megargee, *The United States Holocaust Memorial Museum Encyclopedia*, 1256–1261.

36. Leo Stein, *I Was in Hell with Niemoeller* (New York: Revell, 1942).

37. "Aus einem Brief Pastor Niemöllers DD," *Evangelishes Zentralarchiv in Berlin* (EZA), B. 2/35, 162.

38. Martin Niemöller, addresses at Music Hall, Cincinnati, OH, February 7, 1947; Dayton, OH, February 4, 1947; and University Chapel, Princeton, NJ, March 6, 1947.

39. Martin Niemöller, address, Philadelphia Council of Churches, Philadelphia, PA, March 10, 1947, Presbyterian Historical Society (PHS), 18/16/1.

40. Martin Niemöller, *Briefe aus der Gefangenschaft Konzentrationslager Sachsenhausen (Oranienburg)* (Bielefeld: Ludwig Bechauf Verlag, 1979), 7, 10; Bentley, *Martin Niemöller*, 143.

41. Niemöller, *Briefe aus der Gefangenschaft Konzentrationslager Sachsenhausen*, 23; "Interview with Martin Niemöller," Dorothy Thompson Papers, Syracuse University Library, Special Collections Research Center, box 102.

42. Niemöller, *Briefe aus der Gefangenschaft Konzentrationslager Sachsenhausen*, 11.

43. Niemöller, *Briefe aus der Gefangenschaft Konzentrationslager Sachsenhausen*, 21.

44. Quotations from Niemöller, *Briefe aus der Gefangenschaft Konzentrationslager Sachsenhausen*.

45. Ewart Turner, "Father of Martin Niemöller Dies," *Christian Century*, April 9, 1941, 505–506.

46. Niemöller, *Briefe aus der Gefangenschaft Konzentrationslager Sachsenhausen*, 29–30, 195, 17.

47. Pastor Niemoeller: United Telegram from Church Leaders to Adolf Hitler, March 10, 1938, George Bell Papers, Lambeth Palace Library, London.

48. Leiper to Henry Levy, June 26, 1939, WCC, "Niemöller Visit," YDS 4, mf. 251; "Niemoeller or I," *Time*, July 10, 1939.

49. "For Niemoller," *Time*, March 20, 1939.

50. Albert Viton, "Niemoller or I," *The Nation*, July 1, 1939, 13–14; Dorothy Thompson, *Let the Record Speak* (Boston: Houghton Mifflin, 1939), 148–150, 150.

51. "Prayers for Niemoeller Offered by Chicago Rabbi Group," *The Sentinel*, February 24, 1938, 30; "Rabbi Lists 10 Men Whose Virtue Will Save Civilization," *Brooklyn Eagle*, November 5, 1939, A9; Edgar E. Siskin Papers, Jacob Rader Marcus Center of the American Jewish Archives (AJA), MS-64, box 3, folder 10: "Modern Christian Heroes."

52. "Letters," *Christian Century*, March 15, 1939, 355.

53. Niemöller, *Macht geht vor Recht*, 98.

54. Copies of Niemöller response to *Newsweek*, December 16, 1946, Turner Papers, Temple University; Ben Rose, "An Interview with Pastor Martin Niemoeller," *Christianity and Crisis* 5, no. 21 (December 10, 1945): 4–6, 5.

55. Barth to Bell, December 8, 1939, in Chandler, *Brethren in Adversity*, reprinted in *Watchman-Examiner*, February 22, 1940, 179.

56. Henry Smith Leiper, "His Wife's Story of His 'Offer' to Command U-Boat," *The Churchman*, October 15, 1939, in Henry Smith Leiper Papers, PHS.

57. "German Martyrs," *Time*, December 23, 1940.

58. Niemöller, *Macht geht vor Recht*, 98; Niemöller, *Briefe aus der Gefangenschaft Konzentrationslager Sachsenhausen*, 105, 129, 157, 18; Joseph Goebbels, *The Goebbels Diaries, 1939–1941*, trans. and ed. Fred Taylor (New York: G. P. Putnam's Sons, 1983), 215.

59. See "Sollen wir katholisch werden? Die Auseinandersetzung um Niemöllers Konversionsabsicht," chap. 6 in Schäberle-Koenigs, *Und sie waren täglich einmütig beieinander*, 243–273; Niemöller, *Briefe aus der Gefangenschaft Konzentrationslager Sachsenhausen*, 31, 83, 52.

60. Niemöller, *Briefe aus der Gefangenschaft Konzentrationslager Sachsenhausen*, 83; Schäberle-Koenigs, *Und sie waren täglich einmütig beieinander*, 251; Eberhard Bethge to Dietrich Bonhoeffer, February 8, 1941, in *Dietrich Bonhoeffer Works*, vol. 16, *Conspiracy and Imprisonment, 1940–1945*, ed. Mark S. Brocker, trans. Lisa E. Dahill (Minneapolis: Fortress Press, 2006), 145.

61. Schäberle-Koenigs, *Und sie waren täglich einmütig beieinander*, 261–269; Niebuhr to Turner, April 2, 1941, Turner Papers, Temple University.

62. Niemöller, *Briefe aus der Gefangenschaft Konzentrationslager Sachsenhausen*, 155, 158.

63. Davidson, *God's Man*, 107.

64. Wilhelm Niemöller, *Vater Niemöller: Ein Lebensbild* (Bielefeld: Ludwig Bechauf Verlag, 1946), 59; Else Niemöller, address, Philadelphia, PA, March 10, 1947, PHS, record group 18, box 16, folder 1; Niemöller, *Vater Niemöller: Ein Lebensbild*, 3–4.

65. Niemöller, *Briefe aus der Gefangenschaft Konzentrationslager Sachsenhausen*, 170.

66. Harold Marcuse, *Legacies of Dachau: The Uses and Abuses of a Concentration Camp, 1933–2001* (New York: Cambridge University Press, 2001), 43–44.

67. Christopher Browning, "From 'Ethnic Cleansing' to Genocide to the 'Final Solution': The Evolution of Nazi Jewish Policy, 1939–1941," and "Nazi Policy: Decisions for the Final Solution," in Christopher Browning, *Nazi Policy, Jewish Workers, German Killers* (Cambridge: Cambridge University Press, 2000), 1–25 and 26–57; Karl A. Schleunes, *The Twisted Road to Auschwitz: Nazi Policy toward German Jews 1933–1939* (1970; reprint, Urbana and Chicago: University of Illinois Press, 1990), 62–168; Browning, "Nazi Policy," 40; Doris Bergen, *War and Genocide: A Concise History of the Holocaust* (Lanham, MD: Rowman and Littlefield, 2003), 86–90.

68. Bergen, *War and Genocide*, 101–114.

69. Browning, "From 'Ethnic Cleansing' to Genocide to the 'Final Solution,'" 24.

70. Browning, "Nazi Policy," 36, 40.

71. Megargee, *The United States Holocaust Memorial Museum Encyclopedia*, 442–443; Marcuse, "Dachau," in Merriman and Winter, *Europe since 1914*, 763–766.

72. Megargee, *The United States Holocaust Memorial Museum Encyclopedia*, 443–446.

73. "Interview with Martin Niemöller," Dorothy Thompson Papers, Syracuse University Library.

74. Gerlach, *And the Witnesses Were Silent*, 154–162; Richard Gutteridge, *The German Evangelical Church and the Jews*, 208.

75. Bonhoeffer to Bell, September 25, 1941, in Brocker, *Dietrich Bonhoeffer Works*, vol. 16, 223.

76. Dietrich Bonhoeffer to Erling Eidem, April 11, 1942, in Brocker, *Dietrich Bonhoeffer Works*, vol. 16, 270.

77. Bentley, *Martin Niemöller*, 150.

78. Goebbels, *The Goebbels Diaries*, 133; Hans P. Ehrenberg, *Autobiography of a German Pastor* (London: Student Christian Movement, 1943), 38.

79. Sterik, *Else Niemöller, Die Frau eines bedeutenden Mannes*, 110; Martin Niemöller to Jochen Niemöller, January 3, 1945, in Sterik, *Else Niemöller, Die Frau eines bedeutenden Mannes*, 65.

80. Martin Niemöller, address, Cincinnati, OH, February 7, 1947, WCC Archives, YDS 4, mf. 248–249.

81. Martin Niemöller, *Dachau Sermons* (New York: Harper & Brothers, 1946), 72–73.

CHAPTER 7: GUILT, REPENTANCE, RENEWAL (1945–1946)

1. Marie Vassiltchikov, *Berlin Diaries* (New York: Alfred A. Knopf, 1987), 234.

2. For example, the *Boston Globe* ran an article titled "Rumor Generals Pick Niemoeller to Head New German Republic," January 13, 1942, Turner Papers, Temple University; on Adam von Trott zu Solz, see Ulrich von Hassell, *The von Hassell Diaries, 1938–1944: The Story of the Forces against Hitler inside Germany* (Garden City, NY: Doubleday, 1947), 231–232.

3. See Hugo Gotthard Bloth, "Die Befreiung Martin Niemöllers 1945 aus der Fahrt in den Tod," *Jahrbuch für Westfälische Kirchengeschichte* 78 (1985): 205–210; Sigismund Payne Best, *The Venlo Incident: A True Story of Double-Dealing, Captivity, and a Murderous Nazi Plot* (New York: Skyhorse Publishing, 2009), 237, 222.

4. Best, *The Venlo Incident*, 224–226.

5. Best, *The Venlo Incident*, 228–229.

6. Bloth, "Die Befreiung Martin Niemöllers," 209–210; Best, *The Venlo Incident*, 245; B. A. James, *Moonless Night: The World War Two Escape Epic* (Barnsley, UK: Pen & Sword Military Classics, 2006), 177–197.

7. James, *Moonless Night*, 191.

8. James, *Moonless Night*, 194.

9. "Niemoeller," *Washington Post*, May 13, 1945, B4; Dorothy Thompson, "Pastor Niemoeller on Germany," *Youngstown Vindicator*, May 16, 1945, 8; De-Witt McKenzie, "War Today," *Nashua Telegraph*, May 25, 1945, 14; "Administering Germany," *Christian Science Monitor*, May 18, 1945, 18.

10. Constance Jung to Niemöller, May 8, 1945, ZA EKHN, B. 62/515.

11. Marshall Knappen, *And Call It Peace* (Chicago: University of Chicago Press, 1947), 111; Colonel Earl B. Nichols to Niemöller, May 17, 1945, ZA EKHN, B. 62/1233; Herbert M. Kraus, "Difference Small Between Niemoeller, Other Nazis, Ex-Chaplain Says," *National Jewish Post*, December 20, 1946, 4; opera programs, ZA EKHN, B. 62/1233; Niemöller to Thomas Lovelace, June 19, 1946, ZA EKHN, B. 62/519.

12. Martin Niemöller, "The Position and Prospects of the Evangelical Church," ZA EKHN, B. 62/1016.

13. George Palmer, "Niemoeller Tried to Join the Navy in 1939," *Lewiston Daily Sun*, June 6, 1945, 9; *Time*, "For What I Am," June 18, 1945.

14. *Time*, "For What I Am," June 18, 1945.

15. *Time*, "For What I Am," June 18, 1945.

16. "A Hero with Limitations," *New York Times*, June 7, 1945, 18; "For What I Am," *Time*, June 18, 1945 (emphasis added).

17. Barth and Koechlin to FCC, Hooft, and Bell, June 9, 1945, in *Karl Barth–Willem Adolf Visser't Hooft: Briefwechsel 1930–1968* (Zürich: Theologischer Verlag, 2006), 195–197.

18. Sam Cavert to William D. Hassett, June 12, 1945, and Hassett to Cavert, June 18, 1945, both in Papers of Harry S. Truman, "Confidential Files," Harry S. Truman Library (hereafter Truman Library, "Confidential Files").

19. National Lutheran Council to Niemöller, June 8, 1945, ZA EKHN, B. 62/519.

20. Clemens Vollnhals, ed., *Die evangelische Kirche nach dem Zusammenbruch: Berichte ausländischer Beobachter aus dem Jahre 1945* (Göttingen: Vandenhoeck & Ruprecht, 1988), 21; Dieter Altmannsperger, *Kirche nach der Kapitulation*, vol. 2, *Auf dem Weg nach Treysa* (Stuttgart: Kohlhammer, 1990), 111, 60.

21. Frederic Spotts, *The Churches and Politics in Germany* (Middletown, CT: Wesleyan University Press, 1973), 51; "Knappen: The Niemöller Case," in Altmannsperger, *Kirche nach der Kapitulation*, vol. 2, 60.

22. Atina Grossmann, "A Question of Silence: The Rape of German Women by Occupation Soldiers," in *West Germany under Construction: Politics, Society,*

and Culture in the Adenauer Era, ed. Robert G. Moeller (Ann Arbor: University of Michigan Press, 1997), 33–52.

23. Konrad Jarausch, *After Hitler: Recivilizing Germans, 1945–1995* (Oxford: Oxford University Press, 2006), 23–30; interrogation transcript, ZA EKHN, B. 62/1233, 13–14.

24. Bentley, *Martin Niemöller*, 157.

25. Bentley, *Martin Niemöller*, 158; Else Niemöller, address, Philadelphia, PA, March 10, 1947, PHS, 18/16/1; Else Niemöller, address, Schenectady, NY, February 21, 1947, WCC, "Niemöller Visit," YDS 4, mf. 249; Niemöller to Chinigo, July 4, 1945, ZA EKHN, B. 62/1233; Niemöller to Davis, July 29, 1945, ZA EKHN, B. 62/1233.

26. Vollnhals, *Die evangelische Kirche nach dem Zusammenbruch*, xxiv, xxv.

27. Religious News Service, July 6, 1945.

28. Interrogation transcript, ZA EKHN, B. 62/1233.

29. Interrogation transcript, ZA EKHN, B. 62/1233.

30. Interrogation transcript, ZA EKHN, B. 62/1233.

31. Niemöller to Böhm, July 28, 1945, in Altmannsperger, *Kirche nach der Kapitulation*, vol. 2, 226.

32. Martin Niemöller, "The Position and Prospects of the Evangelical Church," ZA EKHN, B. 62/1016.

33. Matthew D. Hockenos, *A Church Divided: German Protestants Confront the Nazi Past* (Bloomington: Indiana University Press, 2004), chap. 5.

34. "Aus einem Brief Pastor Niemöllers DD," EZA, 2/35, 162.

35. See Murphy's report in Vollnhals, *Die evangelische Kirche nach dem Zusammenbruch*, 120–122; See Gerhard Besier, ed., "Ökumenische Mission in Nachkriegsdeutschland: Die Berichte von Stewart W. Herman über die Verhältnisse in der evangelischen Kirche 1945/46," part 1 in *Kirchliche Zeitgeschichte* 1, no. 1 (1988): 335.

36. Philip A. Adler, "Niemoeller Sermons Show Link to Hitler Philosophy," *Detroit News*, August 8, 1945, 7; Eleanor Roosevelt, "My Day," August 7, 1945. Adler's article mentions a campaign, allegedly by Robert Murphy, to promote Niemöller as president of postwar Germany. Various newspapers picked up on this story in early August 1945, including the *Emporia (KS) Gazette* in "Martin Niemoeller Is Reich's Hot Potato" (August 10, 1945, 7).

37. Vollnhals, *Die evangelische Kirche nach dem Zusammenbruch*, xxvi.

38. Ewart Turner, "Memories of Martin Niemöller," *Christian Century*, April 25, 1984; Turner to Parents, October 18, 1945, Turner Papers, Temple University.

39. Ewart Turner, "Memories of Martin Niemöller," *Christian Century*, April 25, 1984.

40. Gerhard Besier and Gerhard Sauter, *Wie Christen ihre Schuld bekennen: Die Stuttgarter Erklärung 1945* (Göttingen: Vandenhoeck & Ruprecht, 1985), 25.

41. "Military Government," October 14, 1945, Turner Papers, Temple University.

42. Besier and Sauter, *Wie Christen ihre Schuld bekennen*, 29.

43. Ewart Turner, "Memories of Martin Niemöller," *Christian Century*, April 25, 1984, 445; Besier and Sauter, *Wie Christen ihre Schuld bekennen*, 147. Niemöller's sermon is reprinted in Besier and Sauter, *Wie Christen ihre Schuld bekennen*, 145–150.

44. Ewart Turner, "Memories of Martin Niemöller," *Christian Century*, April 25, 1984, 445.

45. William J. Schmidt, *Architect of Unity: A Biography of Samuel McCrea Cavert* (New York: Friendship Press, 1978), 185.

46. Niemöller to Ihrer Durchlaucht der Fürstin von Ysenburg-Büdingen, September 6, 1945, ZA EKHN, B. 62/1233.

47. See Hockenos, *A Church Divided*, chap. 4; Martin Niemöller, *Of Guilt and Hope* (New York: Philosophical Library, 1946), 17, 29–30.

48. Niemöller, *Of Guilt and Hope*, 14–15; Harold Marcuse, "The Origin and Reception of Martin Niemöller's Quotation 'First They Came for the Communists . . . ,'" July 31, 2014, www.history.ucsb.edu/faculty/marcuse/projects /niem/articles/Marcuse2014NiemoellerQuote147gWeb.pdf (accessed January 5, 2015).

49. Niemöller, *Of Guilt and Hope*, 15; "Aus einem Brief Pastor Niemöllers DD," EZA, B. 22/35, 162.

50. Martin Greschat, *Die Schuld der Kirche: Dokumente und Reflexionen zur Stuttgarter Schulderklärung vom 18./19. Oktober 1945* (Munich: Chr. Kaiser, 1982), 184, 188–192; Clemens Vollnhals, *Evangelische Kirche und Entnazifizierung 1945–1949: Die Last der nationalsozialistischen Vergangenheit* (Munich: Oldenbourg, 1989), 174; "Aus einem Brief Pastor Niemöllers DD," EZA, 2/35, 162.

51. Frank Stern, *Whitewashing the Yellow Badge: Antisemitism and Philosemitism in Postwar Germany*, trans. William Templer (Oxford: Pergamon Press, 1992), 307–308.

52. In fact, the death toll on the plaque was wrong. The death toll at Dachau was approximately 42,000, according to Stanislav Zamecnik. See Megargee, *The United States Holocaust Memorial Museum Encyclopedia*, 446, n. 11; Greschat, *Die Schuld der Kirche*, 201–202.

53. Schmidt, *Pastor Niemöller*, 150.

54. Martin Niemöller, address, Geneva, February 20, 1946, in Kathleen Bliss, ed., *The Christian News-Letter*, March 20, 1946, 9–12, 10; Niemöller, address, Memorial Hall, Columbus, OH, January 29, 1947, 15, WCC, "Niemöller Visit," YDS 4, mf. 248.

55. Stewart W. Herman, "Memorandum on Conversation with Pastor Niemöller in Frankfurt on July 31, 1945," in Vollnhals, *Die evangelische Kirche nach dem Zusammenbruch*, 73–77, 75.

56. Robert P. Ericksen, *Complicity in the Holocaust: Churches and Universities in Nazi Germany* (Cambridge: Cambridge University Press, 2012), 169; Ben Rose, "An Interview with Pastor Martin Niemoeller," *Christianity and Crisis* 5, no. 21 (December 10, 1945): 4–6, 5.

57. Vollnhals, *Die evangelische Kircher nach dem Zussamenbruch*, 302.

58. Stewart Herman, *The Rebirth of the German Church* (New York: Harper & Brothers, 1946), 122; Ericksen, *Complicity in the Holocaust*, 168–169, 176–177; Clemens Vollnhals, *Entnazifizierung und Selbstreinigung im Urteil der evangelischen Kirche: Dokumente und Reflexionen 1945–1949* (Munich: Chr. Kaiser, 1989), 118–123.

59. Vollnhals, *Evangelische Kirche und Entnazifizierung 1945–1949*, 41, 58, 286; Ericksen, *Complicity in the Holocaust*, 171–179; on the Catholic and Protestant use of soap certificates, see Ernst Klee, *Persilscheine und falsche Pässe: Wie die Kirchen den Nazis halfen* (Frankfurt am Main: Fischer Taschenbuch-Verlag, 1991); Robert P. Ericksen, "Hiding the Nazi Past: Denazification and Christian Postwar Reckoning in Germany," in *A Lutheran Vocation: Philip A. Nordquist and the Study of History at Pacific Lutheran University*, ed. Robert P. Ericksen and Michael J. Halvorson (Tacoma, WA: Pacific Lutheran University Press, 2005), 137–156.

60. Niemöller to Asmussen, June 22, 1946, ZA EKHN, B. 62/539.

61. Asmussen to Niemöller, July 2, 1946, ZA EKHN B. 62/539; Asmussen to Wurm, November 2, 1946, ZA EKHN B. 62/539.

62. John Conway, "The Political Theology of Martin Niemöller," *German Studies Review* 9, no. 3 (October 1986): 541.

CHAPTER 8: BARNSTORMING AMERICA (1946–1947)

1. Ewart Turner to Martin Niemöller, December 3, 1946, ZA EKHN, B. 62/533; Cavert to Chaplain Rhea, European Theater of Operations, Frankfurt, no date (likely November 22, 1946), PHS, 18/15/24.

2. Acheson to Sherrill, no date, and Cavert to Travers, April 8, 1946, both in PHS, 18/15/24.

3. Acheson to Sherrill, no date, PHS, 18/15/24.

4. Hooft memorandum, August 11, 1946, and Wilberforce to Tomkins, August 22, 1946, both in WCC, General Correspondence (GC), "Martin Niemöller, 1937–48," YDS, mf. 1025.

5. Cavert to Dean E. E. Flack, Hamma Divinity School, Springfield, OH, November 25, 1946, PHS, 18/15/24; Cavert to Rhea, no date (likely November 22, 1946), PHS, 18/15/24.

6. John C. Bennett to Henry Smith Leiper, January 31, 1946, and Cavert to Wise, November 15, 1946, both in WCC, GC, PHS, 18/15/24. Rabbi Wise's November 15 response to Cavert is not in the file, but it is apparent from Cavert's response on November 18 to Wise that Wise remained a critic of Niemöller; Cavert to Wise, November 18, 1946, PHS, 18/15/24.

7. Hooft to Niemöller, May 16, 1946, WCC, GC, "Niemöller," YDS, mf. 1025; Gerhard Besier, "'Efforts to Strengthen the German Church': The Federal Council of Churches of Christ in America and the Representatives of the German Protestant Church after the Second World War (1945–1948)," in *Religion, State, and Society in the Transformations of the Twentieth Century* (Berlin: LIT, 2008), 221–253, 221–226; Stewart Herman to Sam Cavert, May 3, 1946, PHS, 18/15/24.

8. Turner to Cavert, December 8, 1946, PHS, 18/15/24.

9. "Message Sent on Niemoeller," *New York Times*, December 6, 1946.

10. Roosevelt to Oxnam, December 21, 1946, in *The Eleanor Roosevelt Papers*, ed. Allida M. Black (Detroit: Charles Scribner's Sons, 2006), 419; "Masaryk Assails Niemoeller Visit," *New York Sun*, February 11, 1947, PHS, 18/16/1.

11. Ewart Turner, "Procedures Memorandum—Niemoeller Visitation," WCC, "Niemöller Visit," YDS 4, mf. 251.

12. Turner to Cavert, December 10, 1946, PHS, 18/15/24.

13. Turner to Cavert, December 10, 1946, PHS, 18/15/24.

14. Turner to Eleanor Browne, December 19, 1946, PHS, 18/15/24.

15. Turner to Cavert, December 15, 1946, PHS, 18/15/24.

16. Turner to Cavert, December 16, 1946, PHS, 18/15/24.

17. Hertha Niemöller to Martha Turner, February 1947, Turner Papers, Temple University.

18. Martin Niemöller, address, Seattle, WCC, Niemöller Visit, YDS 4, mf. 247.

19. Martin Niemöller, address, Masonic Auditorium, Davenport, IA, December 22, 1946, WCC, "Niemöller Visit," YDS 4, mf. 252; Niemöller, address, First Reformed Church, Schenectady, NY, February 21, 1947, WCC, "Niemöller Visit," YDS 4, mf. 249; Niemöller, address, Music Hall, Cincinnati, OH, February 7, 1947, WCC, "Niemöller Visit," YDS 4, mf. 248–249.

20. Martin Niemöller, address, Masonic Auditorium, Davenport, IA, February 7, 1947, WCC, "Niemöller Visit," YDS 4, mf. 252.

21. Martin Niemöller, radio address, Seattle, December 5, 1946, WCC, "Niemöller Visit," YDS 4, mf. 246.

22. Martin Niemöller, address, Masonic Auditorium, Davenport, IA, December 22, 1946, WCC, "Niemöller Visit," YDS 4, mf. 252; Niemöller, address,

Music Hall, Cincinnati, OH, February 7, 1947, WCC, "Niemöller Visit," YDS 4, mf. 248–249.

23. Martin Niemöller, radio address, WMCA, New York, January 19, 1947, WCC, "Niemöller Visit," YDS 4, mf. 256; Niemöller, remarks at New York press conference, January 20, 1947, WCC, "Niemöller Visit," YDS 4, mf. 256.

24. Harold Marcuse first alerted me to the possibility that a version of the Niemöller quotation might be found in one of his New York addresses; Martin Niemöller, sermon delivered in the Second Presbyterian Church, New York, January 25, 1947, ZA EKHN, B. 62/172.

25. Niemöller to Mrs. Marvin Kane, December 16, 1946, ZA EKHN, B. 62/184.

26. Niemöller to Mrs. S. Paul, Library Department of the *Daily World*, New York, November 17, 1970, ZA EKHN, B. 62/526; Niemöller to Mark K. Stone, January 13, 1975, ZA EKHN, B.62/532.

27. Martin Niemöller, address to FCC, Seattle, December 5, 1946, WCC, "Niemöller Visit," YDS 4, mf. 247; Niemöller, address, Music Hall, Cincinnati, OH, February 7, 1947, WCC, "Niemöller Visit," YDS 4, mf. 248–249.

28. Martin Niemöller, address, First Reformed Church, Schenectady, NY, February 21, 1947, WCC, "Niemöller Visit," YDS 4, mf. 249.

29. Martin Niemöller, address, Rochester, NY, February 25, 1947, WCC, "Niemöller Visit," YDS 4, mf. 257–258.

30. Martin Niemöller, address, Rochester, NY, February 25, 1947, WCC, "Niemöller Visit," YDS 4, mf. 257–258; Niemöller to Forell, *Congressional Record*, April 29, 1947, PHS, 18/16/1.

31. Kurt Meier, *Kirche und Judentum: Die Haltung der evangelischen Kirche zur Judenpolitik des Dritten Reiches* (Göttingen: Vandenhoeck & Ruprecht, 1968), 26.

32. Turner to Cavert, December 10, 1946, PHS, 18/15/24; *New York Times*, January 27, 1947, 3; Rev. Francis T. Cooke to Cavert, December 11, 1946, PHS, 18/15/24; Eleanor Kent Brown to Niemöller, October 23, 1947, ZA EKHN, B. 62/501.

33. Cunningham to Cavert, January 1, 1947, PHS, 18/15/24; Hooft to Niemöller, February 14, 1947, WCC, GC, "Niemöller, 1947," YDS 4, mf. 1026; Cavert to Wurm, April 22, 1947, PHS, 18/9/ 21.

34. Joseph Alliger to Harper Sibley, Treasurer, FCC, January 7, 1947, PHS, 18/16/1; Mrs. George Friedman to FCC, January 9, 1947, PHS, 18/16/1; Frank Matthias to FCC, January 26, 1947, PHS, 18/16/1.

35. "Rabbi Wise Deplores Niemoeller Favor," *New York Post*, January 25, 1947; "Niemoeller Called 'Unfit' as a Leader," *New York Times*, February 3, 1947; Roosevelt to Cavert, January 13, 1947, PHS, 18/16/1.

36. W. B. Spofford, *The Witness*, December 12, 1946, and Cavert to Rev. Emory S. Bucke, *Zion's Herald*, February 6, 1947, both in PHS, 18/16/1.

37. Reinhold Niebuhr, editorial, *Christianity and Crisis*, February 17, 1947.

38. Cavert to Steinberger, January 7, 1947, PHS, 18/16/1; "Sternberger Reverses Position on Niemoeller in Light of Evidence," WCC, "Niemöller Visit," YDS 4, mf. 256.

39. Niemöller to Eleanor Kent Browne, February 27, 1947, Turner Papers, Temple University.

CHAPTER 9: SWORDS TO PLOWSHARES (1947–1956)

1. Niemöller to Gladys Boggess, May 25, 1947, ZA EKHN, B. 62/500.

2. Niemöller to Turner, May 25, 1947, ZA EKHN, B. 62/533.

3. Niemöller to Boggess, September 29, 1947, ZA EKHN, B. 62/500.

4. Else Niemöller to Turner, June 15, 1947, Turner Papers, Temple University; Niemöller to Turner, September 29, 1947, ZA EKHN, B. 62/533.

5. David M. Nichol, "Niemöller Sees Rise of Anti-Semitism in Germany," *Boston Globe*, July 1, 1947, 8.

6. Niemöller to Turner, October 5, 1947, ZA EKHN, B. 62/533.

7. Buchheim, "Ein NS-Funktionär zum Niemöller-Prozess," 312–313; "Nur Judenfreunde," *Der Spiegel*, August 9, 1947; *Christian Science Monitor*, July 30, 1947, 11; "Der nichtverfolgte Verfolgte," *Die Zeit*, August 7, 1947.

8. Freudenberg to Leiper, September 19, 1947, Turner Papers, Temple University.

9. Niemöller to Turner, December 13, 1947, ZA EKHN, B. 62/533.

10. Freudenberg to Leiper, September 19, 1947, Turner Papers, Temple University.

11. Freudenberg's statement can be found in *Juden, Christen, und die Ökumene: Adolf Freudenberg 1894–1994, Ein bemerkenswertes Leben*, ed. Martin Stöhr and Klaus Würmell (Frankfurt: Spener, 1994), 97–98; Constantin Goschler, "The Attitude towards Jews in Bavaria after the Second World War," in Moeller, *West Germany under Construction*, 231–249, 232, 241–244; *Juden, Christen, und die Ökumene*, 98; Niemöller to Leiper, August 15, 1949, ZA EKHN, B. 62/518; on Wolf Meyer-Erlach, see Susannah Heschel, *The Aryan Jesus: Christian Theologians and the Bible in Nazi Germany* (Princeton, NJ: Princeton University Press, 2008), 211–212, 270.

12. For a detailed account of the Darmstadt statement, see Hockenos, *A Church Divided*, chap. 6, and appendix 6 for the statement.

13. For a detailed discussion of "A Message Concerning the Jewish Question" and the Berlin-Weissensee statement, see Hockenos, *A Church Divided*, 153–170, and 195–199 for the statements.

14. Hockenos, *A Church Divided*, 199.

15. Niemöller to Boggess, December 21, 1948, ZA EKHN, B. 62/500; Niemöller to Philip M. Smith, April 25, 1948, ZA EKHN, B. 62/531.

16. Vollnhals, *Entnazifizierung und Selbstreinigung*, 197, 202–203; Spotts, *The Churches and Politics in Germany*, 105; "Niemöller's Stand Condemned by Clay," *New York Times*, February 4, 1948, 13.

17. Niemöller to Turner, February 21, 1948, ZA EKHN, B. 62/533.

18. Martin Niemöller, "How I Became a Pacifist," Swarthmore College Peace Collection, John Nevin Sayre Records (1885–1982), series B, box 16 (hereafter, for example, SCPC, Sayre Records, B/16).

19. Bentley, *Martin Niemöller*, 202.

20. "Interview Notes with Pastor Niemöller," SCPC, Sayre Records, B/16.

21. World Council of Churches, "Minutes and Reports of the Third Meeting of the Central Committee of the World Council of Churches, Toronto (Canada), July 9–15, 1950" (Geneva: The Council, 1950), 27, 91.

22. "Defend Police Action in Korea," *Christian Century*, July 26, 1950, 897. See also Jooseop Keum, "Korean War: The Origin of the Axis of Evil in the Korean Peninsula," in *Peace and Reconciliation: In Search of Shared Identity*, ed. Sebastian C. H. Kim, Pauline Kollontai, and Greg Hoyland (Aldershot, UK: Ashgate, 2008), 109–132, 117; "Out of Darkness, Hope!" *Christian Century*, July 12, 1950; "The UN in Korea," *Christian Century*, July 19, 1950; for the FCC's support, see "Commend UN's Action on Korea," *Christian Century*, August 2, 1950.

23. "FOR Deplores UN-US Policy in Korea," *Christian Century*, July 26, 1950, 885.

24. A. J. Muste, "Theology of Despair: An Open Letter to Reinhold Niebuhr," *Fellowship* (September 1948): 4–8, 7; summary of "Affirmation and Appeal," SCPC, document group 13, box 1, folder: "Conference on the Church and the War, Detroit 1950."

25. Martin Niemöller, "Does the Church Want Peace?" *Christian Century*, July 19, 1950, 866.

26. Muste, "Memo on Conversation with Martin Niemöller," July 21, 1950, SCPC, Sayre Records, B/16.

27. Niemöller to Muste, September 15, 1950, ZA EKHN, B. 62/522.

28. Niemöller, "No German Rearmament Now," *Christian Century*, March 21, 1951, 367.

29. Niemöller, "The Church in Central Europe," *Princeton Seminary Bulletin* (1950): 16–23.

30. Marguerite Higgins, Niemöller interview, *New York Herald Tribune*, December 14, 1949; Niemöller to Leiper, December 8, 1951, ZA EKHN, B. 62/518.

31. Paul Weymar, *Adenauer: His Authorized Biography* (New York: Dutton, 1957), 342.

32. (Ulrich?) Biel to US High Commissioner for Germany (HICOG), Frankfurt, October 17, 1950, US National Archives and Records Administration (NARA), record group (RG) 466 (HICOG), stack 250, row 68, compartment 15, box 124 (hereafter, for example, NARA RG 466, 250-68-15, box 124).

33. Office of Military Government, United States (OMGUS), Office of Intelligence, "Niemoeller and the EKD Council at Spandau," December 29, 1950, NARA, RG 319: "Records of the Army Staff," 270-84-012; Bentley, *Martin Niemöller*, 212.

34. Siegmund-Schultze to Muste, November 25, 1950, SCPC, Sayre Records, B/17; Siegmund-Schultze to Muste, December 7, 1950, SCPC, Sayre Records, B/17.

35. "Agent Report," December 19, 1950, NARA, RG 319, 270-84-012; "Speeches of Hessen Church President Martin Niemoeller in Kassel and Korbach," December 19, 1950, NARA, RG 319, 270-84-012.

36. Martin Niemöller, "Why I Went to Moscow," *Christian Century*, March 19, 1952, 338–340.

37. *Stuttgarter Zeitung*, January 5, 1952; Bentley, *Martin Niemöller*, 207; Jan Niemöller, *Erkundung gegen den Strom: Martin Niemöller reist nach Moskau, Eine Dokumentation* (Stuttgart: Radius, 1988), 113; "German Theologian Resigns from World Council of Churches," Religious News Service, May 13, 1952, 4.

38. "Niemöller Carries His Storms with Him," *Christian Century*, February 6, 1952, 148–149; Dibelius to Taylor, January 30, 1952, Taylor to Truman, February 18, 1952, and Truman to Taylor, February 20, 1952, all in Truman Library, "Confidential Files."

39. Taylor to Truman, April 23, 1952, Truman Library, "Confidential Files"; Eugene Tillinger, "Niemoeller: Germany's 'Red Dean,'" *New Leader*, March 10, 1952, 12–14, 12.

40. Davidson, *God's Man*, 209–210.

41. Reinhold Niebuhr, "The Captive Churches," *Christianity and Crisis*, November 13, 1950, 145–146.

42. "Where Is Wisdom," *Christian Century*, January 16, 1952, 62–63, 63; Reinhold Niebuhr, "Ten Fateful Years," *Christianity and Crisis*, February 5, 1951, 1–4, 3.

43. Douglas Steere, "Visit with Martin Niemöller, Wiesbaden, 1953," Haverford College Library, Haverford, PA, Quaker Collection, Douglas V. and Dorothy M. Steere Papers, collection 1174.

44. Steere, "Visit with Martin Niemöller."

45. Martin Niemöller, "The Way of Peace," *Fellowship* (November 1954): 5–11; Martin Niemöller, "How I Became a Pacifist," SCPC, Sayre Records, B/16.

46. "Program for a Courageous Nation," *New Outlook* 6, no. 3 (March 1953): 44–53, 46; Niemöller, "The Way of Peace," 6–8.

47. Niemöller, "How I Became a Pacifist"; Niemöller, "The Way of Peace," 6.

48. Sayre to Siegmund-Schultze, October 4, 1954, SCPC, Sayre Records, B/17.

CHAPTER 10: AMBASSADOR OF GOD (1956–1984)

1. Niemöller to Philip F. Smith, November 22, 1947, ZA EKHN, B. 62/515; Niemöller to Turner, January 11, 1948, ZA EKHN, B. 62/533.

2. Niemöller to Boggess, December 21, 1948, ZA EKHN, B. 62/500; Heymel, *Martin Niemöller*, 160–161.

3. Schreiber, *Martin Niemöller*, 103.

4. Leiper to Niemöller, February 7, 1957, ZA EKHN, B. 62/518.

5. Martin Niemöller, speech at Boston University, December 22, 1955, ZA EKHN, B. 62/500.

6. Niemöller to Clarissa Start-Davidson, March 13, 1959, ZA EKHN, B. 62/504.

7. Niemöller to Rev. M. W. Howard, June 29, 1962, ZA EKHN, B. 62/513.

8. Amiya Chakravarty to Niemöller, May 7, 1955, ZA EKHN B. 62/502.

9. "Declaration of Conscience: An Appeal to South Africa," African Activist Archive, George M. Houser (Africa collection), Michigan State University Libraries Special Collections, http://kora.matrix.msu.edu/files/50/304/32-130 -FBA-84-Concience%203%20pages%20all.pdf.

10. Niemöller to American Committee on Africa, September 20, 1957, ZA EKHN, B. 62/498; "South Africa Lag?" *Christian Science Monitor*, September 15, 1966, 13.

11. Niemöller to Sayre, March 25, 1959, ZA EKHN, B. 62/530. On the Asbury Howard case, see Martin Luther King Jr., *The Papers of Martin Luther King Jr.*, vol. 5, *Threshold of a New Decade, January 1959–December 1960*, ed. Clayborne Carson et al. (Berkeley: University of California Press, 2005), 205–206.

12. Martin Luther King to Ernest Zaugg, May 25, 1959, MLK Archive, Boston University; Niemöller to King, October 8, 1962, ZA EKHN, B. 62/498.

13. Niemöller to das Nobel-Preis-Kommittee, September 3, 1964, ZA EKHN, B. 62/517; Niemöller to R. N. Maddox, June 16, 1965, ZA EKHN, B. 62/520.

14. "Niemoeller Sees Whites in Peril of Existence," *Los Angeles Times*, August 19, 1957, B1; Niemöller to Mary C. Howeth, October 31, 1957, ZA EKHN, B. 62/513.

15. Samuel C. McMorris, "Rape of Civilization," *African-American Free Enterprise Report* 1, no. 3 (June 1959): 3–4.

16. "White People Held Blame for Current Racial Strife," *Evening Review*, March 31, 1960, 7; Martin Niemöller, "Pazifistische Realpolitik," *Stimme der*

Gemeinde, November 15, 1959; article clipping from *The Pentecostal Testimony* (1957), title and exact date unknown, ZA EKHN, B. 62/501; "White Race in Danger, Says Pastor Niemoeller," *Los Angeles Times*, May 3, 1959, A5.

17. "Replace Hatred with Love, Whites Warned by Dr. Niemoeller," *Afro-American*, April 24, 1965, 1.

18. Bob Friendly, "The Christian and Race Relations: A Question and Answer Session with Martin Niemöller," 1964, ZA EKHN, B. 62/277.

19. See, for example, Terrence Prittie, "Pastor on the Rampage," *Guardian*, July 23, 1961, 9.

20. Sterik, *Else Niemöller, Die Frau eines bedeutenden Mannes*, 146–147; Niemoeller, *Crowns, Crosses, and Stars*, 253–254.

21. Niemoeller, *Crowns, Crosses, and Stars*, 254.

22. Niemöller to Dr. Beyer, October 20, 1961, in Sterik, *Else Niemöller, Die Frau eines bedeutenden Mannes*, 147; Niemöller to Mrs. Judson Webb, November 1, 1961, ZA EKHN, B. 62/535.

23. Henry Koch to Niemöller, May 27, 1964, ZA EKHN, B. 62/517.

24. Eric F. Goldman Papers, Manuscript Division, Library of Congress, Washington, DC, box I/42; Martin Niemöller, "The Real Question Deserves to Be Heard," *Christianity and Crisis*, March 30, 1964, 47–48.

25. On the process of the EKD coming to terms with Christian anti-Semitism in the 1960s and 1970s, see *Der ungekündigte Bund; Neue Begegnung von Juden und christlicher Gemeinde*, ed. Dietrich Goldschmidt and Hans-Joachim Kraus (Stuttgart: Kreuz-Verlag, 1963); *Juden, Christen, Deutsche*, ed. Hans Jürgen Schultz (Stuttgart: Kreuz-Verlag, 1961); "Zur Erneuerung des Verhältnisses von Christen und Juden," in *Die Kirchen und das Judentum: Dokumente von 1945 bis 1985*, ed. S. Rolf Rendtorff and Hans Hermann Henrix (Paderborn: Bonifatius, 1988), 593–596; Matthew D. Hockenos, "Die Kirchen nach 1945: Religiöse Abbrüche, Umbrüche und Kontinuitäten," in *Zerstrittene Volksgemeinschaft: Glaube, Konfession und Religion im Nationalsozialismus*, ed. Manfred Gailus and Armin Nolzen (Göttingen: Vandenhoeck & Ruprecht, 2011), 287–311; Susannah Heschel, "Confronting the Past: Post-1945 German Protestant Theology and the Fate of the Jews," in *The Protestant-Jewish Conundrum*, ed. Jonathan Frankel and Ezra Mendelsohn (Oxford: Oxford University Press, 2010), 46–70.

26. Niemöller to Boggess, July 7, 1965, ZA EKHN, B. 62/500.

27. Niemöller to Boggess, July 7, 1965, ZA EKHN, B. 62/500.

28. Niemöller to Sanford Shetler, December 1, 1964, ZA EKHN, B. 62/531; Niemöller to Boggess, July 7, 1965, ZA EKHN, B. 62/500; Karnick and Richter, *Protestant*, 216.

29. Alfred Hasler, *Saigon, USA* (New York: Richard W. Baron, 1970), 7; on André Trocmé, see "André and Magda Trocmé, Daniel Trocmé," Yad Vashem,

www.yadvashem.org/righteous/stories/trocme. In 1971, Yad Vashem, the World Holocaust Remembrance Center in Israel, recognized André and Magda Trocmé as Righteous among the Nations.

30. "We Have Seen the Anguish of Vietnam," *New York Times*, August 1, 1965, E5.

31. Mary Hershberger, *Traveling to Vietnam: American Peace Activists and the War* (Syracuse, NY: Syracuse University Press, 1998), 84.

32. Hershberger, *Traveling to Vietnam*, 85; "Lasst Diesen Unsinn Endlich Aufhören!" *Der Spiegel*, January 16, 1967.

33. Hershberger, *Traveling to Vietnam*, 86.

34. Martin Niemöller, "Der Vietnamkrieg und die kommenden Geschlechter," *Stimme der Gemeinde*, January 1, 1967; Marcuse, *Legacies of Dachau*, 288.

35. Niemöller to A. Farina, November 13, 1967, ZA EKHN, B. 62/506; Niemoeller, *Crowns, Crosses, and Stars*, 274.

36. "Pastor to Give Award to Hanoi Red Cross," *Bridgeport Telegram*, September 5, 1967; Alistair Horne, *Kissinger: 1973, the Crucial Year* (New York: Simon & Schuster, 2009), 144; Niemöller to Leiper, September 19, 1967, PHS, Leiper Papers.

37. On Communist crimes, terror, and repression, see *The Black Book of Communism*, ed. Stéphane Courtois (Cambridge, MA: Harvard University Press, 1999).

38. Ewart Turner, "Niemoeller's Decision to Remarry Not Sudden," *(Toledo, OH) Blade*, August 26, 1971, Turner Papers, Temple University; Niemöller to Browne, December 10, 1968, ZA EKHN, B. 62/501; Niemöller to Leiper, September 19, 1967, Henry Smith Leiper Papers, PHS; Niemöller to Browne, November 16, 1969, ZA EKHN, B. 62/501.

39. Niemoeller, *Crowns, Crosses, and Stars*, 213–214.

40. Ewart Turner, "Niemoeller's Decision to Remarry Not Sudden," *(Toledo, OH) Blade*, August 26, 1971, Turner Papers, Temple University; Niemoeller, *Crowns, Crosses, and Stars*, 263.

41. Niemöller to Turner, January 6, 1972, Turner Papers, Temple University; Niemoeller, *Crowns, Crosses, and Stars*, 271–272.

42. Niemöller to Turner, January 6, 1972, Turner Papers, Temple University.

43. Niemoeller, *Crowns, Crosses, and Stars*, 280.

44. Hertha Niemöller to Turner, December 15, 1977, Turner Papers, Temple University.

45. Niemöller to Invite, April 27, 1960, ZA EKHN, B. 62. 526; Niemoeller, *Crowns, Crosses, and Stars*, 282.

Index

ERIN COVEY

MATTHEW D. HOCKENOS is the Harriet Johnson Toadvine '56 Professor in 20th-Century History at Skidmore College. The author of *A Church Divided: German Protestants Confront the Nazi Past*, he lives in Round Lake, NY.